Here's what readers are saying:

"No other product or web development tool provides the level of flexibility and power provided by HTML/OS. I'm glad there's now a book on this amazing product."
> —Charles J. Cangialosi, VP, Electronic Communications,
> Cooper Leder Marketing, www.cooperleder.com

"Nothing else comes close to the performance, flexibility and easiness of use of HTML/OS. *Advanced Web Sites Made Easy* is simple, clear, and easy to understand with lots of examples and exercises."
> —Yann Rapetto, Chief Information Officer,
> Alese Technology, Inc., www.alese.com

"*Advanced Web Sites Made Easy* is a wonderful tool for connecting the programming dots. The book covers a good range of topics and areas, is well documented, contains illustrations, good exercises to implement what you learn and has a lot of meat. There is something for everyone, touching on topics useful for programmers at different levels and skills."
> —Marvin Ellis, President,
> www.Equestrian.com

"This first book covering Aestiva HTML/OS provides a long-needed resource and a solid stepping-stone to the world of HTML/OS programming. The novice will find grounding in the first four introductory chapters, and subsequent chapters build the reader's confidence by introducing simple (and not-so-simple, but easy) tasks, then encouraging learning through experimentation by presenting possibilities and thorough exercises, to which end the reader receives a 30-day online trial of the software—ample time to learn to develop sophisticated applications."
> —Brigitte Botnick, Owner,
> Fauna Art Studios, www.fauna-art.net

"*Advanced Web Sites Made Easy* is right on target. Not only does it cover the ins and outs of using HTML/OS but it serves as a great introduction and review of basic programming concepts and methods. It is invaluable to anyone who wants an advanced web site."
> —D. Schuyler Kuhl, Computer Assistance Services,
> www.computerassistanceservices.com

Here's what HTML/OS users are saying:

"When I got HTML/OS, I had no knowledge of HTML or programming. Now I have one of the largest vitamin stores on the Web. And I built it myself."

—David Greenwalt, President,
www.ThePowerStore.com

"Our real-time tracker allows tens of thousands of people to simultaneously monitor runners in our marathon. Thanks to HTML/OS and its high-speed database engine our Web site and race day options are number one in the world."

—Alice Schneider, VP Computing,
The New York City Marathon, www.nyrrc.org

"Because of HTML/OS, I've leapfrogged my competitors."

—Curtis Palmer, Web Developer,
www.palmerinternet.com

"I built a content management system for Globix.com, one the backbones of the Internet. I saved them about a quarter of a million dollars."

—Khanh Vo

"We've been in business for over 100 years. We chose HTML/OS for one reason and one reason only. It's more powerful, easier to use, and more reliable than anything else on the market."

—Tom Sweet
www.kingarthurflour.com

"I built an entire computer retail business powered on the HTML/OS engine and then sold it for over $10,000,000. I can sincerely say it would not have happened without HTML/OS."

—Bryn Kaufman, Former Owner,
CMP Express

"You could spend hundreds of thousands of dollars on SQL Server 7, ColdFusion and a team of Web developers. But why do that when you get more power and more reliability with HTML/OS. Plus you can do the development yourself."

—Don Nicholes, President,
The Diamond Lane

ADVANCED WEB SITES MADE EASY

The Simple Way to Build Databases and Other Applications with HTML/OS

by

D.M. Silverberg

TOP FLOOR
PUBLISHING

Advanced Web Sites Made Easy:

The Simple Way to Build Databases and Other Applications with HTML/OS

SAN#: 299-4550
Top Floor Publishing
8790 W. Colfax #107
Lakewood, CO 80215

Feedback to the author: feedback@topfloor.com
Sales information: sales@topfloor.com
The Top Floor Publishing Web Site: http://TopFloor.com/
The HTML/OS companion Web site: http://dev.aestiva.com/advanced/

Library of Congress Catalog Card Number: 2001099698

ISBN: 1-930082-17-7

ACKNOWLEDGMENTS

The road leading to this book has been in the making since 1995, when the seeds of HTML/OS were first sown. Along the way hundreds of friends, colleagues, customers, vendors, and associates have provided invaluable suggestions, criticisms, ideas, challenges, and labor. I thank everyone who has offered a suggestion, presented a criticism, volunteered an idea, challenged me, or committed time and labor to the cause of Web-based computing and HTML/OS.

A special thanks goes to the talented team who helped me create *Advanced Web Sites Made Easy*. My heartfelt thanks goes to: Missy Ramey whose executive decisions, artistic creativity and industry experience made this book magically come together; J.W. (Jerry) Olsen whose impressive leadership as project manager and development editor made this book exceed expectations; Syd Jones whose hard work ensured chapters made sense; Pablo Collins, Paul Forsyth, and Matt Esquivel for their invaluable proofing of the endless number of code examples; Joann Woy for her indexing work; Susan Woolfolk for proofreading; Steve Winterkorn, Pamela Punzulan, and Don Nicholes for their help in the construction of the companion Web site for this book.

Finally, I would like to thank Peter Kent whose support and suggestions made this book possible.

ABOUT THE AUTHOR

Dave Silverberg is a founding member of Aestiva, the maker of HTML/OS. Dave is currently the Director of Technology for Aestiva, overseeing commercial product groups and Web technology research. Prior to founding Aestiva, Dave managed a consumer-oriented online serviced called LA ONLINE. He has been involved in online technology development since 1985. Dave has an undergraduate degree in physics from Clarkson University and a graduate degree in physics from the University of California, San Diego.

CONTENTS AT A GLANCE

TABLE OF CONTENTS

PREFACE

This is the first book on a new technology known as HTML/OS. The technology promises to popularize the construction of advanced Web sites. HTML/OS may be the most exciting technology since the advent of Java by Sun Microsystems.

The HTML/OS technology is the first major technological innovation of the post-Web era. It is not a marketing ploy or a repackaged idea. It is an original, easy-to-use technology that stands out from otherwise confusing, complex, and costly alternatives. The HTML/OS engine single-handedly eliminates the need for database servers and complex integration tools such as ASP, JSP, and PhP. It eliminates the need for programming languages to handle protocols such as XML, Corba, and DCOM. It replaces all of these complex legacy-centric technologies with a *simple BASIC-like language you type into HTML documents*.

At the same time, HTML/OS provides new capabilities such as Web networking. It empowers Web developers, allowing them to rise to new heights. Again, (excuse the mantra), all with *a simple BASIC-like language you type into HTML documents*.

As you'll learn, HTML/OS slashes complexities by more than a factor of 250. Suddenly the world is your oyster. What can you do with HTML/OS? Use it to build database applications, e-commerce sites, dynamic HTML forms, Web-based software, database search pages, portals, Web-based associate programs, remote learning programs, intranets, text editors, staff pages, chat systems, e-mail systems, Web-based forums, shopping cart bureaus, Web shopping malls, CRM (Customer Relationship Management) systems, Web-based accounting systems, application service providers (ASPs), Web-based shells, tracking systems, and industry-specific applications that run across the Web—all with a *simple BASIC-like language you type into HTML documents*.

HTML/OS is available on multiple platforms including FreeBSD, Linux, MacOS X, Sun Solaris, and Windows. It can be installed on standalone Web servers and in standard hosting accounts. In many ways, HTML/OS is what server-side Java should have been. On one hand Java is cross-platform making it extremely appealing. But Java is not easy to use like high-school BASIC. It does not run in standard hosting accounts. And it does not eliminate the need for a database server.

HTML/OS is cross-platform. It runs through a browser, making it available to virtually anyone. It includes a built-in database engine. It runs in standard hosting accounts. And most of all, you do your development with a *simple BASIC-like language you type into HTML documents.*

Aestiva, the company behind HTML/OS, is independent and radically pro-Web. Aestiva's belief that old legacy technologies are responsible for today's complexities is why its HTML/OS technology is *not* rooted in legacy technologies. It's rooted in HTML, the backbone of the Web. HTML/OS exemplifies a fundamental change in thinking that places the Web first and legacy second. It is based on solid engineering principles developed with the cooperation of thousands of Web developers, hosting providers, and Web-site owners. It is the successful result of five years of continuous innovation, engineering, testing, and development.

Is This Book for You?

This book was written for Web designers, computer programmers, and commercial product developers in all industries seeking a common-sense approach to advanced Web development. It's a must-read for every Web professional who wants an advanced Web site.

The book is useful to anyone who wants to move beyond simple HTML development. Because the book assumes no more than a basic knowledge of HTML and some simple programming or scripting skills, it is suitable to just about anyone. Unlike many books on Web development, this book moves beyond the theoretical into the practical. *Advanced Web Sites Made Easy* includes over one hundred useful examples and explanations of advanced Web-based components.

Most importantly, HTML/OS technology is refreshingly devoid of unnecessary learning barriers. While many computer technologies celebrate their complexities and mind-bending abstractions, HTML/OS celebrates the simplicity, elegance, and power it brings to Web development.

If you are a graphics designer you will want this book on your shelf to complement your HTML design skills. You'll find HTML/OS the tool you need to satisfy all of those requests for database-driven applications. HTML/OS is the tool that gets you to the next level.

If you're a serious Perl or ASP programmer, you will want to switch to HTML/OS so you can complete your work faster and master more challenging projects. You may also want to use HTML/OS to get involved in the new and exciting world of Web-based commercial application development as explained in Appendix C, *The Next Generation: Web-Based Products.*

If you're a small business owner you will want HTML/OS so you can build out a Web site that meets your organization's needs. If you're an MIS manager you'll want this on your shelf to remind you of all the things departments within your organization can accomplish without employing costly DBAs or system integrators. At the very least, you'll want to loan this book to the departments you support so you can minimize requests to your department. (But don't count on getting the book back!)

How This Book Is Organized

The book is designed to get you up and running quickly and at the same time give you the foundation you need to succeed as an advanced Web developer.

Part I of *Advanced Web Sites Made Easy* introduces the world of HTML/OS. A Web-based development world opens up as you get online and write your first Web-based computer program. This book includes a 30-day trial copy of HTML/OS preinstalled for you on the Web. There's nothing to install on your own PC, so you can be up and running in minutes. All you need is a browser connected to the Web.

Once online, you'll access the HTML/OS desktop. You'll learn how to use the HTML/OS File Manager and Web-based text editor. Part I is about getting a feel for the Web-based development environment. You'll complete a few simple programs.

Part II is where you'll uncover how HTML/OS works. Fundamentals are described in detail. The first two chapters of this part are a must-read. You'll also learn how to debug Web-based programs. The last half of Part II walks you through example after example of advanced Web-based components you can build and test. You'll learn how to build a variety of Web-based text editors, login screens, and Web pages that process HTML forms.

In Part III you'll learn about Web database programming. You'll learn how to use dbConsole, a point-and-click database-management tool included with HTML/OS. You'll learn how to place tags in documents that read, write, and search databases. The last half of Part III is filled with examples and explanations of useful database-driven applications.

Part IV focuses on the world of e-commerce. You'll learn how to build a shopping cart and a lot more—you'll learn how to build advanced shopping systems. The chapters in the part are filled with numerous examples of features and components you would expect to find in the most advanced e-commerce sites on the Web. You'll learn about real-time inventory, how to "cookie" shopping carts, and how to build back-end systems and order-management systems.

The appendixes include HTML/OS resources, a crash course on HTML (in case you're not yet conversant in it), a reference on the HTML/OS tags used in this book, and a discussion of how to bundle commercial Web-based products.

Using This Book

There is nothing special you need to learn to use this book. But you will want to read it while on the Web with your copy of HTML/OS. To get online read Chapter 1, *Introduction*. It includes instructions for activating your preinstalled copy of HTML/OS.

This book is best read from beginning to end, but in any case you should read the first six chapters thoroughly. Plus you should read Chapter 11, *The Web Database*, so you know how to set up and program HTML/OS databases.

If you're a seasoned Web designer with little or no skill in programming, read Part II. *Programming Basics,* carefully and do the exercises in the first two chapters in that part to acquire a solid foundation in HTML/OS programming.

If you're an experienced programmer, perhaps with background in Fortran, Pascal, or C, but you have little or no HTML experience, then it is important that you bone up on your HTML before reading this book. Appendix C, *Major HTML tags*, is a must-read for you. It shouldn't take you more than a few minutes to review the tags and another hour online to set up Web pages that use these HTML tags so you can give yourself hands-on experience. You need to think in HTML when you program in HTML/OS.

Getting Support

Web sites offering free support on HTML/OS are beginning to pop up around the Web. And Aestiva maintains a User Center, with a knowledge base, sample code, a freeware library, and tutorials that you can access free of charge. The free forum for purchasers of this book is also a handy resource. A wealth of additional support, online and by voice, is available to licensees of the Professional edition of HTML/OS.

Conventions Used in This Book

This book describes how to build advanced Web pages containing HTML and HTML/OS programming tags. In this book HTML tags are written in lower case whereas HTML/OS tags are written in upper case (although HTML/OS tags can be written either way). HTML tags, HTML/OS tags, variables, and all programming content is written in Courier type as in this example:

```
IF age < 18 THEN GOTO "underage.html" /IF.
```

Exercises

At the end of each chapter you'll find useful exercises. The exercises are provided as an aid to instructors using this book in courses on e-commerce, Web development, or how to build Web-based applications.

Completing the exercises is not a requirement for using this book, but we recommend you attempt a few of the exercises in each chapter. The answers to the exercises provide a supplemental resource of code examples. Answers are posted on the companion Web site for this book at http://www.dev.aestiva.com/advanced/.

PART I

Getting Started

## CHAPTER 1

Introduction

This book is about bringing sanity to the world of advanced Web-site construction. Now that the dot-com mania is over, it's time to simplify your outlook on building advanced Web sites. It's no longer acceptable to employ 10 or 20 people to build a business Web site. During the dot-com days money flowed from well-financed venture capitalists like water down the Nile. But those days are toast. Today's, advanced Web development has the same goals, but this time it's not rich dot-coms knocking on the door. Millions of small businesses and fiscally responsible corporations are running the show.

Making advanced Web development straightforward for the legions of people wanting advanced Web sites is what *Advanced Web Sites Made Easy* is all about. Large development staffs are over. Whether you're a graphics designer, business owner, computer consultant, or programmer, you want to know how to single-handedly build sites with databases, shopping carts, download and upload areas, staff areas, membership areas, discussion areas, and sites with high degrees of functionality.

And that's not all. You may also want to build Web-based applications. After all, the next generation of programs will be on the Web. You might want to build a Web-based sales and contact-management system, a document-management and workflow system, an intranet with file management and collaborative messaging, a Web-based accounting package, a financial reporting system, a company portal, or any number of industry-specific, Web-based applications.

You might want to build that Web site for yourself, a customer, or your boss. You might want to build a commercial product and sell it to thousands of people. Or maybe your goal is simply to advance your Web-development capabilities. Whatever it is you want to do, you need a development environment that's easy to understand and deployable all across the Web.

Most people believe these kinds of projects are way over their head—even the professionals. You probably do too. If you're like most people, you've put off building advanced Web sites. It seems every day you need to learn another new technology. The whole endeavor seems far too complicated. In fact, I wouldn't be surprised if you're a bit suspicious of the title of this book. After all, you might wonder how the word "advanced" and the word "easy" could be in the same book title. A walk down the computer aisle of any bookstore reinforces the notion that advanced Web construction is complicated. A peek inside any book on the subject will tell you so. A talk with a friend or colleague would support your conclusion too.

But advanced Web site construction isn't complicated if you're using the right approach. You don't need to be a highly experienced programmer. You don't need to learn the latest technologies. If you follow the approach detailed in this book, you'll be able to build sites as advanced and even more advanced than those dot-com Web developers of yore. You'll be able to satisfy the development requests of all of those small businesses and fiscally responsible corporations knocking on your door.

In this chapter, I'll explain the overall approach used by HTML/OS, the product described in this book, and compare it to the approach most people follow. You'll see why HTML/OS simplifies advanced development. You'll also see why the approach produces sites more powerful than ever. The dot-com days may be over, but advanced Web development has just begun.

The Legacy Beast

Let's start with a misconception: Building advanced Web sites has to be tough. This notion is accepted as gospel in most Web development circles. Why? Because most Web developers still use the approach popularized by the dot-com era, which indeed is tough. The approach is called systems integration. It requires you to be well versed in intricate and complex technologies, many of which can be understood only be those trained in computer science.

The systems-integration approach is about building Web sites by integrating multiple software packages: a database engine, integration tools, programming tools, and so on. The approach is based on the belief that it's smart to link legacy (pre-Web) systems directly with newer Web-based systems. Otherwise, the argument goes, you'd have to throw out the legacy systems, which would cost you more than integrating them with new, Web-based systems.

But this point of view doesn't take into account the high cost and complexity of systems integration. The systems-integration road is filled with potholes. System and version incompatibilities, hosting compatibility problems, the need to learn interface languages and protocols, potential upgrade nightmares, and the need to learn the intricacies of multiple products are just some of the challenges. Writing applications in these environments is incredibly complicated. The systems-integration approach is not elegant, simple, or beautiful. It's not a smart way to build an advanced site. Sites built this way are typically 50 times the cost, less reliable, and harder to maintain. So much for saving a couple of bucks. It's the brute force way to build advanced sites, and because Web developers are told over and over they have no other option, the systems-integration approach is still the dominant way advanced Web sites are constructed.

The systems-integration approach is so complicated it has single-handedly given rise to dozens of new technologies and well over a thousand books on various aspects of the subject, all designed to tame the beast; but the beast has not been tamed. If anything, systems integration has become more complex as new technologies are introduced on top of, underneath, and along side the others. It's become a multibillion-dollar business backed by many of the world's largest software powerhouses. Divide and conquer should be their motto. Thankfully, nobody is forcing you to follow the systems-integration approach.

A Web Approach

As you may have guessed, this book is not another attempt to simplify the world of systems integration. It is not a patch or a fix to what should be obvious to most—that systems integration is a dead end. There is no sense in spending so much money and time saving old systems or integrating them with the Web. It's a lot easier and less costly for customers to simply transfer their data to new Web-based systems and ready themselves for a new Web-based world.

This book readies you for the next generation of the Web and, at the same time, frees you from the systems-integration nightmares that poison Web development. Your future is simple once you leave the legacy world behind and enter the Web world. Web-based business applications, advanced Web sites, e-commerce systems, even commercial products are much easier to build and more powerful when there's no legacy stuff to muck up everything. Using HTML/OS, you can build a customer login page with five lines of code. You can build a Web-based text editor with 10 lines of code. You can build a Web-based database editor with 15 lines of code. This book includes such code examples. When the Web is set free to do its thing, it blows away the old school.

Advanced Web Sites Made Easy disregards systems integration. Words used in the systems-integration world, such as DCOM, CORBA, .NET, SOAP, SQL, and OLE, aren't solutions. They're the reasons why everything is so complicated.

Here, you'll learn how to place HTML/OS tags in HTML documents. That's the crux of it. And the beauty is you won't be any worse off than had you spent months learning the systems-integration approach. On the contrary, you'll gain capabilities surpassing those using these complex systems-integration technologies.

You'll find the single-product, Web-centric approach of HTML/OS so easy, you'll be amazed as you wander your way through discussions of applications you previously thought too tough to build on your own. Armed with only knowledge of HTML tags and some rudimentary programming skills, you'll find you already have the ability to build sites more advanced than those being built by people with far more education and experience.

Your first step will be to access your preinstalled copy of HTML/OS. (For those purchasing a copy of HTML/OS, it's no more difficult. HTML/OS installation is included with purchase.) This step is described in Chapter 2, *Logging into Your Copy of HTML/OS*. You'll be provided a URL that accesses your preinstalled copy of HTML/OS over the Web. Once on that copy of HTML/OS, you'll have everything you need. You won't need external database engines, because HTML/OS includes its own high-performance database engine. You don't need integration tools either. It'll just be you, your HTML documents, and your copy of HTML/OS.

One of the first things you'll discover about HTML/OS is that it's Web based. You don't install software on your own PC. You work over the Web. When you log into your copy of HTL/OS, you'll see a desktop with icons. The icons launch Web-based programs you've built and others included with the desktop for building and maintaining Web-based products. HTML/OS is a Web computer. You can add icons to your desktop, install products, and write programs, as with a computer, only everything is Web based.

Another nice feature of HTML/OS is you don't need to be a server administrator or to know anything about Web servers. You don't need FTP or Telnet either. You can do everything through the HTML/OS desktop over the Web.

What will really get you excited, however, is the way HTML/OS simplifies advanced Web development. To drive home the point, consider the case of building a database-driven shopping-cart system. In the world of Web development, shopping carts are considered advanced applications. Consider the difference between building one with Perl, perhaps the most popular language on the Web, and building one with HTML/OS. A basic database-driven shopping-cart system written in Perl takes 5,000 or more lines of intricate programming spread across dozens of program libraries and program files. With HTML/OS, you'll need a few dozen lines of easy instructions placed in the half-dozen HTML documents needed for the site. That's a 250-to-1 ratio. You might say advanced Web development with HTML/OS is more than 250 times as easy as Perl. And that doesn't include the benefits that come from not having to set up a database server and maintain it, or that HTML/OS is a lot easier to write.

HTML/OS is simplicity itself. It gives you the ability to go where you haven't been able to go before; it gives you the ability to do your work faster, and the ability to build sites and complete projects you would never have otherwise attempted. If you're learning HTML/OS to help with your own business, HTML/OS means new business opportunities, because with it you can build features you would not have otherwise built. If you're learning HTML/OS because you want to become a better Web developer, you'll be able say "yes" to almost anything asked of you. It also means you can single-handedly compete against systems-integration teams by simply offering your potential customers custom features they would be reluctant to provide.

Placing HTML/OS Tags in Documents

Developing advanced Web sites is a matter of placing HTML/OS tags inside HTML documents. The HTML/OS tags are also called *Otags*, which stands for Overlay tags. You'll see why in a moment. An example Web page is shown here:

```
<html>
<title>Test Page</title>
<font size=5><b>My Dynamic Web Page</b></font><br><br>
<font size=4>Did you know...<ul>
<li> 345 multiplied by 12 is equal to <<345*12>>.
<li> We're <<TIMEFROM("01/01/2000","days")>> days into the new
millenium.
<li> It's <<IF ISWEEKDAY(TODAY) THEN DISPLAY "not" /DISPLAY /IF >>
the weekend.<br>
</ul></font>
</html>
```

This Web page is a standard HTML document except for the programming that appears in bold. HTML/OS programming instructions are placed within << and >> characters. These program segments are called *Overlays*. The tags within them are called *Overlay tags*. The page shown here has three Overlays, each containing a single HTML/OS tag, called an *Otag*. Building dynamic Web pages is a matter of adding Overlays to them. The first Overlay does a math calculation. The second calculates the number of days since Jan 1st, 2000. The last displays the word "not" in the document if the current day is a weekday.

The Spreadsheet Analogy—*Overlay programming is somewhat analogous to spreadsheet programming. Whereas spreadsheets are composed of one or more spreadsheet pages containing macros applied to specific cells, HTML/OS Web sites are composed of one or more Web pages containing macros applied to specific locations within the HTML document.*

You can use Overlays to program any part of a Web page. You use them to change the content of any HTML document sent to a visitor of a site at the instant the page is requested. This ability to change documents as they're requested by browsers is what separates simple Web sites from advanced ones. Advanced Web sites, for this reason, are also known as on-the-fly Web sites.

In the current example, three Overlays calculate some numbers and text. Overlays can also generate HTML tags, links, and any content you want to place dynamically in an HTML document. You can even use them to change the parameters you pass to Java applets or place Javascripts in documents or exchange data with Flash applications.

In addition, Overlays can execute in response to a user clicking a hypertext link or a button in an HTML form. For example, suppose you have a Web page with an order form. When the user clicks the Complete Order button on the form, you want to add an entry to a database and send out a confirmation e-mail. To accomplish this, you add an Overlay to the HTML document that includes instructions for performing these two tasks. You'll learn how to perform these kinds of tasks, and more, later in this book.

The ability to transform a static Web site into an on-the-fly Web site by merely placing Overlays in HTML documents, is one of the elegant aspects of HTML/OS. No matter how advanced your site becomes, the process of creating the site is still a matter of placing Overlays in HTML documents.

Overlays can contain HTML/OS tags that read, write, and search databases. They can send out e-mail. They can perform calculations and display images. They can move files around on the server. They'll do anything you program them to do. You can define all the dynamic tasks that need to be performed as a user navigates a Web site by placing instructions in the Overlays you put in your Web pages.

Once you know the rules for placing Overlays in HTML documents and know how to write the instructions contained inside them, you can begin building advanced Web sites. A detailed description of the different ways to place Overlays in documents appears in Chapter 5, *Underlays, Inlays, and On-Click Overlays*. Writing instructions is covered in Chapter 6, *Working with Variables*.

Simplicity Is Power

The single-product, Web-centric approach used by HTML/OS has many benefits. As you'll see in the sections that follow, HTML/OS is more than an easy-to-program environment. It's not just a pretty face. It's also fast and well suited to the server environments prevalent on the Web. The baggage of the systems-integration world has been dropped. You're in the Web world now.

Speed

HTML/OS runs fast. By eliminating the overhead of inter-product communication, speeds are actually increased. And HTML/OS uses a high-level language, not a low-level language, so code runs faster.

Let's say, for example, you have a database with 500,000 records and you want to write a Web page that searches the database and displays the first 20 results. When using HTML/OS, this task requires two tags: DBFIND to search the database and LAYOUT to lay out the results on the page. That's it. You type these high-level tags directly into the HTML document used to display the page. Exactly such a page is discussed in Chapter 4, *Your First Web Database Program*. You can write the code for the page in a minute. Because the page contains only two tags, most of the processing occurs inside the HTML/OS engine, a highly efficient, compiled C++ application—the language of choice for the fasted products in the world. You'll be happy to know HTML/OS renders search results in about 10 or 20 milliseconds. (A millisecond is one-thousandth of a second). Of course, the transfer of the document from the server to your browser will take a lot more time. Since HTML/OS is so fast, chances are you won't feel the time HTML/OS takes to perform the search.

Compare this to systems integration, in which case the program needs to compose a database message and pass it to the remote database. Then it must wait for the reply. Sockets need to be opened and closed. Transaction limits may need to be tested. Database drivers need to be accessed. (Separate database engines need to be set up, tested, and maintained too.) Multiple messages may need to be passed to the database server, so this process might have to be repeated. The overall speed of the page depends on many factors. The efficiency of a driver, the speed of the external database engine, how well the database programming is written, and the efficiency of the integration product selected, are all important factors. The systems-integration approach can take 100 times as long.

Unlimited Transactions

The HTML/OS database engine has no built-in transaction limits. Most database servers limit the number of users at the same time. The limitations stop you from taking full advantage of the capabilities of your hardware, unless you purchase special licenses often costing more than the computers on which the database servers run. HTML/OS has no built-in transaction limits. You're limited only by the capacity of your hardware.

Web Compatibility and Portability

Another advantage of HTML/OS is its superior Web-compatibility and portability. Web-compatibility is the ability to run a Web application in the various environments popular on the Web. Not only must an application be compatible with the various browsers on the market, it should also be compatible with the heterogeneous array of server environments. Most Web sites run on servers using some version of Unix, Linux, or Windows. Many hosting accounts are shared. On a practical note, many server administrators don't give their hosting clients the ability to reconfigure their servers to fit their specific needs. All of this leads to problems for organizations using multiproduct solutions.

Web sites built with systems integration rarely run at shared hosting accounts except when the hosting service is the one providing the products you must integrate to. The simpler single-product approach used by HTML/OS suffers no such limitation. HTML/OS applications run in shared hosting accounts.

Product Sharing—*Some hosting services provide you with database engines and integration products you can share with other customers. While this offers a temporary solution you can use until you get your own database engine, the solution locks you into the hosting service. The large amount of systems integration needed to link to the various products installed at the hosting provider often creates an insurmountable cost if you decide to move your site later. In addition, hosts reserve the right to upgrade or suspend the maintenance of those products at any time. Furthermore, shared products can be adversely affected by others using them. This puts your site at constant risk. It's best to control your own server-side software and build sites so they can be moved, if necessary.*

Portability is also a concern. Portability, means the ability to move a Web site from one kind of hardware or operating system to another. The systems-integration approach requires the matching of hardware and software components. Each software component must be compatible with the other and each must be compatible with the hardware. The result is a system of hardware and software that is best left alone. The Web site is difficult to move, because changes in hardware and operating systems require the intervention of experts, a change in software components, and most often, a reprogramming of the Web site. The HTML/OS single-product approach frees the owner of a Web site from the loss of Web compatibility and the loss of portability. HTML/OS sites run in standard hosting accounts. No special configuration requirements are placed on the server administrator. The servers can use almost any kind of server, such as Unix, Linux, Windows, and MacOS X.

Moving an HTML/OS site from one setting to another is much like moving Web sites with no programming or dynamic elements. It's a matter of copying the files, documents, and databases in the site to a new hosting account. The only difference is that you need to install an HTML/OS engine on the new site. This high level of portability and cross-platform compatibility are not possible when Web sites are built from multiple, integrated products.

Server-Configuration Independence

The HTML/OS engine is not only portable and cross-platform. It's also immune to server-configuration dependence. Applications built with HTML/OS have no connection to the underlying server. As a result, you can install applications with the point-and-click method. For example, suppose you take an HTML/OS application, pack it up, and move it to some other hosting account with an HTML/OS engine. When you unpack the application, it would run the same way. The two servers could be completely different. Their internal file directories, hardware, and operating system could be different. One server could be Windows. The other could be MacOS X.

This ability to move HTML/OS applications between different kinds of servers, without modification, gives you the ability to build and maintain a single application but sell it to people on Unix, Linux, or Windows server platforms. The topic of building commercial products with HTML/OS is discussed in Part VI, *Building Commercial Products*.

Web Networking

The single-product approach used in this book means you'll be able to enjoy some capabilities not available before—not even to those in the systems-integration world. One of the new things you'll be able to do is take advantage of Web networking, which is a technology that allows you to network multiple copies of HTML/OS. Unlike traditional networking, Web networking implies the nodes of the network (a copy of HTML/OS is called a node) can be anywhere on the Web and use any kind of hardware or operating system. In other words, Web networking is wide-area and cross-platform.

HTML/OS allows you to set up Web networks. The capability is built in. Once you set up a Web network, files and databases on one Web site can be accessed from another site by preceding the name of files and databases with node names. For example, if site A, located on a Linux system in India, has a product database called /db/products, site B, located on a Sun Solaris system in Texas, could access it by using the name A:/db/products in the HTML documents on their site.

You set up Web networks by using the Control Panel included with each copy of HTML/OS. The Control Panel gives you the ability to define levels of security, set a node identity for that copy of HTML/OS, and define links to other nodes in your Web network. Setup is point and click.

Web networking is appropriate in a variety of situations. As an example, consider an international company with multiple copies of HTML/OS spread throughout the world. If the human resources department needs access to data stored on a copy of HTML/OS used by the sales department, the human resources users can use Web networking to access the data. As another example, a company may want to share data between its intranet and Web site. Web networking provides an easy solution.

Distributed Execution

With HTML/OS, you can take advantage of the automatic way in which applications can be distributed across multiple servers. For example, suppose you have an existing Web-based ordering system you want to modify. You would like to place the order page on a new Web site and leave the rest of the Web site on the original server. You want to do this because you're developing an intranet on the new Web site that will be taking over the ordering function. A developer using systems integration would have a tough time adapting to the new requirements. Distributed execution is extremely complicated in multiproduct environments, even for the experts. A developer thinking about satisfying such a request might say the task is impossible, unrealistic, or too much trouble, or recommend reprogramming the site from scratch.

Distributed execution is built into the HTML/OS engine. When you spread documents between different servers, they continue to run as if it they were placed on a single server, because HTML/OS is a *distributed state-persistent system*, a fancy way of saying HTML/OS doesn't loose its variables as users on a site move from page to page, even when the pages are on different servers. Distributed execution gives you, as the HTML/OS developer, the ability to spread applications across multiple servers when one server can't take the volume of hits, or is simply not convenient.

Summary

In this chapter, we've reviewed the major differences between the systems-integration approach to building Web sites and the single-product approach taken in this book. As you have seen, the topic of advanced Web sites has many facets; but the construction process discussed in this book is simple and powerful. Now you know why this book is titled *Advanced Web Sites Made Easy*.

In the next chapter, you'll get on a copy of HTML/OS. You'll use its Web-based development environment. You'll review the tools available to you and begin experiencing for yourself the beauty of advanced Web development.

## CHAPTER 2

Logging into Your Copy of HTML/OS

As you use this book, you will want HTML/OS in front of you. This chapter tells you how to log on and run your personal copy of HTML/OS. Then, the chapter acquaints you with the HTML/OS File Manager and Web-based text editor, two of the applications reviewed in this chapter that you will use throughout this book. You'll get an overview of the HTML/OS desktop, take a look at the File Manager, a tool for navigating the files and directories, and learn to use the Web-based text editor. After that, you'll build some simple Web pages and learn to provide access to them. The chapter also describes the HTML/OS Control Panel and other programs included with your copy of HTML/OS.

Let's Get Started

Advanced Web Sites Made Easy has reserved a copy of HTML/OS just for you. The copy runs on the Web, so there's nothing to install on your own PC. All you need is a connection to the Web and the HTML/OS registration number printed on the HTML/OS Free-Trial Card in the back of your book. Follow these instructions to activate your copy of HTML/OS:

1. Open up a browser.
2. Go to the HTML/OS Free-Trial Web page at http://dev.aestiva.com/freetrial.
3. Click the **Free Trial Account Signup** button.
4. Enter the 10-digit reservation number on your HTML/OS Free-Trial Card along with your e-mail address and any optional information requested.

Seconds after you sign up a new-account letter will be e-mailed to you. It will contain a URL and password. Pick up your e-mail and use the URL and password to access your copy of HTML/OS. The URL goes directly to the login screen of your preinstalled copy of HTML/OS. You're now ready to work online.

Usage Limitations—*You can use your copy of HTML/OS as a place to sharpen your design and development skills and as a demonstration site for existing and potential customers. But you cannot use the copy to host a Web site. It's strictly an Aestiva Developer account, a limited hosting account with no FTP or Telnet, no e-mail accounts, and 100 MB of hard disk space. See your sign-up agreement at* http://dev.aestiva.com/freetrial/policies *for details, limitations, and usage policies.*

You can access your copy of HTML/OS from anywhere. Share it with friends or use it to show off your HTML/OS applications. Your copy of HTML/OS will be available to you for a period of 30 days from the date you first log in. If after 30 days you wish to extend the hosting of your free copy, you can purchase additional 6-month blocks for a nominal charge of $25.

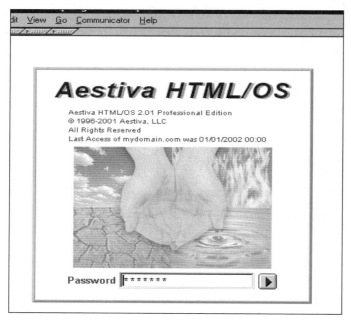

Figure 2.1: This is your HTML/OS login screen.

First Looks at Your Copy of HTML/OS

To log into your copy of HTML/OS go to the URL provided in your new-account e-mail and enter your password. Then press Enter. You will see the HTML/OS desktop as shown in Figure 2.2. The desktop is your personal administrative area. It somewhat resembles a computer desktop, but of course, it runs in a browser. In the next section, you'll read about the HTML/OS desktop and learn how to use it.

Your HTML/OS Desktop

Your HTML/OS desktop has two horizontal options bars and a set of application icons. The top options bar includes the options **Menu, New, File Manager,**

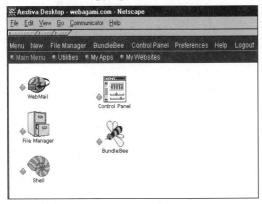

Figure 2.2: The HTML/OS desktop...

Control Panel, Preferences, and **Logout.** The bottom options bar includes a list of application menus. When you first log in, you're placed on the Main menu.

Your HTML/OS desktop is where you place applications and run them. Use it to organize applications and store bookmarks to other Web sites. The desktop also comes with a number of useful utilities and programs preinstalled that help you, the Web developer. We'll discuss them later in this chapter.

The Top Options Bar

Your top options bar contains fixed links and programmable links you can add and edit. The fixed links are as follows. They're discussed individually in the sections that follow.

- Menu
- New
- File Manager
- Control Panel
- Preferences
- Help
- Logout

Menu

The **Menu** link gives you the ability to add or delete menus from the menu bar. A menu is a set of icons that launch applications or locations on the Web.

New

The **New** link is for creating new icons. When you click **New,** a small window will pop up allowing you to create a new icon in the menu you are viewing. An example is shown in Figure 2.3. Note that icons can be links to applications or bookmarks.

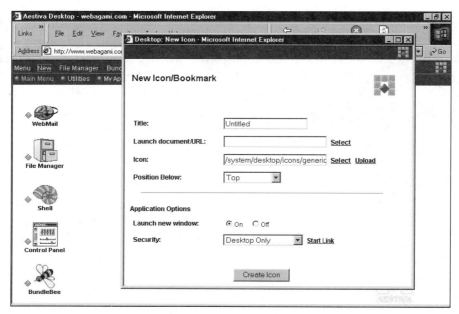

Figure 2.3: Creating a new icon or bookmark.

To set up an application icon, enter a title for your icon and the full name of an HTML document to run. Click **Select** if you need to browse your file system. Note that every application icon has an entry HTML document that runs when it's clicked. This is called the application Launch document.

To set up an icon to a remote Web location, in other words a bookmark, enter a title for your icon and the full URL of the Web site. Click the **Create icon** button at the bottom of the page when you are done.

The New window also includes options to position your icon relative to the others on your menu, select an image for your icon, and determine how it should be launched. An icon can launch in a new browser window or in the same window, displacing your desktop when it runs. If your computer has enough memory and is fast, you will want icons to launch in new windows.

Just below the **Launch New Window** option is the Security drop-down list. It should be set to **Desktop Only** unless you want the application to be accessible to others on the Web. In this case, set security to **Allow Public Access** and click **Start Link** to view the URL you can give out to anyone wishing to launch the application from the Web

File Manager

The **File Manager** link gives you the ability to navigate the directories in your system, edit and run HTML documents, perform uploads and downloads, and perform file-management tasks. A description of the File Manager is provided in the "File Manager" section later in this chapter.

Control Panel

You use the **Control Panel** link to install applications, set up networking to other copies of HTML/OS, configure e-mail settings, and set up system-wide settings used by HTML/OS. The Control Panel is also described in the "Building Your First Web Pages" section later in this chapter.

Preferences

The **Preferences** window allows you to change the appearance of your HTML/OS desktop to fit your individual tastes. The window is shown in Figure 2.4. It contains a variety of settings, from determining how to display the titles of icons on your screen to setting screen colors. The settings are summarized in the following list:

Background Themes—Use this to set up different desktop backgrounds and color combinations. Select from themes already installed or create your own.

Shortcuts—You can set up these special links to launch specific applications. Shortcuts are positioned between the File Manager and Control Panel on your top options bar. To modify your shortcuts, click **Select** and choose one or more icons from those installed. Note that shortcuts must relate to an existing icon. Use shortcuts only for highly used applications, because the top options bar is visible, regardless of which menu you are in.

Launch Windows—Use this setting to choose how windows are launched. HTML/OS launches windows in either of two ways. They can be launched as a new browser window or as an adjustable JavaScript window. JavaScript windows give you greater control over the size of the window launched; but sometimes, depending on the computer you use, they can open slowly. HTML/OS is delivered with JavaScript windows off. Feel free to change this setting to see what works best for you.

Font and Font Size—These two settings allow you to change the type of font and font sizes used in icon titles.

Maximum Rows and Maximum Columns—These two settings give you the ability to organize how icons appear on a menu. Use the settings to ensure icons do not fall off your desktop.

Help

Help launches an on-line Help window with information about how to use the HTML/OS desktop. Refer to this pop-up facility when you have questions.

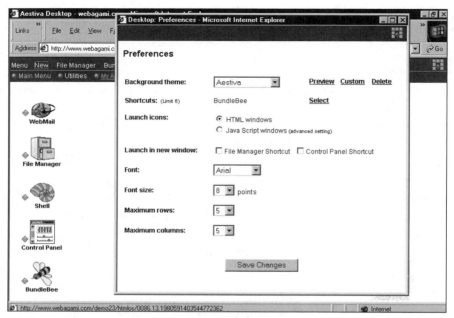

Figure 2.4: You use the Preferences window to change desktop preferences.

Logout

Click **Logout** to log out of your HTML/OS desktop.

The Bottom Options Bar

Your bottom options bar contains the names of menus of icons. Menus give you a way to organize the bookmarks and applications you use. Create and delete menus as needed. When you first log into HTML/OS, you'll see it comes with the following four menus preinstalled:

Main Menu—Place general-purpose applications here.
Utilities—Place utilities here.
My Apps—Place the applications you create here.
My Websites—Place bookmarks to your popular Web sites here.

Each menu on your bottom options bar is marked by a small globe. The globes preceding your current menu selection serve a function. Click them to toggle your display between a listing of icons and a text-based display of listings.

Your Icon Marker

Each icon or listing in your display is preceded by a globe or a diamond. They have meaning. Globes tell you the icon is a bookmark, in other words, a link to a Web site. Diamonds tell you the icon is an application, in other words, a link to an HTML document.

Diamonds can be red or orange. Red means the public can access the application with a Start-link. Start-links are explained in the "Start-links" note later in this chapter. The red color warns you the application is accessible by the public. All other application icons are orange.

Icon Preferences

The **Icon Marker** is also a link. Click it to edit the preferences for the icon. A window, like that shown in Figure 2.5, will open.

The Edit Icon screen is similar to the screen you see when you click **New** on the top options bar on the desktop. It includes the same options as the New window with additional options to delete the icon or move it to another menu. The New Icon screen was described in the "Top Options Bar" section earlier in this chapter.

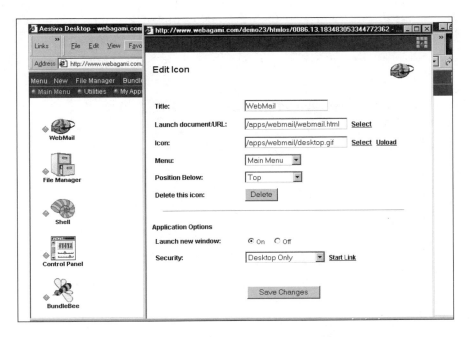

Figure 2.5: In the Edit Icon window you can delete or move icons.

Desktop Applications

Your HTML/OS desktop includes useful applications for managing files, editing and running HTML documents, packing and unpacking files, creating and managing databases, bundling products, and changing the settings used by HTML/OS. The two applications you'll be using the most throughout this book are the File Manager and Web-based editor. To a lesser degree, you'll be using the Control Panel, discussed later in this chapter, and dbConsole, discussed in Chapter 11, *What Is a Web Database?*

In preparation for creating your first Web page, let's review how to use the HTML/OS File Manager and its Web-based text editor. We'll also be discussing Start-links and the Web File System (WFS) used by HTML/OS. If you find these a bit confusing, don't worry. They're not essential at this point. They will make more sense later in this chapter when the topic comes up again in the "Giving Access to Your Three-Page Application" section.

File Manager

The HTML/OS File Manager is a file-management utility that allows you to select, copy, rename, create, delete, upload, download, and list files on your Web site. You can launch it by clicking **File Manager** on the top options bar on your desktop. The File Manager also includes an online help utility, a search utility, and a Web-based text editor. (See Figure 2.6.)

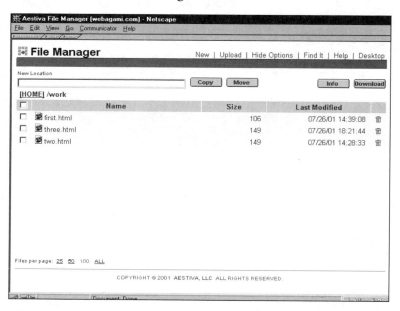

Figure 2.6: From the File Manager, you can access documents on your Web site, edit them, and run them.

Using the File Manager, you can perform tasks on single files or entire groups of files. The top options bar has links for creating new files and directories, uploading files, and finding files. You'll also find a link to an online help utility and a link to show or hide options. When options are hidden, the options area, just below the options bar, is not shown on the screen.

The options area includes a New Location box and buttons to copy, move, download, and obtain information on selected files or directories. Buttons in the options area will perform tasks on one file or on all the files and directories you check.

Your current directory path is listed just below the options area. Below that is your file and directory list. To copy, move, download, or obtain information on one or more items, place a checkmark beside the items and click the button for the action you want to perform. To create a new file or directories or upload a file, use the appropriate link in the options bar.

Multi-File Tasks

As mentioned in the preceding section, the File Manager can copy, move, download, and display information on multiple files and directories. For example, if you wanted to copy or move some files and directories into the directory /mywork, you would place a checkmark beside the files and directories you wanted to copy or move, type /mywork in the New Location box, and click the **Copy** or **Move** button. All the files and directories would copy or move across. Note that the File Manager, when it copies or moves directories, copies or moves the entire directory tree, meaning all files and directories inside the specified directory, and all files and directories inside that, and so on.

If you need to download or display information on multiple files, place a checkmark beside each file, and click **Download** or **Info**. When downloading multiple files, a download list will be provided to you. Click each name you want to download. When getting information on multiple files, each information section will be listed, one after the next, on the same screen.

File List Sorting

At the top of your file list, you'll see headings for each filename, size, and last date modified. Click these column headers to sort files by filename, size, or date modified. Click again to reverse the sort order. Note that directories always appear above files regardless of how you sort your file list.

Navigation

The File Manager gives you access to the files in your Web site. The root directory of your Web site is called Home or /. It can contain files and other directories, which can contain other files and directories, and so on. To view the contents of a directory, click the directory name on your screen. To exit a directory, click any directory link in the current directory path.

File Viewing and Editing

When directories and files are listed in the File Manager, each is preceded with an icon. Click the icon to display the document in the browser. Click the document name to open it in the HTML/OS File Manager's Web-based editor. The icon preceding a filename tells you the kind of file it is. Directories are preceded with an icon that looks like a folder. Other icons tell you whether the file is an HTML document, a text file, an image, a database, a Pack file, a bundled application, or an unknown file type.

Information

To retrieve information on one or more files and directories, select them and click the **Info** button in the options area. You'll see a screen similar to that shown in Figure 2.7. The following information is provided for each file requested:

   File Path—The full path to your selected file or directory. The file path is the full location and name of the document. For example, the full path of index.html is `/index.html`. The full path of a file called cart.html located in the directory apps is `/apps/cart.html`.

   File Size—The size of your file.

   Type of Document—A document type, such as image or database. The Type of Document tells you whether HTML/OS recognizes your file as an image, HTML document, or a special file.

   Last Modified—The date and time the file was last changed.

   File Area—The internal storage area of the file (*Public*, *Private*, or *Mirror*). The File area tells you where your file is located in the Public or Private tree of the server. See explanation in the accompanying "Internal Files Areas" note.

   Start-link Access—A security setting (**Allowed** or **Not Allowed***)*. Start-link Access tells you whether the public has access to your Web page. Start-link URL is the URL users would use to launch HTML/OS and run the page. See the accompanying "Start-links" note.

   Start Link—The URL to run the document (if Start-link Access is allowed).

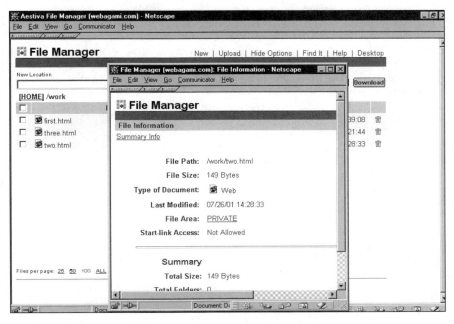

Figure 2.7: You can view file information from the File Manager.

***Internal File Areas**—Web sites use a Web File System (WFS) that's a subdirectory of the server's file system. When using HTML/OS from the Web, you don't need to think about the underlying directory structure of the server. However, if you work directly on the server, you should know that a single directory in HTML/OS has two directories on the server. One is in the Public tree and the other is in the Private tree. Files are stored in either side, but directories are mirrored in both sides. The Public tree is usually the server's DocumentRoot (where the index.html file is located). The Private tree is a directory outside the DocumentRoot. When HTML/OS creates a new directory, two directories on the server are created, one on the public side and one on the private side. You can move documents between these two directories by using the Info option. A conventional Web site has only a single directory tree, called the DocumentRoot, which causes file security problems, because all files are, by default, open and public. In HTML/OS, most files are private. Specifically, if the extension used by a file is in the HTML/OS Private Extensions List, which is defined in the Control Panel, it is private. Otherwise it is public. All database files, text files, and HTML files are, by default, private. GIFs and JPEGs are, by default, public. A technical description of the WFS can be found in the Knowledge Base on Aestiva's Web site.*

Start-links—*Start-links are URLs that can be placed in static Web pages or used over the Web. They launch the HTML/OS engine and run a specified Web page. When using HTML/OS on a Web site, whether for the entire site or only an application in a site, a Start-link accesses the first page in HTML/OS. For security reasons, Start-links cannot be used until they're allowed in the Control Panel.*

Find It

The File Manager's options bar includes the **Find It** link. Click this to find a file. Multiple search options are provided. Searches can be case sensitive; they can span the content of all files, or only filenames, and you can restrict searches to only files with specific extensions.

Help

Click the **Help** link on File Manager's options bar to access the File Manager's on-line Help system. Use **Help** to find detailed information on using any options in the File Manager. Explanations of the HTML/OS directory structure and how to use the Web-editor are included.

Web-Based Editor

The Web-based editor used by the File Manager is a text editor for your HTML documents and any kind of text document. The Web-based editor is launched when you click a filename. It has options to save, reload, and run your Web page. If you're working over the Web, you'll be using this editor for much of your work.

Text Box Resizing

Before using the Web-based editor, you'll want to adjust it for your computer screen. To resize the text area, click the **Resize** icon at the bottom right under the text box. A window will appear giving you options to change the width and height of the text area. (See Figure 2.8.) The following table shows the recommended settings:

Monitor Size	Recommended Columns and Rows Settings
640 X 460	Width 73, Height 12
800 X 600	Width 92, Height 20
1024 X 768	Width 120, Height 20

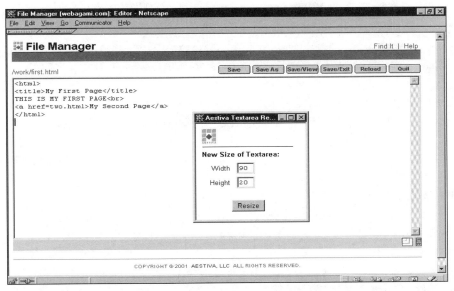

Figure 2.8: Your Web-editor is used to edit HTML documents and try them out.

Reverting to Previous Pages

To revert to a previous version of a page you have been working on, take advantage of your browser. Use the **Back** button of your browser or your browser's **History** feature to find the page you want. When you find it, click the Web-based editor's **Save** button (not your browser's Save feature). If you simply want to revert to the last saved version of a page, click the Web-based editor's **Reload** button. Your text area will be filled with the previous version, overwriting all changes.

Running Your Page

The HTML/OS Web-based editor includes a **Save/View** button. Use this to run your page. Clicking the **Save/View** button saves your data and runs it. Click the **Back** button in your browser to return to your editor after running your page. The **Save/View** button comes in handy as you write and test the documents you create. The ability to make a change to a page, test it, and return to edit the page in just a few clicks makes programming a snap. Note that your page is saved before it is viewed (run), because until it's saved, it's stored in your browser, not on the server, where it runs.

If you want to run your page in one window and edit it in another, do the following: Edit the preferences for your File Manager's icon. Set it to launch as a new window. Then Click the **File Manager** icon twice to launch two different windows. Use one window to edit and one to view.

Also note that you can view (run) any HTML document from the File Manager by clicking the icon to the left of the document's name.

Quitting the Web-Based Editor

Use the HTML/OS **Save/Exit** button to save what you're working on and return to the File Manager. Click **Quit** to quit what you're working on and return to the File Manager, discarding changes made since the last save or save/exit.

Building Your First Web Pages

Now that you've seen how to use the File Manager and Web-based editor, you can build your first Web pages. You'll create three simple Web pages that do little other than link to each other. Building these pages is a good way to learn your way around HTML/OS. Think of these pages as a simple Web application. Later you'll add a Start-link to the first page so the set of pages can be accessed from the Web.

Click **File Manager** and click **New**. It's a good idea to set up a directory to work in. Enter the directory name /work and click the **New Dir** button. Click **New** again, enter /work/first.html, and click the **New File** button. You're ready to create your first page. Enter the following code into your page:

```
<html>
<title>My First Page</title>
THIS IS MY FIRST PAGE<br>
<a href=two.html>My Second Page</a><br>
<a href=three.html>My Third Page</a>
</html>
```

Click **Save** to save your work. Then click **Save As** and enter the filename /work/two.html and click **Save** again. This will create a new file using your first file as a starting point. Edit the document so it looks as follows:

```
<html>
<title>My Second Page</title>
THIS IS MY SECOND PAGE<br>
<a href=first.html>My First Page</a><br>
<a href=three.html>My Third Page</a>
</html>
```

Click **Save**. Then click **Save As**, enter the filename `/work/three.html` and click **Save**. Edit the document so it looks as follows:

```
<html>
<title>My Third Page</title>
THIS IS MY THIRD PAGE<br>
<a href=first.html>My First Page</a><br>
<a href=two.html>My Second Page</a>
</html>
```

Click **Save/Exit**. You have now created three Web pages that link to each other in your `/work` directory. To run the first page, click the icon to the left of `first.html`. Test the pages. Go back and edit if you've made some mistakes.

Giving Access to Your Three-Page Application

Think of your three Web pages as an application. After all, on the Web that's exactly what applications are—sets of HTML documents. The entrance page of your application, the first page entered by users, is `first.html`. This page has links to `two.html` and `three.html`. Although your three Web pages are accessible from the HTML/OS desktop, they are not accessible by the public. But what if you want to attach these three pages to your site? To accomplish this, you need to give access to the entrance of your application with the Control Panel.

Click the link back to your desktop. On the top options bar, click the link that launches the Control Panel. In the Control Panel, select **Security**. A number of options will appear under Security. Select **Start-link Allow**. You'll see an input area like that shown in Figure 2.9.

Type the entry `/work/first.html` on a new line and click **Save Settings**. Now the page is accessible with a Start-link. As mentioned in the "Start-links" note earlier in this chapter, a Start-link is a URL anyone on the Web can use to access the `/work/first.html` page. The URL starts HTML/OS and runs the page. There are two ways to determine the URL. First, you can look at the help screen provided in the Control Panel. Click **Turn Help On** to do that. I can't tell you exactly how to write a Start-link in this book, because Start-links depend on how your copy of HTML/OS was installed. On the other hand, your Help screen knows. It shows you exactly how Start-links are written for your installation.

Another way to find your Start-link is to use the **File Info** option in the File Manager. Exit the Control Panel and click **File Manager** on the HTML/OS desktop. Find `/work/first.html`, place a checkmark beside it, and click **Info**. The Properties screen for the document will give you the Start-link for the page. To test it, enter the URL in the location line of your browser.

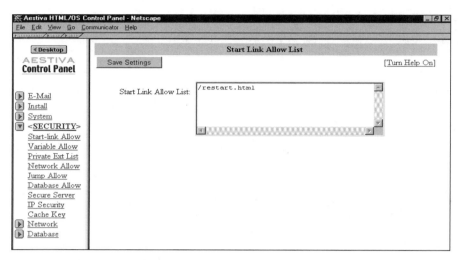

Figure 2.9: Start-links are allowed using the Control Panel.

Now that you know how to build Web pages and give users access to them, how about setting up an icon on your desktop for it too? To do that, exit to your desktop and select **New** on the top options bar. Enter a title for your icon and enter the name of your launch document—the document that runs when the icon is clicked. In this case, it would be /work/first.html. You can type it into the box manually or use the **Select** option to navigate your Web site and find it. At this point, you can click the **Create Icon** button. If you want to use a different icon as the default, then before clicking **Create Icon**, click the **Select** link located to the right of the Icon entry box. Select an icon and then click **Create Icon**. Now you have a new icon that, when clicked, launches your three-page application in a new window.

The Control Panel

Your Control Panel is where you install new applications, change or view your system settings, set up networking, and manage your copy of HTML/OS. Control Panel options are organized as follows:

E-mail—Configure outgoing e-mail settings and defaults
Install—Install, register, and uninstall products
System—Change or view system settings
Security—Set up access and database security settings
Network—Configure Web networking
Database—Access special files and logs used by databases

You can open or close each category by clicking it. Open categories are followed by a list of options. The options are summarized in the following sections. The Control Panel is shown in Figure 2.9.

E-mail

This is where you can test and configure your outgoing e-mail defaults. Autoresponders and HTML/OS mail tags will not send out e-mail until the outgoing mail server is configured here. You also configure related e-mail settings here.

Install

HTML/OS applications can be bundled, using a program called Bundle Bee, into application files known as bb files (pronounced bee-bee). Once bundled, an application can install by using point-and-click into any copy of HTML/OS, regardless of the hardware it is on. This category is for installing and managing these bundled HTML/OS applications. The category includes the following four options:

Install Product—Use this to install bundled applications, also known as bb files. To install, select a highlighted product from your file list and install. Products may be installed in any directory of your choice. In general, it is best to use the install directory provided by the product or a subdirectory of /apps.

Registration—If your product needs to be registered, type in the product code and registration key provided by the vendor of your product here. Make sure your product vendor gives you both a product code and key. Both are necessary.

Product Uninstall—Use this to uninstall a product. Use it carefully. This option will uninstall icons on your desktop and will empty all files and subdirectories in the install directory of the application.

History—This screen allows you to review products you have installed or uninstalled on your Web site.

System

Over 15 system-wide settings are stored in this section—the most important being the password to your HTML/OS desktop! Step through each, with Help turned on, to learn about each system-wide option.

Security

Unlike standard Web sites, where pages are accessible from the Web until you make them inaccessible, HTML/OS keeps everything inaccessible from the Web until you explicitly make it accessible from the Web or from a page (by virtue of typing a hypertext link or an HTML form) that is already accessible. This Security category contains access lists for Start-links and variables, secure server (HTTPS) access information, settings related to Web-network security, and other security measures.

Network

This category has options for setting your *node* (a node is a copy of HTML/OS) identity, and configuring the nodes that can access you. The HTML/OS network is a peer-style, wide-area network. There is no central point of failure. Every node has full control over whom it can see and who can see it. This category also includes a network error log and testing utilities that come in handy when setting up Web networks.

Database

This category contains miscellaneous database options. An error log that logs problem database requests and an option to set up database handles (aliases to databases) is provided. For further information on database error logging or database handles, see the on-line help included in this section or the knowledge base on Aestiva's Web site.

Other Applications

At first, you'll see many HTML/OS applications that are unfamiliar to you. The following sections provide a brief introduction to the more popular applications. Use the pop-up help system included with each application in addition to the cross-references provided here to educate yourself further about these products.

Bundle Bee

Bundle Bee is an application for bundling commercial products. It can take a series of Web pages and convert them into a single, compressed, copy-protected application (a bb file), which can be sold and installed on any copy of HTML/OS. The application is discussed in Chapter 35, *Using Bundle Bee*.

dbConsole

dbConsole is an application used to create databases and import data into them. If you're a developer, you'll find this program invaluable. dbConsole is discussed in Chapter 11, *What Is a Web Database?*

Packit 2.0

If you've heard of Stuffit on the Macintosh, Zip on Windows, or Tar on Unix or Linux, then you already know what Packit does. This utility allows you to pack multiple files into a single file for storage or transfer. Packit 2.0 is shown in Figure 2.10.

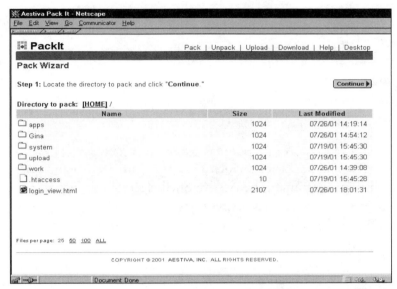

Figure 2.10: Packit backs up files and directories or transports large sets of documents between copies of HTML/OS.

Packing files is accomplished through an easy-to-use wizard. First, you select a directory from which to extract files. All files in your Pack file will be specified relative to this directory. Then you select the files and subdirectories you want to place in your Pack file. Then you pack it. Like Stuffit, Zip, and Tar files, Pack files can be e-mailed and copied from one location of the Web to another. They can be unpacked on any copy of HTML/OS. Note that HTML/OS applications are server-independent. HTML documents packed on one system can be unpacked and run on another.

Note for Packit 1.0 Users—*Packit 1.0 provided a mechanism to attach desktop icons to a pack file. This option is not supported in Packit 2.0. Instead, the option is available in Bundle Bee, a complete application-packaging tool that's included with HTML/OS. Bundle Bee is described in Chapter 35.*

Aestiva Shell

Aestiva Shell is a Web-based version of the shells that have become the primary command-line interface for Unix and Linux systems. If you prefer command-line interfaces to point-and-click interfaces, you'll enjoy this shell.

Aestiva Shell supports many of the features found in Unix and Linux shells including the following:

- On-line Help
- Redirection and pipes
- Command aliasing
- Program execution
- Command history

Aestiva Shell supports over 20 popular commands such as `ls`, `cat`, `diff`, `cp`, `mv`, `mvdir`, `rm`, `rmdir`, and `help`. It also includes a text editor (edit) and gives you ability to run HTML/OS programs. The Aestiva Shell is shown in Figure 2.11.

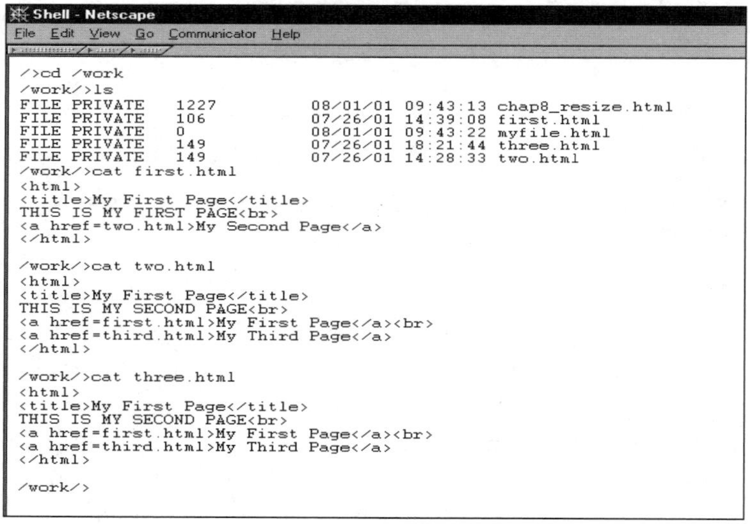

Figure 2.11: Aestiva Shell is an optional command-line interface for those who want to keep their fingers on the keyboard.

Tracer

Aestiva Tracer is a utility that works with the HTML/OS programming tag, TRACE. The application is described in Chapter 7, *Debugging Techniques*. Tracer allows you to analyze trace files filled with history information accumulated during program execution.

WebMail

WebMail is a Web-based e-mail program. The full-featured application can read e-mail from multiple e-mail boxes, direct e-mail into specific folders (filters), search your e-mail, and maintain a list of e-mail addresses.

Using Freeware

In addition to the applications listed in the preceding sections, numerous freeware applications are available. Aestiva Freeware Library, which is located in **Aestiva's User Center** (http://www.aestiva.com/support) features dozens of applications that can be downloaded and installed using the **Install Product** option in your Control Panel.

Exercises

Exercises 1 and 2 test your knowledge of the desktop and using Packit 2.0. Exercises 3 and 4 are about variable passing —a topic related to the three-page application you created earlier in this chapter. These latter two exercises show you how variables work with those Web pages and how they pass between pages or can be passed into them from the Web. Answers to all exercises are provided on this book's companion Web site as described in the book's Preface.

Exercise 1

Create a desktop menu called `mywork`. Move any icons you've created into this menu.

Exercise 2

Pack up the `/mywork` directory into a Pack file. Download it and save to your local computer. Then take the file and upload it back to your copy of HTML/OS. Unpack it into the directory `/mywork2` and access it from the File Manager. Then create a new icon that launches the page `/mywork2/first.html`.

Exercise 3

This exercise is about passing variables between pages. Take the three-page application you created in this chapter. Place the instructions just below the `<html>` tag on each page. Place `<<abc=1>><<abc>><br>` on the first page. Place `<<abc=abc+1>><<abc>><br>` on page two, and `<<abc>>` on page three. Run the application from the desktop and move between the pages. In HTML/OS, you display single variables by placing them in `<<` and `>>` brackets. You also run instructions by placing them in `<<` and `>>` brackets. This topic will be expanded on in the coming chapters. Follow abc as you move from page to page. What happens?

Using the instructions here as a model, write new instructions that reset abc to 0 when first.html is accessed, adds 2 to abc when two.html is accessed, and adds 3 to abc when three.html is accessed.

Exercise 4

This exercise is about passing variables to applications when they are launched. You do this by adding *name=value* pairs to Start-links. You'll see an example in this exercise. In Exercise 3, you placed the instruction <<abc=1>><<abc>>
 in first.html. Delete this instruction so the variable abc is not initialized to 1 when the page is accessed.

Access first.html using a Start-link. The default value of all variables, including abc, is ERROR. Note how abc displays as ERROR and how abc plus 1 equals ERROR1. This is Okay. It happens because the plus (+) character is also used to paste text together.

Add to the end of the Start-link the six characters, ?abc=5. Use this extended Start-link to access first.html. This is what we meant by adding a *name=value* pair to a Start-link. What happens?

Now enable access to the variable abc in the Control Panel. To do this go into the Control Panel, click **Security** and select the option **Variable Allow**. Type the variable name abc on a line by itself and click **Save Settings**. Now try the extended URL again. What happens this time?

Next, change the example so abc is initialized to 100 when the page is launched and is decreased by 1 every time any of the pages first.html, two.html, or three.html is accessed.

CHAPTER 3

Your First Program

In the previous chapter, you got online with HTML/OS. Now you build your first program. Your first program is simple since the purpose of this chapter is to give you a taste of programming on the Web. In this chapter, you will build a program that's an adaptation of a computer program called Hello World.

Hello World is typically the first program students learn in computer science classes. Students learn how to write a program that displays the words *Hello World* on the screen.

In keeping with tradition, in this chapter you'll also write a program that prints the words *Hello World* on the screen. However, you'll do more. After all, anyone with knowledge of HTML can display *Hello World,* because you can do that by simply typing the words into an HTML document. Instead, you'll write a program that displays *Hello World* in different colors depending on the color a user selects. See Figure 3.1. If a user selects Red, *Hello World* displays in red; if the user selects Blue, it displays in blue; if the user selects Green, it displays in green.

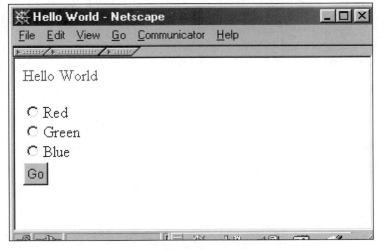

Figure 3.1: Hello World is your first Web-based computer program.

Your first step is to create an HTML document with the look you want. This is because developing programs with HTML/OS is top down. In other words, first you design your Web pages, then you add the programming. Using the Web editor in the File Manager (see Chapter 2, *Logging into Your Copy of HTML/OS,* for an explanation of how to use the File Manager), enter the following code into a Web page:

```
<html>
<font color=[Location1]>Hello World</font>
<form action=[Location2]>
<input type=radio name=color value=red>Red<br>
<input type=radio name=color value=green>Green<br>
<input type=radio name=color value=blue>Blue<br>
<input type=submit name=mybutton value="Go">
</form>
</html>
```

This page displays the words *Hello World* on the screen and includes a set of three radio buttons the user can use to select a color. In this code example, [Location1] and [Location2] appear where you need to insert the dynamic content. [Location1] is positioned where the contents of a variable containing a color value is needed. [Location2] is where you should link your HTML form. When the user clicks the **Go** button, you want the color selected to appear at [Location1]. That way, when the page is redisplayed, the words *Hello World* appear in the color the user selected.

Don't Know HTML?—*If the HTML tags in the accompanying Web page are unfamiliar to you, you will want to bone up on your HTML. Luckily, HTML is not difficult. It's not necessary to understand most HTML tags. You only need to learn about 15 tags. Most others work only with Netscape or Internet Explorer browsers, or in only the latest browsers. By sticking to a small set of tags, you'll be able to learn HTML fast and you'll be learning the same tags used by sites like amazon.com and yahoo.com that design their sites so they can be used by anyone on the Web. A list of these tags can be found in Appendix B,* Major HTML Tags.

To complete the Hello World program, you need to know a few things about HTML/OS programming. First, when using HTML/OS, you create dynamic content in documents by placing Overlays in them. An Overlay is one or more programming instructions surrounded with << and >> characters. For example, the Overlay <<DISPLAY color /DISPLAY>> prints the contents of the variable color in the page. The Overlay can also be written as <<color>>. You'll learn more about Overlays in chapter 5, *Overlays, Inlays, and On-click Overlays.*

The second thing you need to learn about HTML/OS is that you link HTML forms to Web pages by setting the ACTION parameter in the HTML form. When users submit their form, the selections they made are automatically saved to the variable names specified in the HTML form and the user is directed to the page specified by the ACTION parameter. The page can be written explicitly or you can use an Overlay to dynamically set it.

In your program, you want to redisplay the page after the user clicks the **Submit** button. To accomplish this, set ACTION to <<page>>, which is a tag in HTML/OS that contains the name of the current Web page. Alternatively, you can set ACTION explicitly to the current page. For example, if your HTML document is called mypage.html then you can write ACTION="mypage.html" in the header of your HTML form. You are now ready to complete your first program. Edit the page so it looks as follows:

```
<html>
<font color=<<color>>>Hello World</font>
<form action=<<PAGE>>>
<input type=radio name=color value=red>Red<br>
<input type=radio name=color value=green>Green<br>
<input type=radio name=color value=blue>Blue<br>
<input type=submit name=mybutton value="Go">
</form>
</html>
```

This revised page has Overlays where [Location1] and [Location2] once stood. An Overlay that displays the value of the variable color replaces [Location1]. An Overlay that displays the value of the current page replaces [Location2]. The page tag contains the value of the current page. Click the **Save/View** button in your Web-based editor to run your program. Select different colors and click the **Go** button. The page will redisplay with the words *Hello World* in the color you select.

Understanding the Inner-Workings of Web Programs

It is important to understand the steps that occur in the split second you run a Web page. Unlike computer programs that aren't Web-based, programs running on the Web are distributed between the Web server and a browser. The Overlays run on the Web server. The HTML tags are run on the browser.

When a user clicks a link on a Web page, a request is transmitted from the browser to the Web server for a specific Web page. The page is then scanned by the HTML/OS engine on the Web server. HTML/OS reads the document from top to bottom. As it encounters Overlays, it runs them and uses them to build an HTML-only document, which is then transmitted to your browser. The original document containing Overlays stays on the server. The browser reads the HTML-only document received from the Web server and displays it on the screen.

When a user clicks a button in an HTML form, a similar sequence of steps occurs:

1. The variable names and values placed in the HTML form, along with a request for a Web page are transmitted to the Web server. Notice that each radio button contains a variable name and a value. When an HTML form is submitted, a variable name and value pair is transmitted from the browser to the Web server (only the one selected, of course).

2. The HTML/OS engine on the server takes those values and places them inside the variable names specified in the HTML form.

3. The HTML/OS engine reads the Overlays in the document and uses them to build an HTML-only document. It then transmits the document back to your browser. The browser reads the HTML-only document and displays it on your screen.

As you can see, Web pages with HTML tags and Overlays contain instructions for both the Web server and the browser. Web programs behave differently than programs not on the Web. They're double-pass, meaning first the server passes across the document and then the browser passes across the document. Computer programs not on the Web are single-pass.

The server-side tasks defined in Overlays are performed before client-side tasks. They are used to change the contents of HTML documents dynamically. By the time the HTML document is rendered by HTML/OS and transmitted to the browser, the document contains only HTML tags. It no longer contains Overlays.

To witness this, run your Hello World page using the **Save/View** button in your Web-based editor. Then view the source of your Web page with your browser. All the Overlays will be gone. In their place, you will see the standard HTML. URLs, such as the one you defined for the ACTION in the header of your HTML form will be replaced with encoded URLs that link back to the Web site. You will not see any Overlays, because HTML/OS used them on the Web server to render the page. They are not transferred across to the browser.

This is a good thing. Browsers are finicky, and the way they interpret tags can vary from browser version to browser version, which is why it's best to stick to the most basic HTML tags. On the other hand, servers browsers do not interpret Overlays, so that Overlays can be used reliably. Reliability is a necessity when it comes to building advanced Web sites. Although you can depend on Overlays to work as advertised, you will need to use HTML tags sparingly and cautiously.

The HTML Document as a Template

As you also see, Web pages stored on the Web server are not the same as those received by the browser. The pages on the Web server act as templates. A single page on the Web server can render thousands of different pages, because it can include Overlays that extract data from variables and databases and merge it with the page when requested by a browser.

Such pages will look different depending on the record from the database used or the contents of a variable. On the other hand, the HTML tags in the page are constant. A single change to the HTML in the page will change the rendering of any page it produces.

Summary

Although you have only created your first program, you are beginning to see why HTML/OS is so powerful. It gives you the ability to fully define the dynamic nature of your Web pages, an important component of advanced Web sites. The HTML outside your Overlays is the fixed portion of the page. The HTML produced by your Overlays is the dynamic portion of the page. The page stored on the server acts as a template. The pages transmitted to the users are the pages rendered by HTML document stored on the server, not necessarily the document itself.

In this chapter, you learned about Hello World, a simple program that's educational but not particularly useful. In the next chapter, you will write your first database program. There you learn how to extract data from a database and merge it with an HTML document.

Exercises

After completing the three exercises in the following sections, you will have a better feel for programming with HTML/OS. As you complete your exercises, you'll see that HTML/OS programming is different from programming off the Web. You can build sophisticated programs quickly and with less effort than with conventional off-the-Web (legacy) programming techniques. Answers to all exercises are provided on this book's companion Web site as described in the book's Preface.

Exercise 1

The program in this chapter uses radio buttons. Exchange the radio buttons with a pull-down select box. Note that the code for a pull-down Select box is written as follows:

```
<select NAME=variable_name>
<option value=value_one>Selection One
<option value=value_two>Selection Two
<option value=value_three>Selection Three
</select>
```

Exercise 2

Exchange the radio buttons with three hypertext links. Note that HTML/OS allows you to place *name-value* pairs in standard hypertext links. For example, you can write the following:

```
<A HREF=some_page.html NAME=var_name VALUE=var_value>Selection One</A>
```

When the user clicks the link `var_name` is set to `var_value`.

Exercise 3

Build a Hello World program where both the color and font size can be varied by the user. Use two pull-down select boxes in a single HTML form to accomplish your goal.

CHAPTER 4

Your First Web Database Program

After you write the program Hello World, you're ready to go one step further. In this chapter, you will build a program that allows users to search a contact database and display a search result. Your program does not require many Overlay tags—only a few; but it does require that you learn how HTML/OS stores and displays variables, how to use an Overlay tag called DBFIND that searches databases, and how to use LAYOUT, an Overlay tag for reorganizing information in variables.

This chapter introduces you to the concept of two-dimensional data, an important concept used throughout HTML/OS. You'll learn how to create a database with a program called dbConsole. You'll then learn how to write the tag to fill a variable with multiple rows and columns of search results and how to reorganize that variable so it displays nicely on the page. Figure 4.1 illustrates the program you will build.

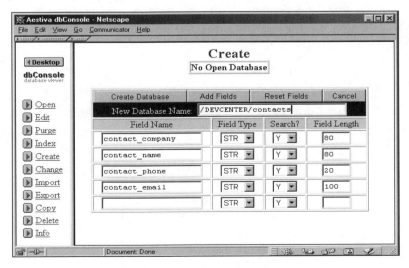

Figure 4.1: Creating a Web database is point and click.

You start by creating a database and populating it with sample data. You use dbConsole, a point-and-click Web application for creating and managing databases, as described in the next section.

Creating a Database

To create a database, click the **dbConsole** icon on your HTML/OS desktop. Then select **Create**. You should see a screen like that shown in Figure 4.1.

A First Look at HTML/OS Databases—*The following list contains a quick introduction to the basic concepts of HTML/OS databases:*

1. *The HTML/OS database engine is a high-performance engine capable of serving thousands of users simultaneously.*
2. *HTML/OS databases look like spreadsheets placed on their sides. Instead of columns, they have fields. Instead of multiple rows, they have multiple records. HTML/OS databases can contain over a million records each. Each record can contain hundreds of fields.*
3. *The first field of an HTML/OS database record is called* record. *It contains a number that uniquely identifies the record. The* record *field is followed by the fields you set up.*
4. *In HTML/OS, databases and database tables are the same things, because HTML/OS database tables do not need to be linked together with schemas, a technique used by relational databases off the Web to join multiple database tables together. HTML/OS can join multiple database tables together at program time, a feature not typically found in database engines. This topic is discussed in further detail in Chapter 20,* Database Joins.
5. *The HTML/OS database engine works with your Web server. It does not need a separate database server like off-the-Web database engines. There is no database server to maintain, and you can manage the database engine easily through a Web-based program called dbConsole.*
6. *The HTML/OS database engine is built directly into the HTML/OS engine. To access the database from within your HTML documents, you use tags such as* DBADD, DBEDIT, *and* DBFIND. *No SQL (a widespread database query language) is needed. Unlike SQL-based solutions, HTML/OS is a type of Fourth Generation Language (4GL). When using 4GLs, database programming is simplified, because you need to use only one tag per database operation. HTML/OS databases are discussed in further detail in Chapter 11,* What Is a Web Database.

To set up your contact database, specify the names of the fields you want in the database along with the field type and field length for each. In the example here, you use a database with four fields: contact_company, contact_name, contact_phone, and contact_email (excluding the field record, which is created automatically).

Set the field type of your fields to STR. STR stands for *string*, which is computer talk for text. Specify a field length for each of your fields. Use the values shown in Figure 4.1. Set the database name to /mycontacts, and click the **Create Database** button. You have created your first database.

Open the database by clicking **Open** in the left column of dbConsole. Your database is in the Home directory because you named it /mycontacts. (Names beginning with a slash are in the Home directory.) Then click **Edit** in the left column to edit a new or existing record. Add a contact to the database. Enter the contact data for your fields, and click the **Save** button above the record. Click the **New** button above the record to start a new record. Repeat until you have entered four or five records.

Creating your Web Page

You're ready to build a Web database program. Just as in Chapter 3, *Your First Program*, you design your program from the top down. Exit dbConsole and use the File Manager to create a new file. Fill it with the following HTML code:

```
<html>
<form method=post ACTION=[Location1] >
<font size=2>Enter Search:</font><br>
<input type=text name=mysearch size=15>
<input type=submit value="Find">
</form>
Search Results:
[Location2]
</html>
```

To view the Web page, click the **Save/View** button in your Web-based editor. You should see an HTML page that has a search box with a Find button and a place for a search result.

Adding the Overlays

In the code you entered previously, the parameter ACTION is set to [Location1] and [Location2] is placed where search results should be displayed. To complete your program, you need to write code for [Location1] and [Location2]. Since you want to redisplay your Web page when the user clicks the Find button on the page, you need to set [Location1] to the page name by replacing ACTION=[Location1] with ACTION=<<page>> or ACTION="/mypage.html" assuming your page is called "/mypage.html".

[Location2] is where you insert an Overlay that searches your contact database and displays a message or a search result. What you display depends on the value of mysearch. The first time the user accesses the page, the variable mysearch is equal to ERROR, because variables in HTML/OS default to the value ERROR. On the other hand, if a user enters a search, mysearch is equal to the value the user typed into the input box. In this second case, you want to conduct a search of your database and display a table of results.

The Overlay at [Location2] needs to take into account these two cases. By using an IF-THEN statement, you can selectively perform a search when mysearch is not equal to ERROR and display a text message when it is not. Your Web page, with [Location1] and [Location2] swapped out for the proper code, is shown here:

```
<html>
<form method=post ACTION=<<page>> >
<font size=2>Enter Search:</font><br>
<input type=text name=mysearch size=15>
<input type=submit value="Find">
</form>
Search Results:
<<IF mysearch="ERROR" THEN
DISPLAY "Please enter search above. " /DISPLAY
ELSE
sstr = 'contact_name ~ ' + '"' + mysearch + '"'
mydata = DBFIND("/mycontacts",sstr,1,20,
"contact_company,contact_name,contact_phone,contact_email")
mynewdata = LAYOUT(mydata, [1], " - ", [2], " - ",[3], " -
",[4], "<BR>")
DISPLAY mynewdata /DISPLAY/IF>>
</html>
```

The tags that perform a search are placed between the ELSE and the /IF in the IF-THEN statement. The tags DBFIND and LAYOUT are used. The tag DBFIND searches a database and places a subset of the records it finds into mydata. The LAYOUT tag is used to format the data in mydata so it can be displayed with the DISPLAY tag. The remainder of this chapter gives you a detailed explanation of how this application works.

Understanding Your Application

The following sequence of steps occurs when a user runs the Web page presented in the preceding section:

1. When a user enters a value in the search box and clicks the **Find** button, the text that user entered into the input box is transmitted to the Web server and saved into the variable `mysearch`.

2. The HTML/OS engine scans the Web page from top to bottom. As it moves through the file, it creates an HTML page for the user. The first Overlay it encounters is `<<PAGE>>`. HTML/OS adjusts the HTML form so it links back to the current page. `<<PAGE>>` is a tag that contains the name of the current document.

3. The next Overlay HTML/OS encounters is below the words `Search Results`. The `IF-THEN` statement in the Overlay runs the instructions between the `ELSE` and the `/IF` in the event `mysearch` is not `ERROR`. In this case, the Overlay fills the variable `sstr` with a query string. The instruction uses plus (+) signs to paste text together. If `mysearch` is equal to `george`, the instruction would fill `sstr` with `contact_name ~ "george"`. HTML/OS uses the variable `sstr` as the input of the `DBFIND` tag on the following line.

4. HTML/OS runs the `DBFIND` Overlay tag. The tag fills `mydata` with a table of information. It can do this because HTML/OS variables are two-dimensional. They have one or more columns and one or more rows. The accompanying "Understanding HTML/OS Variables" note discusses how HTML/OS stores variables. A more thorough discussion is provided in Chapter 5, *Working with Variables*.

The five parameters in `DBFIND` define which database to search, which records to retrieve, and which search results to place in `mydata`. Like all HTML/OS tags, parameters are separated from each other with a comma. Parameters can be literal text, expressions, other tags, or variables. The first parameter of `DBFIND` is the name of the database. The second parameter contains the search criterion, also known as the Boolean query. If the Boolean query is empty, it means you want to extract records from the entire database. If that parameter contains a value like `contact_name ~ "J"`, `DBFIND` extracts only those records in the database with contact names beginning with the letter "J". Boolean queries are discussed in greater detail in Chapter 12, *Boolean Queries*.

The third, fourth, and fifth parameters tell `DBFIND` which records to put into `mydata`. The third and fourth parameters tell `DBFIND` to fill `mydata` with the first up to the tenth search result. If it finds less than ten results, it places only what it finds in `mydata`. If `DBFIND` finds no results, it sets `mydata` to an empty string—a one-row-by-one-column cell that's empty. If it finds more than ten records, it puts only the first ten items it finds into `mydata`. The last parameter is a list of field names. It tells DBFIND what to put in each column of `mydata`. The columns of `mydata` are filled from left to right in the same order as the fields you specified in the parameter. DBFIND is discussed in further detail in Chapter 14, *Building a Database Search Page*. It is also defined in Appendix C, *Major HTML/OS Tags*.

5. After running the DBFIND tag, HTML/OS runs the LAYOUT tag. The tag is used to reorganize `mydata`, so when the results display on the screen, the HTML you see is ordered the way you want. This formatting is needed, because displaying the contents of `mydata` on the screen produces an ugly presentation. The LAYOUT tag is described after Step 7, which is the last step taken when this Web page runs.

6. The line DISPLAY `mynewdata` /DISPLAY runs, placing the contents of `mynewdata`, the table of search results, into the Web page.

7. The Web page generated by HTML/OS is transferred to the user's computer and displayed with a browser.

***Understanding HTML/OS Variables**—HTML/OS variables are two-dimensional. Most of the time, variables have one column and row; they never have less. You may want to think of HTML/OS variables as mini-spreadsheets with a minimum size of one column by one row. For example, the instruction* `myvariable = 5` *creates the variable* `myvariable` *with one column and one row containing the value 5. When HTML/OS variables are only one column by one row, you don't think much about their two-dimensionality. You work with them without regard to their ability to have more rows or columns; but when you need tables of well-organized values, HTML/OS' two-dimensionality becomes indispensable. Searching databases is a prime example. (For a more comprehensive discussion of databases, see Chapter 11,* What Is a Web Database.*) A database search typically yields multiple records, and each record has multiple fields. Because HTML/OS variables are two-dimensional, you can place the results of a search in a single variable. Field values are placed in different columns of a single row. The variable is filled, one record per row. As another example, suppose you want to work with a comma-delimited file containing login names and passwords. (A more comprehensive discussion of delimited text files is provided in Chapter 6,* Working with Variables.*) You can load the delimited file into the cells of a variable with a single* COPY *tag. Or suppose you want to add up the values in a column of a variable; again, only a single tag is needed. HTML/OS variables are discussed in further detail in Chapter 5.*

Using the *LAYOUT* Tag

When HTML/OS displays multicell variables, it displays each cell, one after the other, left to right, top to bottom, with nothing between each cell. Suppose `mydata` contained the following data:

John	Smith	212-555-1212
Janet	Jones	310-555-1212
Jack	Chen	415-555-1212

The code `DISPLAY mydata /DISPLAY` would generate the following text in your HTML document:

```
JohnSmith212-555-1212JanetJones310-555-1212JackChen415-555-1212
```

This is not acceptable. You want your search results to appear as they do in Figure 4.2. The HTML code for such a search result looks as follows:

```
John Smith - 212-555-1212<br>Janet Jones - 310-555-1212<br>Jack
Chen - 415-555-1212<br>.
```

Working backwards, since you know that HTML/OS displays data in cells of a variable left to right and top to bottom, displaying the following six-column variable produces a page like that shown in Figure 4.2.

John	-	Smith	-	212-555-1212	\
Janet	-	Jones	-	310-555-1212	\
Jack	-	Chen	-	415-555-1212	\

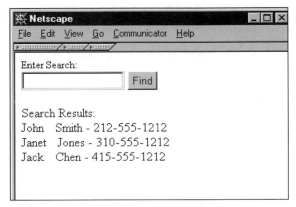

Figure 4.2: Your Web database program with search results will look like this.

To create this variable from `mydata`, use the `LAYOUT` tag, which is designed to take a variable with many columns and rows and produce a new variable with just as many rows but with columns filled in according to the parameters you specify in the tag. In this case, you want to build a six-column variable called `mynewdata` from `mydata`. The first, third, and fifth columns in `mynewdata` come from `mydata`. The second, fourth, and sixth columns in `mynewdata` are filled with a space, a dash and a `<BR>` respectively. The instruction `mynewdata=LAYOUT(mydata,[1]," ",[2]," - ",[3],"<BR>")` is what you need.

The `LAYOUT` tag works as follows: Its first parameter is the input variable. All other parameters specify what to place in each column of its output. The `LAYOUT` tag works from left to right, creating columns in an output variable as it reads its own parameters. It starts with its second parameter and moves right until there are no more parameters. If a parameter contains quoted text, the entire column in the output variable is filled with the text. If the parameter is a column number in square brackets, the column in the output is copied from the specified column of the input variable.

In your example, the first parameter of `LAYOUT` is `mydata`, the three-column variable containing the result of your search. The remaining parameters define what you want to appear in each of the six columns of `mynewdata`. Note how you are using two kinds of parameters. To specify a column from the starting variable, you include the column number in square brackets. On the other hand, to fill a column with text, you specify the value explicitly.

Reformatting Your Report

The code in the "Adding the Overlays" section in this chapter produces a report with fields separated by dashes. (Refer to Figure 4.2.) You will more likely want to format your search result in columns using an HTML table. You may want to add column headers too. To accomplish this, you should change the parameters in `LAYOUT` so the tag displays multiple HTML table rows, each beginning with a `<tr><td>` and ending with a `</td></tr>`. You need to place the tags, `<table>` and `</table>` around the rows as well to delineate them. Rewrite your page as follows:

```
<html>
<form method=post ACTION=<<page>> >
<font size=2>Enter Search:</font><br>
<input type=text name=mysearch size=15>
<input type=submit value="Find">
</form>
Search Results:
<< IF mysearch="ERROR" THEN
DISPLAY "Please enter search above." /DISPLAY
ELSE
sstr = 'contact_name ~ ' + '"' + mysearch + '"'
```

```
mydata = DBFIND("/mycontacts",sstr,1,20,
"contact_company,contact_name,contact_phone,contact_email")
DISPLAY
"<table border=1>" +
"<tr><td>Company</td><td>Name</td><td>Phone</td></tr>"
/DISPLAY
mynewdata = LAYOUT(mydata,
"<tr><td>", [1],
"</td><td>", [2],
"</td><td>", [3],
"</td></tr>")
DISPLAY mynewdata /DISPLAY
DISPLAY "</table>" /DISPLAY
/IF
>>
</html>
```

This code displays a report in table format as shown in Figure 4.3. You can experiment with the parameters in LAYOUT to vary the look of your report. Alternatively, you can control your display by using FOR loops, which are discussed in Chapter 6, *Working with Variables*.

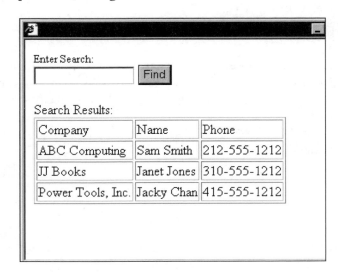

Figure 4.3: Your Web database program looks like this with nicely formatted search results.

Summary

In this chapter, you created your first Web database program. Unlike the previous chapter where you learned the Hello World program, here you set up and accessed a database, worked with two-dimensional data and did some programming. Unfortunately, you did this without any fundamental understanding or description of how HTML/OS works.

In the next two chapters, you return to the basics. You learn more about variables, how to place Overlays in documents, and how to use the most important Overlay tags. The next two chapters serve as a solid foundation for those chapters that follow them dedicated to specific areas of advanced Web development.

Exercises

The following exercises give you a feel for working with the LAYOUT tag. The last exercise builds on what you learned in the previous chapter regarding select boxes and the ability to use them to vary the value in a variable. Answers to all exercises are provided on this book's companion Web site as described in the book's Preface.

Exercise 1

Extend your report so it displays `contact_email`. You need to modify the LAYOUT tag to accomplish this.

Exercise 2

Add a select box to the HTML form that gives the user the ability to select a page size of 20, 40, or 100. Hint: Set the variable name of the select box to `page_size` and substitute the 20 in DBFIND with the variable.

PART II

Programming Basics

CHAPTER 5

Underlays, Inlays, and On-Click Overlays

In this chapter, you learn the fundamentals of placing HTML/OS Overlays in ordinary HTML documents. The title of this chapter refers to the three kinds of Overlays you can use. You start by learning how Overlays are written. Then you will learn the different ways you can place them in documents and when to use each kind of Overlay.

The end of this chapter discusses the Web-centric perspective—the perspective Web developers should take when building advanced Web sites and Web-based applications.

The HTML Document

The HTML document is the center and foundation of Web-based computing. Text, images, sound, video, data stored on the Web server (in files and databases), as well as JavaScript, Java applets, and links to other HTML documents are controlled by the HTML document. In essence, the HTML document is the "control" document of the Web pages. In fact, one could say HTML documents, at least those run in browsers, are the Web.

Static Web sites are built from pure HTML documents. These HTML documents are limited in that they have no connection to data and files stored on the server, because HTML documents are run on the browser, not the server. Static Web sites do little more than store documents prepared in advance and pass them to users who request them. On static Web sites, the HTML document stored on the server is the same document that is delivered to the user's browser.

By contrast, dynamic Web sites have the ability to deliver on-the-fly HTML documents to browsers. Although they must still deliver pure HTML documents to users, the documents stored on the server can contain instructions that reference data and files on the server. In HTML/OS, the instructions you place in HTML documents are called Overlays.

What Is an Overlay?

Overlays are special instructions that are actually program segments. Specifically, an Overlay is a set of << and >> brackets around programming code. Overlays can contain calculations, instructions, and Overlay tags. They may contain only a single variable, an instruction, or hundreds of instructions.

An *Overlay tag* is a programming function or word used to perform a specific task. For example, the Overlay `<<mynumber=RANDOM(10)>>` contains the Overlay tag RANDOM. The tag selects a random number between one and ten and places it in the variable `mynumber`. Overlay tags are also referred to as *Otags, HTML/OS Tags,* or *Reserved Words.*

There are two kinds of Overlays. Some Overlays contain one or more instructions, and some Overlays contain a single calculation.

Overlays Containing One or More Instructions

The following Overlays are examples of Overlays containing one or more instructions:

`<<DISPLAY A /DISPLAY>>`	Prints the contents of A.
`<<DISPLAY A + B /DISPLAY>>`	Prints the result of A + B.
`<<A="<font color=red>" B=6 C=7>>`	Assigns values to A, B, and C.
`<<IF A > 5 THEN B=6 /IF C=7>>`	Executes a conditional and sets a value for C.

An Overlay can contain as many instructions as you want. You separate instructions from each other with one or more spaces or a new line. Like HTML, HTML/OS ignores multiple spaces and new lines, and it isn't *case-sensitive,* meaning that it doesn't matter whether you write a tag in upper case, lower case, or a mix of the two. For instance, the following three instructions are the same:

```
1. <<DISPLAY A /DISPLAY>>
2. <<DiSpLay      a        /DiSpLaY >>
3. <<
   display
   A
   /display
   >>
```

Overlays Containing a Single Calculation

The following Overlays are examples of Overlays containing a single calculation:

`<<A>>`   Prints the contents of a variable labeled `A`.

`<<A + B>>`   Prints the result of `A + B`.

`<<TODAY>>`   Prints today's date.

An Overlay with a single calculation is a shorthand way of displaying the results of the same calculation using a `DISPLAY` instruction. For example, the three previous Overlays can also be written as follows:

```
<<DISPLAY A /DISPLAY>>

<<DISPLAY A + B /DISPLAY>>

<<DISPLAY TODAY /DISPLAY>>
```

Positioning Overlays in a Document

For a browser to be able to read an HTML document, the document should begin with an `<html>` tag and end with an `</html>` tag. The documents stored on the server, however, do not need to begin with a `<html>` and end with a `</html>`. They can begin or end with Overlays. In HTML/OS, the portion of the document sitting between the `<html>` and `</html>` tags is the display portion of the document. Outside of this area, nothing can be displayed, but instructions can be executed. For example, when a Web page is requested, instructions above the `<html>` tag can direct the user to another Web page if the user has not logged in. In general, you can place Overlays above, inside, and below the display portion of the document. You'll see how this works in a moment.

When a user requests a Web page, HTML/OS reads the page from top to bottom. If the first thing it finds in a Web page is an Overlay (even before it encounters the `<html>` tag), it runs the Overlay. This kind of Overlay is known as an Underlay. *Underlays* can contain any number of instructions and any of the Overlay tags in the HTML/OS arsenal, with the exception of those tags that change the content of the page. Instructions, such as `DISPLAY a /DISPLAY` are not allowed, because Underlays are not in the display portion of the page.

Overlays you place between the `<html>` and `</html>` tags are called *Inlays*, because you place them in the display portion of the Web page. The Overlays you used in Chapters 2, *Logging into Your Copy of HTML/OS*, and 3, *Your First Program*, were all Inlays.

Because you place these Inlays in the display portion of the page, you can use them to change the document on the fly. Like Underlays, they too can run most of the Overlay tags in the HTML/OS arsenal. However, although Inlays can run tags like DISPLAY, they can't run the GOTO tag, because HTML documents are contiguous—a fancy way of saying they must remain whole. Once within the display portion of a page, it makes no sense to tell HTML/OS to stop rendering the page and begin rendering some other page.

The third and last kind of Overlay is called the on-click Overlay. You place *on-click Overlay*s below the `</html>` tag. They are different from Underlays and Inlays, because on-click Overlays are not executed as HTML/OS reads a document from top to bottom. On-click Overlays run in response to a user clicking a hypertext link or a Submit button—hence the name on-click Overlay. You also write them differently. On-click Overlays have names since they need to be specified. Hypertext links and HTML forms that call the on-click Overlays specify which on-click Overlay to run. For example, the hypertext link `<A HREF=dostuff>Do Some Stuff</a>` calls the on-click Overlay `dostuff` when it is clicked. The on-click Overlay placed below the `</html>` tag in the document, begins with the word Overlay, followed by the word `dostuff`, the name of the on-click Overlay.

An example page with all three kinds of Overlays follows this paragraph. The Overlay at the top of the Web page is an Underlay. It contains four instructions. The last of the four instructions contains a GOTO tag. The instruction tells HTML/OS to stop reading the page and read `home.html` instead (in the event `tryno` is larger than `max_tries`). This use of the GOTO tag is appropriate since page rendering has not yet begun. The second Overlay displays the value of the variable `tryno`. It's an Inlay. It changes the document on the fly, printing `tryno` where it's placed.

Just below the display portion of the page is an on-click Overlay called `test_password`. It runs when a user clicks **Go**, which is the Submit button defined in the HTML form on the page, because the ACTION parameter in the HTML form references `test_password`. Examine the following code to pick out the various Overlays:

```
<< max_tries = 5
   mypass = ""
   IF tryno="ERROR" THEN tryno=1 /IF
   IF tryno > max_tries THEN GOTO "home.html" /IF
>>
<html>
```

```
Try number <<tryno>><br>
Enter Password:
<form method=post ACTION=test_password>
<input type=password name=mypass size=10>
<input type=submit value="Go">
</form>
</html>
<<OVERLAY test_password
  IF mypass="LetMeIn" THEN
    GOTO "private.html"
  ELSE
    tryno = tryno + 1
    GOTO PAGE
  /IF
>>
```

The on-click Overlay here was referenced from an HTML form. As an example of referencing an on-click Overlay in a hypertext link, suppose you added the following hypertext link to the document:

```
<A HREF=test_password name=tryno value=0>Clear Counter</a>
```

The link, when clicked, sets the value of `tryno` to `0` and runs the on-click Overlay `test_password`. If you add this hyperlink to the previous document, the instruction `tryno = tryno + 1` would run (since `mypass` would not be equal to `LetMeIn`. When the page redisplays, it would print *Try number 1* on the page.

Overlay-HTML Rules

Adding what you just learned about the three types of HTML/OS Overlays to a basic understanding of HTML tags and how to write the instructions and use variables gives you everything you need to build advanced Web sites. The combination of HTML and Overlays gives you a complete development environment. When mixing Overlays with HTML also keep in mind the following rules:

Overlays *can* display HTML. For example, consider this hypertext link:

```
<A HREF=done.html name=abc value=0>Reset Me</a>
```

Its effect is the same as that of the following:

```
<<DISPLAY "<A HREF=done.html name=abc value=0>Reset Me</a>"
/DISPLAY>>
```

HTML tags *can* contain Overlays. For example, you can write the following:

```
<A HREF=<<PAGE>>>Redisplay</a>
```

The Overlay tag PAGE is a predefined tag that contains the name of the current document. Clicking this link directs the user to the current page.

Overlays can *not* contain other Overlays. For example, you can't write the following:

```
<< a = a + <<b>> >>
```

Instead, you would write

```
<<a = a + b>>.
```

Overlay names can *not* contain a dot. For example, you can write the following:

```
<<OVERLAY myprocessing
    instructions here
>>
```

You can't reference the same Overlay if it were written as follows:

```
<<OVERLAY myprocessing.data
    instructions here
>>
```

Overlay tags are *optional*. An HTML document does not need to contain Overlays. It can be a standard HTML document, created with any HTML editor, with no programming in it. For example, the following page is valid:

```
<HTML>
Hello World
</HTML>
```

HTML tags are *optional*. An HTML document does not need to contain any HTML either. It can be a single Underlay. For example, the following page is also valid:

```
<< myvariable = "Hello World"
   GOTO "home.html"
>>
```

These last two rules, that Overlays and HTML tags are both optional, mean that documents can be either pure HTML documents or pure programming. This duality is an essential component of the Web perspective, which is discussed in the following section.

The Web-Centric Perspective

The Web is a fusion of three worlds: the publishing world, the programming world, and the database world. HTML/OS carries this fusion to its logical conclusion, allowing the publishing (HTML) world, the programming world, and the database world to become one. In this chapter, you've seen how the first two worlds merge. Later, in Chapter 11, *The Web Database*, you see how the database world is also "one" with the HTML document.

Recall that when using HTML/OS, the fundamental programming document is the HTML document—as stored on the server. The document can be all programming, all HTML, or a combination of the two.

***Web-Based Computing Demands HTML Centrism**—Whereas the center of the PC world is CPUs—hardware such as video cards, and operating systems such as Linux, Windows, and MacOS—the center of the Web computing world is the HTML document—a simple document that doesn't care about the CPU you use, the kind of video card you have, or the operating system your PC uses. Unfortunately, companies often apply PC programming techniques to the Web-programming world. Whether due to habit or special interest, the techniques direct you away from the HTML document and lead you in the direction of hyper complexity.*

If you're a programmer, the Web-centric view demands that the notion of an external API (Application Program Interface) be dropped, because API's are defined to work with hardware and computer screens, not the Web. The HTML document is your API. You can place most of your programming directly in these documents. Does this mean there's no room for old-style programming? Not at all. If necessary, you can drop compiled modules into HTML/OS as system extensions. (This topic is not discussed in this book. It's reserved for C and C++ programmers.) You're also free to use function libraries. (See the knowledge base on the **Aestiva** Web site at http://www.aestiva.com/support/.) But these are side issues. The HTML document is now your primary source document.

Summary

In this chapter, you learned how to place Overlays in documents. You learned they can be in the display portion of the document (Inlays), above the `<html>` tag (Underlays), or—when they're activated in response to a user clicking a button in an HTML form or a hypertext link—below the `</html>` tag (on-click Overlays). You've seen that Overlays allow you to think of HTML documents as pure HTML, pure programming, or a fusion of the two.

This chapter did not discuss how you write specific instructions, how you handle variables, or how you write the more common Overlay tags. Those topics are discussed in depth in the next chapter, *Variables, Conditionals, and Loops*.

Exercises

The two following exercises are designed to get you used to using Overlays to build highly dynamic Web pages. Answers to all exercises are provided on this book's companion Web site as described in the book's Preface.

Exercise 1

Create a simple calculator using an HTML form with two input boxes and a select box containing the options Add, Subtract, Multiply, and Divide. Link the form to an on-click Overlay on the bottom of the page. Calculate the result and return to the same page to display the result. You will only need an IF-THEN statement.

Exercise 2

Create a guess-my-number game. Have the user click a link to start the game. The link should go to an on-click Overlay that sets a variable between one and ten. Place an HTML form on the page. When the user submits the form, see whether the number matches the game selection. If it does, display a message saying the user won. If not, display a message asking the user to try again. You will need to use a RANDOM tag and IF-THEN statements. You will need two on-click Overlays; one to run instructions when users click a Begin Game link and one for running instructions when the users click the Submit button in the HTML form, after entering their guess.

CHAPTER 6

Variables, Conditionals, and Loops

Variables are the life-blood of applications. You use them in tags, calculations, and most everything you do. The HTML/OS development environment uses variables to carry data between HTML forms, Overlay tags, calculations, fields in databases, and files. The same variable environment is used throughout. In this chapter, we review the rules, requirements, limitations, and conventions used when working with HTML/OS variables. We also discuss how to use IF-THEN conditional statements and FOR loops, how to work with two-dimensional data, how to load comma-delimited text files into variables, and how to work with variables in HTML forms.

The information you learn in this chapter is used throughout this book, because advanced Web development is mostly about moving data between variables, files, and HTML documents. Along with the fundamentals discussed in Chapter 5, *Overlays, Inlays, and On-Click Overlays*, these two chapters give you most of the foundation you need. The only major area missing from this discussion is the topic of databases, which is discussed in Part III, *Database Programming*.

If you're comfortable with BASIC programming, feel free to skip over the sections that appear trivial. But take a look at the sections on FOR loops, because they introduce you to a new kind of FOR loop used in HTML/OS with which you may not be familiar. Also it is important that you look at how HTML/OS works with HTML forms. You'll also see code examples that introduce you to some of the more popular Overlay tags used in HTML/OS. You may want to take note of them.

Regardless of your familiarity with BASIC programming, you will want to be online as you go through this chapter so you can try the code examples provided.

Variable Names

Starting with how to write a variable name, you need to adhere to the following rules:

- Variable names are *case-in*sensitive.

- Variable names can *not* begin with a number.
- Variable names can contain only letters, numbers, a dot (period), and an underscore. Other characters, including spaces, are *not* allowed.
- Variable names can *not* be the same as the name of a tag or function.

The following list includes examples of valid variable names:

- `data14`
- `cart_price`
- `myfolder`
- `acct.name.first`

The last variable example in the list, `acct.name.first`, shows a variable containing dots. Note that dots in variable names are treated like other characters. Object-oriented languages, such as JavaScript, Java, and C++ use the dot as a special character. HTML/OS is a functional language similar to those found in spreadsheet macros. The dot has no special meaning.

The following list contains examples of *in*valid variable names:

- `14data`*
- `cart-price`
- `my folder`
- `acct$name$first`

The first example in the previous list, `14data`, is invalid, because it begins with a number. The second, `cart-price`, is invalid, because it includes a hyphen (which, when interpreted by HTML/OS, means subtract `price` from `cart`). The third, `my folder`, contains a space, which is not allowed. The last, `acct$name$first`, contains dollar signs, which are special characters and are not allowed.

When naming variables, it is best to use words with meaning. It makes your programming more readable. Also, it's a good idea to prefix your names with the name of your application and an underscore. This ensures your variables don't conflict with Overlay tags, because Overlay tags don't contain underscore characters. As an example, when building a shopping-cart application, use variable names like `shop_cart`, `shop_taxrate`, `shop_shippingrate`, and so on.

Default Value of Variables

The default value of variables in HTML/OS is ERROR. To be more specific, the default value of all variables is a one-cell table with the word ERROR stored in it. For example, suppose you added the following Overlay to your Web page:

```
<< DISPLAY my_error_message /DISPLAY>>
```

If you previously set a value for the variable `my_error_message`, it would display on the page where the Overlay was positioned. If you did not previously set a value for the variable, the word ERROR would display on the page.

Since you don't want ERROR to appear on Web pages, you should place the instruction inside an IF-THEN conditional, as follows:

```
<<
IF my_error_message!="ERROR" THEN
DISPLAY my_error_message /DISPLAY
/IF
my_error_message="ERROR"
>>
```

Two-Dimensionality

When using HTML/OS, it is important to remember that variables are two-dimensional. In other words, all variables contain one or more cells organized in columns and rows. The simplest of all variables, the empty string, has one row and one column with nothing in it. The instruction `abc=""` sets a variable to an empty string.

A variable can never have less than one row or less than one column. The two-dimensionality of variables does not change the way you perform simple calculations; but it gives you powerful capabilities that come in handy when working with databases and delimited text files and when performing operations on large sets of information. Figure 6.1 shows an assortment of variables.

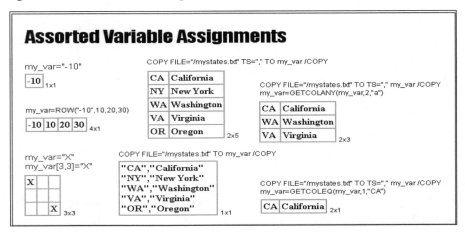

Figure 6.1: The size of **my_var** varies depending on what you place in it.

Specifying Variables

When working with variables, you may specify the entire variable or only a specific cell. To specify the entire variable, write the name of the variable. To specify a specific cell, follow the variable name with the column and row number in square brackets.

For example, `cart_products` refers to all the cells in the variable `cart_products`; whereas `cart_products[1,3]` refers to the first cell in the third row of `cart_products`. Note also that you don't need to specify both the column and the row. You may specify only the column number. When you do not specify the row, the row number equals 1. For example, `cart_products[3]` and `cart_products[3,1]` both refer to the cell in the third column of the first row of `cart_products`.

The Math Convention

When using HTML/OS, you specify cell positions by column and row, not by row and column. Also, the first cell in a variable is at position 1,1, not at position 0,0. This is called the *math convention*. It's intuitive, unless you were trained as a computer programmer. Many computer languages define the upper-left column and row number of a table as position 0,0 and most often, they require that you specify the row number ahead of the column number. If you are familiar with programming languages, you will want to remember that HTML/OS uses the conventions from mathematics, not computer science.

Variable Assignment

The following list contains example valid variable value assignments:

- `my_var = "-10"`
- `my_var = ROW("-10","10","20","30")`
- `my_variable [3] = "-10"`
- `my_var[3,4]  =  "-10"`

The first example, `my_var = "-10"`, creates a new variable with one column and one row containing a negative 10. Any data previously stored in `my_var` is lost.

The second example, `my_var = ROW("-10","10","20","30")`, creates a variable four columns wide and one row in height containing the specified cells. As in the first example, any data previously stored in `my_var` is lost. The example uses the tag ROW to build the one-row variable. For additional information on ROW, see Appendix D, *HTML/OS Tag Reference Guide*.

The third example places a negative 10 in the cell at column 3, row 1 of `my_var`. Values in other cells are preserved.

The fourth example places a negative 10 in the cell at column 3, row 4. Values in other cells are preserved.

In the last two examples, if my_var were less than three columns wide, my_var would be automatically expanded to have more rows and columns. Other cells would have been left unchanged. Although the default value of a variable is a one-column, one-row cell containing the word ERROR—when expanding the size of a variable, undefined cells are left empty. For example, if you were to run the two instructions my_var="X" and my_var[3,3]="X", the cells in my_var at locations other than 1,1 and 3,3 would be empty.

Data Types

Each cell of a variable can store numbers, fractions, dates, times, logical values (TRUE or FALSE), small pieces of text, or large pieces of text (such as a text file). You don't need to write tags telling HTML/OS how many rows or columns you need in a variable. And you don't need to declare the type of data you put in each cell or how much data you expect to put in a cell. This feature is known as *auto-data-typing*. For example, suppose you want to create a variable called stooges containing three columns and one row with the cells containing the names Larry, Moe, and Curly. You would write it as follows:

```
stooges=ROW("Larry","Moe","Curly")
```

Or suppose you have a text file called mydoc.txt containing 10,000 characters that you wish to load into the variable mytext. You would write the following code:

```
COPY FILE="mydoc.txt" TO mytext /COPY
```

As you see, to create or use a variable, you simply use it.

Using Different Kinds of Variables

Although variables are auto-data-typed, you must still write them according to predefined conventions, and they must have values within predefined limits. A summary of those limits and conventions is shown in the following sections.

Text

You are free to write text almost any way you want. Text stored in a variable can be 0 to 100,000 characters long. It can contain non-English (eight-bit) characters. It can contain special characters such as tabs, linefeeds, and carriage returns, and it can contain HTML codes, programming tags, e-mail messages, XML code, and complete or partial text documents.

Integers

Integers are whole numbers—positive or negative—up to 11 characters in length. When storing integers in a variable, do not place special characters (such as $) or commas in them. If you wish to reformat the number, do so when you display it. For example, consider the following statement:

```
price = "50000"
price_with_tax = price * (1.0825)
DISPLAY FORMAT(price_with_tax,"comma",2) /DISPLAY
```

The price is stored properly. Formatting is applied when the variable is displayed. The example uses the FORMAT tag. In this case, the tag reformats the number with two decimal places, placing commas in it if needed. For additional information on FORMAT, see Appendix D, *HTML/OS Tag Reference Guide.*

Other Limits—*When working with variables keep in mind the following facts about variables:*

- *HTML/OS variables may have up to 1000 columns and up to 100,000 rows.*
- *Unless otherwise specified, text searches, tags and comparisons are case-insensitive. The one exception is when specifying files because Unix and Linux and MacOS X systems are case-sensitive.*

Fractions

Fractions are numbers—positive or negative—with one or more decimal places. When writing fractions, make sure the total number size, including the decimal point, is less than eleven characters in length. As with integers, do not store commas or special characters in your fraction.

Logicals

A *logical* is simply the word TRUE or FALSE (case-insensitive). Some instructions, such as IF-THEN statements, use these words to perform conditional operations. Other instructions produce these words. For example, the tag ISFILE returns a TRUE or a FALSE depending on whether it finds a specified file. Consider the following instructions:

```
myimage="someimage.gif"
IF ISFILE(myimage)="TRUE" THEN
  DISPLAY "<img src=" + myimage + ">" /DISPLAY
ELSE
  DISPLAY "<img src=default.gif>" /DISPLAY
/IF
```

The IF-THEN conditional runs what's within the THEN and the ELSE if the test between the IF and the THEN is true. If it is not true, it runs the instructions between the ELSE and the /IF. Note that the test placed between the IF and the THEN could also be written as follows:

```
<< myimage="someimage.gif"
    IF ISFILE(myimage) THEN
       DISPLAY
          "<img src=" + myimage + ">"
       /DISPLAY
    ELSE
       DISPLAY
          "<img src=default.gif>"
       /DISPLAY
    /IF
>>
```

Here the test is simply a calculation that returns the value TRUE or FALSE. You can write IF-THEN tests both ways. Read more about Conditions in the accompanying "The Conditional" note.

The Conditional—Like standard IF-THEN *conditionals, HTML/OS* IF-THEN *statements run instructions based on a test appearing between the* IF *and the* THEN. *The tests can be calculations that calculate to* TRUE *or* FALSE, *or they can be tests that compare calculations to other calculations. The following comparisons operators can be used:*

=	*Equal*	<	*Less than*	
!=	*Not equal (Same as <> operator)*	<=	*Less than or equal*	
>	*Greater than*	~	*Begins with*	
>=	*Greater than or equal*	~~	*Contains*	

You can combine multiple tests together in a Boolean test to build more complex tests. For example, consider the following IF-THEN *statement:*

```
IF (balance > 0 AND user_level >= 3) OR super_user="YES"
THEN
     Your Instructions
/IF
```

It performs Your Instructions *conditionally—if* super_user *is equal to* YES *or if the user's* balance *is positive and have a* user_level *of* 3 *or above. When combining tests, use the words* AND, OR, *or* NOT, *placing parentheses around each test.*

Dates and Times

You must write dates and times in a specific format or they will not be interpreted correctly. In general, they are written as: MM/DD/YYYY HH:MM. The MM stands for a two-digit month. DD stands for a two-digit day. YYYY stands for a four-digit year. If the time HH:MM is dropped, midnight (00:00) is assumed. If the day MM/DD/YYYY is dropped, 01/01/2000 is assumed. This date format is the only date format used in HTML/OS. Use it when working with cookies and databases, and when performing date and time calculations. Date calculations work on dates going back to 1970.

Overlay tags are available for displaying dates and times in multiple formats; but when stored they should be in the format HTML/OS uses. For example, consider the following Overlay:

```
<< expire_date = ADDDAYS(TODAY,5)
   DISPLAY
     "Your demo will expire " + GETDATE(expire_date,"long")
   /DISPLAY
>>
```

The expiration date is stored properly; but formatting is applied when you display the variable. The GETDATE tag used here formats the number in a *long* format, meaning that a date, such as 05/01/2002, would display as May 1, 2002.

Y2K Convention—*A Year 2000 convention in HTML/OS helps with two-digit year ambiguities. When specifying a two-digit year less than 20, the current millennium is assumed. When greater than 20, the millennium beginning with 1900 is assumed. Note that this Y2K convention will be changed in future releases of the product to enable use of 2-digit years for dates after 2020. If you are referencing dates in the distant past or distant future it is best to use 4-digit dates.*

Global Variables

Variables in HTML/OS carry their values from Web page to Web page. For example, if you write the instruction myname="Yoshi" on one Web page, five Web pages later, myname will still be equal to Yoshi. On the Web, this is called state-persistence. In off-the-Web environments, this is called a global variable environment. Whatever you call it, variables in HTML/OS automatically save from page to page.

The exception to this rule is the case of *local variables*, which are variables that you can define inside functions. Local variables persist while inside the function, but disappear outside of it. Local variables give programmers the ability to build advanced algorithms. This topic is beyond the scope of this book; but it is useful to know local variables are available to you if you need them. For information on setting local variables in functions see the knowledge base on the **Aestiva** Web site at http://www.aestiva.com/support/.

Clearing Variables

To clear a variable, set it to ERROR. Clearing variables is useful if you are concerned about the total size of your variable environment. Since variables pass from page to page, they are saved on the Web server as users leave and return to the site. The larger the variable environment you use and the more users you have visiting your site, the more hard disk space you need. It is a good idea to clear variables larger than 50,000 bytes if you do not need them. If you clear a variable before the end of a page, HTML/OS won't store it.

State Persistence across the Network

Variables in HTML/OS save from page to page, even as page control moves across a network. For example, suppose you write the instruction myname="Yoshi", and the user moves from one copy of HTML/OS to another, which is known as *server jumping*. Then myname will still be equal to Yoshi. Server-jumping and other topics relating to Web-networking are discussed in Chapter 15, *Database Networking* and Chapter 16, *Distributed Systems.*

Using Variables in Calculations

Calculations in HTML/OS can use operators to perform mathematical calculations. Operators include the four main math operators, plus (+), minus (-), multiply (*), and divide (/) and dozens of predefined Overlay tags for performing math, logical, and geometric calculations. These tags are listed in Appendix D, *HTML/OS Tag Reference Guide*. Here are some examples of calculations:

- c=SQRT(SQUARE(a)+SQUARE(b))
- a=c*SIN(myangle)
- cart_subtotal=SUMCOL(cart_products,"4")

In the first two examples perform mathematical calculations. The first is the calculation of the length of a diagonal of a triangle using the Pythagorean theorem. The second is a trigonometric calculation using the sine function. In the third example, the tag SUMCOL sums the cells in column 4 of the variable cart_products. This is how, for example, you would sum the price of products in a shopping cart.

Variables, Literals, and Parameters

As you write your Overlays, sometimes you want to pass data you type into an instruction. At other times, you wish to reference data stored in a variable. This data may be used as a setting to an Overlay tag or it may be used in a calculation. Here we review how to specify data. You learn what variables, literals, and parameters are. Consider the following instruction:

```
shipping_cost = SUMCOL(cart_products,"4")
```

The tag SUMCOL has two parameters. The first is a variable. The second is a value, known as a literal. It is in quotes. When writing tags, it is important to know how to differentiate between literal values and variables, and how to place them in tags. The following rules apply:

- Literal values should always be surrounded with single or double quotes except when the value is a positive integer, in which case quotes are optional.

- A literal value containing a single quote must be quoted with two double quotes. A literal value containing a double quote must be quoted with single quotes. A literal value containing both must be broken up into smaller sets of letters and pasted together. Here are some examples:

Literal	**Value stored in myvar**
`myvar="Can't You See?"`	`Can't You See?`
`myvar="-100"`	`-100 (negative one-hundred)`
`myvar='He said,` `"' + "Can't you See?"`	`He said, "Can't You See?"`

- Variables cannot be surrounded with quotes, or else they'll look like literals.

- Parameters of Overlay tags can be variables, literals, or complete calculations. Each must be separated from the next with a comma. The ability to replace a parameter with a calculation, which itself may contain other Overlay tags with parameters, is called *nesting*. Overlay tags are nestable. For example, you use the tag REPLACEALL to perform a search and replace on a variable. It has three parameters; the first is the name of the variable being searched, the second is what you are searching for, and the last is what you replace it with. To eliminate < characters from a variable and replace them with < characters (the HTML code for a less than sign), you write the following code:

```
myvar=REPLACEALL(myvar,"<","&lt;")
```

Now suppose you want to replace not only the less than sign, but also the greater than sign. You could write it as follows:

```
myvar=REPLACEALL(myvar,"<","&lt;")
myvar=REPLACEALL(myvar,">","&gt;")
```

Or, taking advantage of nesting, you could write the following:

```
myvar=REPLACEALL(REPLACEALL myvar,"<","&lt;"),">","&gt;")
```

Using Variables in HTML

HTML/OS variables are also called *names*. The nomenclature is borrowed from the use of the word *name* in HTML. For example, the HTML input tag can contain *name-value* pairs, as in the following example:

```
<input type=text name=country value="USA" size=15>
```

HTML/OS is an *integrated environment*, meaning the names in HTML forms and the variables in HTML/OS are related. HTML/OS variables fill values in HTML forms. Names in HTML forms, when submitted to the server, fill HTML/OS variables. It's automatic. Suppose, for example, an HTML form, like the following one, is stored on the Web server:

```
<html>
<< IF firstname="ERROR" THEN
      firstname="John"
      Lastname="Smith"
      Gender="M"
   /IF
>>
<form ACTION=<<page>>>
First Name: <input type=text name=firstname size=15><br>
Last Name: <input type=text name=lastname size=15><br>
Gender: <select name=gender><option value="M">Male<option
value="F">Female</select>
</form>
</html>
```

Before the Web page runs, the variables have the default value ERROR, so when the page runs, they are set to initial values as specified in the IF-THEN statement at the top of the file. The HTML form takes on the values of those variables. When the HTML page is provided to the user, the values appear in the HTML form. The page transmitted to the browser contains the initial values even though you never needed to program them into your HTML form. Run the page and, using the options in your browser to view the HTML page as seen by the browser, click **View** and then, depending on your browser, **Source** or **Page Source**. Note how the *name-value* pairs appear in the HTML source. The page rendered by this code and its source are shown in Figure 6.2.

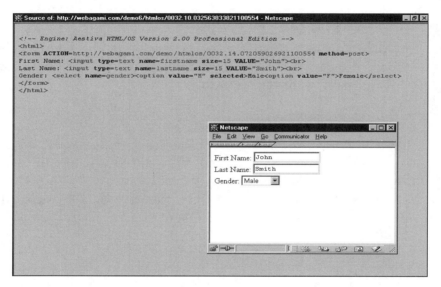

Figure 6.2: The View Source option of your browser allows you to view the HTML-only document rendered by HTML/OS.

The automatic filling of HTML form elements gives you the ability to integrate HTML forms into the applications you write. It also allows you to span HTML forms across multiple documents. For example, suppose you have a lengthy form that would be better off spread across multiple documents. Divide the form into multiple forms, placing each of the smaller forms on a single page. Then add Next and Previous hypertext links to the pages to give users the ability to navigate between the pages containing the forms. The automatic filling of HTML forms by HTML/OS ensures the forms still retain their information and behave like HTML forms placed on a single page.

It is a good habit to avoid setting values in HTML forms explicitly. If you need to place a value in an HTML form component, set the value prior to displaying the form. If you do specify a value in an HTML form, the HTML form will show the value as expected. But the HTML/OS variable will not change to the value specified in the HTML form until it is submitted. This topic is discussed in greater detail later in this book. See the "Further Reading" note.

***Further Reading**—The subject of HTML forms is such an important topic in the world of advanced Web sites that we dedicate an entire chapter to the subject. See Chapter 10,* HTML Forms Processing, *for an in-depth look at the world of HTML forms.*

Working with Delimited Text Files

Delimited text files are text files containing data organized in columns and rows. Most often, the files are exported from databases and spreadsheet programs. The character used to separate one cell from the next is called the *delimiter*. End-of-line characters are used to separate one row from the next. The following example is a delimited text file containing the state codes and names of five U.S. states.

```
"CA","California"
"NY","New York"
"WA","Washington"
"VA","Virginia"
"OR","Oregon"
```

As you see, the delimiter is a comma. The character surrounding each piece of data is called the *quoting character*. Here the quoting character is a double-quote. Almost all database programs and spreadsheets give you the ability to export your data to some kind of delimited text file. Most often, the delimiter is a comma or a tab character. Sometimes the cells of each row in the text file are surrounded with quote marks, sometimes not. To load a delimited text file into a variable use the following instruction. (We have assumed your delimited text file is called /mystates.txt.)

```
COPY FILE="/mystates.txt" TS="," TO mydata /COPY
```

This will load the five states in /mystates.txt into mydata, creating a two-column by five-row variable. The TS parameter (TS stands for Table Separation.) is a comma that tells HTML/OS the file is comma-delimited. (For more information, see "The TS Parameter" note in this section.)

If you do not set the TS parameter, the file will be loaded into mydata like any other text file. Remember to specify the TS parameter. Otherwise, the COPY tag will create a single-column by single-row variable containing the entire contents of the file.

You can also use the COPY tag to create delimited text files. For example, suppose you wish to load the comma-delimited file shown previously and then save it to a new tab-delimited file, with the same data. You could write the following two instructions:

```
COPY FILE="mystates.txt" TS="," TO mydata /COPY
COPY mydata TO FILE="mystates2.txt" TS=TAB /COPY
```

The first COPY instruction loads the comma-delimited text file into mydata. The second takes the variable and saves it to the new file mystates2.txt.

The TS Parameter—*The TS parameter can contain between one and three characters. It can contain the delimiter, the delimiter and a quoting character, or a delimiter, quoting character, and an "escape" character. Most often you need to define only a delimiter, as shown in the example used in this section. In special cases, you can add other characters. The nuances of dealing with special cases are beyond the scope of this book. For further information, access the Knowledge Base on the Aestiva Web site at* http://www.aestiva.com/support/.

Working with Loops

Anyone familiar with high-school BASIC is familiar with WHILE and FOR loops. The same kinds of loops work in HTML/OS too. WHILE loops allow you to repeat a set of instructions while a particular condition is TRUE. FOR loops repeat sets of instructions while a predefined variable (with one row and column) steps between two values.

When working with HTML/OS, you have the same loops; but you also have a FOR loop that repeats sets of instructions as you move across the different rows of a variable. This last kind of loop is the most popular loop that HTML/OS developers use.

In this section, we'll review standard WHILE and FOR loops but spend most of our time explaining the FOR loop which is used most often.

WHILE Loops

Suppose you want to write a set of instructions that copies files in a folder to a backup folder. You could use a WHILE loop that uses the following algorithm. First, you generate a list of files to be copied. Then, one at a time, you copy each to the backup folder. After each copy, you delete the file copied from a list of files that remain to be copied. You do this until no files are left. The instructions could be written as follows:

```
myfilelist = SYSLS("/folder1")
```

```
myfile_in = "/folder1/" + myfilelist[1]
myfile_out ="/folder2/" + myfilelist[1]
WHILE ISFILE(myfile_in) DO
  COPY FILE=myfile_in To FILE=myfile_out /COPY
  myfilelist=DELROW(myfilelist,1)
  myfile_in = "/folder1/" + myfilelist[1]
  myfile_out ="/folder2/" + myfilelist[1]
/WHILE
```

The first statement uses the Overlay tag SYSLS to place a list of filenames in /folder1 into myfilelist. SYSLS is a predefined tag in HTML/OS that creates a variable with multiple rows, one row for each file found in a specified folder. Filenames are placed in column one. For additional information on SYSLS, see Appendix D, *HTM/OS Tag Reference Guide*.

The next two instructions build filenames for input and output files respectively. The plus (+) sign pastes text together. The WHILE statement contains the test ISFILE(myfile_in) so it will run the instructions between the DO and the /WHILE as long as myfile_in contains the name of a file that exists.

In the WHILE loop, the COPY tag copies myfile_in to myfile_out. The tag DELROW removes the first line of myfilelist; then myfile_in and myfile_out are set again using the first row of myfilelist, and the loop is repeated. For additional information on COPY and DELROW, see Appendix D, *HTM/OS Tag Reference Guide*.

As you see, WHILE loops in HTML work identically to those used in other languages. The instructions between the DO and the /WHILE execute repeatedly, until such time that the test between the WHILE and the DO is no longer true—at which time, execution shifts to the next instruction following the WHILE tag.

FOR Loops

Another way to perform the operation shown in the previous code is to use a FOR loop. FOR loops, like you find in high-school BASIC, are not popular in HTML/OS. They are clunky for the programmer. You write them as follows:

```
FOR NAME=variable_name VALUE=begin_value TO end_value
STEP=step_value DO
  instructions here
/FOR
```

These old-style FOR loops require that you determine beginning and ending points of the loop, which is cumbersome and can lead to errors. We will not use them here. Although HTML/OS supports these old-style loops, the more popular FOR loop is written as follows:

```
FOR NAME=variable_name ROWNAME=row_name DO
  instructions here
/FOR
```

This style loop takes advantage of the two-dimensionality of HTML/OS variables. To perform a loop, you need to specify only the name of a variable (to loop across) and the name of a variable to fill with a slice of that variable, as you loop across it.

You do not need to calculate beginning or ending values, because the loop knows to run once for each row of your specified NAME. Each time the FOR loop loops, it places the next row of your specified NAME in the specified ROWNAME.

Once again, suppose you wish to write instructions to copy files in a folder to a backup folder. Using a FOR loop, you would write the following code:

```
myfilelist = SYSLS("/folder1")
FOR NAME=myfilelist ROWNAME=myfilerow DO
  myfile_in = "/folder1/" + myfilerow[1]
  myfile_out ="/folder2/" + myfilerow[1]
  COPY FILE=myfile_in To FILE=myfile_out /COPY
/FOR
```

This example uses SYSLS, once again, to create a two-dimensional variable called myfilelist. The FOR loop fills myfile with the next row in myfilelist each time through the loop. Within the loop, you set myfile_in and myfile_out using the COPY tag; the file myfile_in is copied to the file myfile_out.

As an example, suppose "/folder1" contained the three files albert.txt, bobby.txt, and cindy.txt. SYSLS would create myfilelist, a variable that would look as follows:

```
albert.txt   22916 07/02/02     08:37:33      FILE
bobby.txt    12027 06/30/02     15:00:47      FILE
cindy.txt    34200 07/05/02     18:07:10      FILE
```

The first time through the FOR loop myfilerow looks like this:

```
albert.txt   22916 07/02/02     08:37:33      FILE
```

The second time through the loop myfilerow looks like this:

```
bobby.txt    12027 06/30/02     15:00:47      FILE
```

These FOR loops work by filling the variable specified by the ROWNAME parameter with a one-row slice of the variable specified by the NAME parameter. Each time through the loop, the FOR loop fills the variable specified in the ROWNAME parameter with the next row. The instruction `myfile_in="/folder1/"+myfilerow[1]` (remember that `myfilerow[1]` is the same as `myfilerow[1,1]`) calculates the source file, `myfile_in`. The instruction immediately after this one calculates the destination file, `myfile_out`. That instruction is followed by the instruction that actually copies the file.

Summary

In this chapter, you learned about variables, how they work with HTML forms and how to use IF-THEN conditionals, WHILE loops, and FOR loops. They are the fundamental building blocks of Overlays, which you learned how to place inside HTML documents in Chapter 5, *Underlays, Inlays, and On-Click Overlays*. You now have a solid foundation in HTML/OS programming.

The remaining chapters in Part II, *Programming Basics*, are dedicated to applied issues. The next chapter covers debugging techniques—an important topic for the user of any development environment. If you have been going through the code here, typing it and running it, you have already encountered little problems and error messages along the way. The next chapter will shed light on this extremely practical topic and provide valuable advice on how to diagnose and solve development problems as they arise.

Exercises

The following exercises are designed to accustom you to working with two-dimensional variables, IF-THEN statements, and FOR loops. Answers to all exercises are provided on this book's companion Web site as described in the book's Preface.

Exercise 1

Create a file counter. When the user reaches the file counter page, see if the file contains a number. If not, set it to 1. If it does, increment it. Display the counter value on the screen along with a Redisplay link. You will need to use the COPY and ISINTEGER tags, and an IF-THEN statement.

Exercise 2

Create a page that displays a random message at the top of the page. To do so, each time the page loads, copy a file containing multiple messages, one per line, into a variable. Then randomly select a line from the variable and display it. You will need to copy from a delimited file. (Note that delimited text files with only one column still need a delimiter. Set your delimiter to any character not in the file, such as a vertical bar.) You will need to use the RANDOM and COPY tags. To calculate the number of rows in a variable, use the tag ROWS.

Exercise 3

Use a FOR loop to read a list of HTML pages in a folder and display a list of HREF links. When users click a link, they should be directed to the page.

Exercise 4

Use a FOR loop to read a list of files in a folder and display a pull-down select box with the filenames. Add a Submit button so, when users select a file they are directed to the page.

Exercise 5

Use a FOR loop to read a two-column file containing names of states (like the example shown in this chapter). Using a FOR loop, display a pull-down select box on the page. Hint: Use the FOR loop to display multiple <option>..</option> lines, one for each state. Use standard HTML to display the <select> and </select> tags.

CHAPTER 7

Debugging Techniques

The programs presented in this book illustrate many facets of Web development. Although we hope you find these programs helpful, they are not a substitute for the experience gained by sitting down and using your copy of HTML/OS to program Web pages. The experience of writing a program, line by line, is different from looking at how programs are written. In sample programs, you see intermediate results and the end product—programs that run without errors and behave as intended. During development, however, programs are not likely to behave exactly as planned. You rarely write them correctly the first time. The most experienced programmers make mistakes in the first writing of their programs. In fact, making mistakes is an accepted part of the process of writing Web applications—or any computer programs, for that matter. The process of building a program is intertwined with the activity of fixing mistakes.

As you typed the example Web pages in this book into your Web-based editor, you most likely encountered mistakes. You may have encountered parsing errors reported to you on the Web page when you ran these example programs.

You may have used these reports to fix the problem, find the missing line, or correct the misspelled word. In a Web page with only 10 or 20 lines, mistakes are easy to identify. But as you write longer and longer pages, the potential to make careless typing errors and mistakes in your logic increases. Finding the mistakes also becomes more difficult.

In general, you test and debug advanced Web pages, like those discussed in this book differently than static or pure HTML pages. When working with pure HTML, you are mostly interested in the "look" of the page. You need to see if the look works in the popular browsers on the Web. This is called cross-browser compatibility testing. While you must still pay careful attention to cross-browser issues, it is not the topic of this chapter. In this chapter, you learn about debugging the functionality of Web pages.

As you test Web pages you want to give them a wide range of input to make sure they run as intended. If a page comes up with an error or does not behave as intended, you must debug it. *Debugging* is the process of identifying errors and correcting them. This chapter reviews commonly used debugging techniques. You also learn about the automatic error messaging provided to you by HTML/OS and you learn about a program called Tracer for tracking down programming bugs.

The beginning of this chapter explains the kinds of error reporting provided by HTML/OS.

Errors Reporting

The HTML/OS engine issues three kinds of error reports; full-page error reports, in-page error reports, and HTML/OS tag-specific error results. Full-page and in-page error results are also known as *parse errors*. Tag-specific error results are placed in variables by HTML/OS tags in response to improper data. The following sections describe the different kinds of errors and reports.

Parse Errors

Parse errors occur as the HTML/OS engine *parses*, or interprets your document. Deciphering parse errors reported to you on Web pages is easier if you understand how HTML/OS parses Overlay tags. HTML/OS scans Overlay tags from left to right and immediately stops interpretation when it encounters an error—that is if HTML/OS is unable to continue. In some cases however, it can continue its interpretation.

If a tag is misspelled or HTML/OS does not recognize it, it will assume you have an undefined tag or function and stop its interpretation. If you write your tag properly but place an incorrect number of parameters in the tag, HTML/OS reports it to you and continues its interpretation.

Full-Screen Reports

When an error occurs and HTML/OS is unable to render the HTML document, it issues a full-screen error report. For example, consider the following page, which is a simple calculator. The first IF-THEN statement has no THEN, so HTML/OS is unable to render the page.

```
<html>
<title>Five-Line Math Calculator (with Error)</title>
<<
IF ISNUMBER(a+b)="FALSE"
  z=1 a=0 b=0 result="?"
/IF
```

```
IF z=1 THEN result = a + b /IF
IF z=2 THEN result = a - b /IF
IF z=3 THEN result = a * b /IF
IF z=4 THEN result = a / b /IF
>>
<form method=post action=<<Page>>>
My First Calculator:<br>
<input type=text name=a size=5>
<select name=z>
<option value="1">+
<option value="2">-
<option value="3">*
<option value="4">/
</select>
<input type=text name=b size=5>
<input type=submit value=" = ">
<b><<result>><br>
</form>
</html>
```

Running this page produces the screen shown in Figure 7.1. A similar screen would be reported if, for example, you forgot an IF or if the tag misspelled ISNUMBER

The disadvantage of full-screen error reports is that they do not explicitly identify the location in the file where the error occurs. Usually however, using the error report, you can identify the location by the nature of the problem reported. If this does not work, you can use other methods to identify and fix the problem. One method is called commenting out code, a topic discussed in the "Commenting Out Code" section later in this chapter. Another method is to use a program called Tracer. The program allows you to mark a document, so you can find the last instruction in the document that ran before it failed. Tracer is discussed in the section "Using Tracer," located at the end of this chapter.

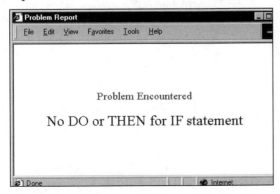

Figure 7.1: Full-screen error reports occur when HTML/OS cannot render a Web page.

In-Page Reports

Not all errors cause full-screen reports. Often, when an error occurs, HTML/OS is still able to render the HTML document. In these cases, HTML/OS issues an in-page report. In-page reports are text messages surrounded by [[and]] characters. For example, suppose in our previous program you mistakenly wrote the instruction

```
IF z=1 THEN result = a + b /IF
```

as

```
IF z=1 THEN result - a + b /IF
```

Note the second equal sign in the instruction is a minus sign. Running this instruction renders the Web page screen shown in Figure 7.2. The page includes the in-page error report:

```
[[HTML/OS Error: parse error 1 a=0 b=0 result="?" /IF IF z=1
THEN result -]]
```

When encountering this kind of error report, read it right to left. The last character

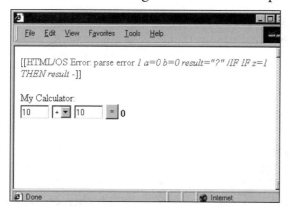

of the message is a minus sign. That's where HTML/OS failed to interpret the instruction. The minus sign should have been an equal sign.

Use the message inside brackets ([[ ]]) to identify the location of the error in the file. The last characters of the message tell you exactly where HTML/OS could no longer interpret the instruction. The left most part of the error report, HTML/OS Error parse error, provides a general description of the error HTML/OS encountered.

Figure 7.2: HTML/OS provides in-page error reports when it can render the Web pages despite the error.

Tag-Specific Results

Not all errors cause error reports. If, for example, a calculation is out of range or has an incorrect input, the most likely result is for HTML/OS to return the value ERROR as a result for your calculation. The following calculations, for example, place the value ERROR in myresult:

```
myresult = 5 / 0
myresult = 12345678 * 12345678
myresult = ROUNDUP("Two Hundred")
myresult = ADDDAYS(TODAY,"Two")
myresult = LEFT("Hello World","-9")
```

The first two examples produce numbers that are too large, so HTML/OS returns ERROR. The third and fourth examples contain text parameters that should be numbers. Again HTML/OS returns ERROR. The last example contains a parameter that's a negative number but it requires a positive number. If you get a value of ERROR in a variable, it's likely to cause errors in other variables based on that variable. If you find a variable with the value ERROR when it should have some other value, work your way back in the code until you find the first HTML/OS tag that caused a value to come up as ERROR.

TAGRESULTS—Many HTML/OS tags place additional error messages in a special variable called TAGRESULTS. *If an HTML/OS tag does write to* TAGRESULTS, *it uses the following convention; it places one of the values—*TRUE, FALSE, *or* ERROR—*in column 1, row 1 of* TAGRESULTS. *It also places an English-like error message in column 1, row 2 of* TAGRESULTS *(or places the word* OK *in this cell if it finds no error). It fills other cells of* TAGRESULTS *with supplementary information depending on the specific tag. Consult your HTML/OS Reference on the specific tag to see whether to fill* TAGRESULTS *and what information to place in each cell.*

Debugging Your Code

The techniques used to hunt down a problem vary according to the problem you encounter and the kind of error message you get. For example, if you run a Web page and see a blank screen, you would follow one set of steps to debug the problem. If you run a Web page and see a full-screen error report, you would follow a different set of steps. If you get an in-page error report, you would follow yet another path to hunt down the error.

The best way to debug is to debug little at a time. If you find yourself encountering many bugs as you write your code, write smaller amounts of code at a time before you test the code on the page. The Web-based editor gives you a single-click **Save/View** button. Use it to test your code as you program. If you're a beginner, it may make sense to write only four or five lines of code at a time, each time viewing the page, fixing the problems that arise, and then returning to write additional lines of instructions. When you encounter the bugs, you should adhere to the rules outlined in the following sections.

Verify and Repeat

Regardless of how you hunt down a bug, you should avoid jumping to conclusions. When you encounter a bug or problem, the first thing to do is repeat the bug so you understand the circumstances that give rise to it. If your bug is not repeatable, edit your page until it is. Problems that are not repeatable (also known as intermittent) are difficult to solve.

Location, Location, Location

Once you have a repeatable problem, you need to identify where the problem occurs in the code. This step is almost always a matter of narrowing down the general location of the error until you can isolate its exact location. Then, and only then, can you move on to find out why the problem occurred. This is the most important step in resolving any bug. In fact, this is what good debugging is about. It doesn't make sense to rethink your entire program. That would be too much to wrap your brain around. It makes sense to rethink only that portion of the program where the mistake occurs.

Viewing Document Source

If you are having difficulty localizing your bug, try looking at the HTML source of the document. It may help you tell whether the problem is HTML, code, data, or logic. Sometimes HTML/OS error messages get stuck inside HTML brackets and are not visible until you view the source of the page as the browser sees it. For example, suppose your Web page has a text box that is not rendering properly. Suppose the code is as follows:

```
<textarea cols=<<mycols>> rows=<<myrows>> name=mytext ></textarea>
```

A look at the HTML document source in your browser might uncover the following line:

```
<textarea cols=5 rows=ERROR name=mytext ></textarea>
```

This tells you that `<<myrows>>` rendered to the value ERROR. Now you know to look in your instructions to see why the variable `myrows` is equal to ERROR.

Viewing the actual HTML text rendered by HTML/OS gives you more clues than simply viewing the page rendered by the browser.

The Bug Hunt

Start your hunt for the location of a bug by determining the exact page causing the problem, and whether the problem is in your HTML or in an Overlay. If the problem is in an Overlay, you need to determine which Overlay or HTML tag is causing the problem. Keep in mind bugs are not always caused by an incorrect use of an Overlay tag. That's just one possible cause. Bugs are also caused by problems in the following areas:

Your data—If your data is the cause of a bug, narrow down the specific data that's causing the problem. After you do this, go back and see how that particular data is handled.

Poorly deployed Overlay tag—If the problem is in the way an Overlay tag is used, investigate the behavior of the Overlay tag to see exactly how it works.

Incorrect algorithm—If the problem is in an algorithm, step through the algorithm to verify it is doing what you believe it should be doing.

Incorrectly launched Web page—If the problem is in the way you are running your Web page, look at the values of the variables the Web page uses when it is first launches to see how that compares with what you expect.

Displaying Intermediate Values

Often, you can locate a bug by viewing the changes in one or more variables used in the Web page. To track the contents of the variable `my_var`, for example, sprinkle your page with debugging instructions like `dbg1=my_var`, `dbg2=my_var`, `dbg3=my_var`, and so on. Then, at the bottom of the page, just above the `</html>` tag, display the `dbg` variables with instructions like `dbg1=<<dbg1>><br>` and `dbg2=<<dbg2>><br>`. Then rerun the page. Compare the values of these `dbg` variables with what you expect. When you find values that don't match your expectations, use the locations of the debugging instructions to narrow down the location in your code causing the problem. Once you locate the problem delete the debugging instructions.

Commenting Out Code

In some cases, you comment out code as a way to locate a problem. For example, suppose some variable has the value ERROR, but you do not know why. You know the variable is calculated in a large section of code. Try commenting out this code by using the # and /# tags. Placing these tags around instructions tells HTML/OS to ignore them. Remember that these tags only work inside Overlays. If you need to comment out HTML tags, surround them with <!– and –> tags.

If commenting out code fixes the bug, reduce the amount of code you comment out and try again. Repeat this process until the commented out code is a small segment that identifies the location of the problem.

The Mind Is a Funny Thing—*Debugging a problem is often a battle between your mind and your program. The time you spend debugging can be frustrating, because most problems are the result of careless mistakes and errors in logic. But writing a program without making at least a few mistakes is a rarity.*

Most often, mistakes happen because it doesn't make sense to be 100% thorough when you write a program. It's usually faster to write a program the best you can and then go back and debug it. Debugging a program is a mind game you must play with yourself. During the debugging process, you must rethink some of the steps you took when writing the program. If you skip over the steps that got you into trouble in the first place, you won't be able to solve your problem.

When you are debugging, your mind might repeatedly skip over the piece of information causing the problem, because you think something is obvious when it is not. Do not trust yourself too much when debugging. Use systematic approaches rather than hunches and guesses. At the very least, you should use systematic approaches when other methods fail.

Using Tracer

You can solve most programming problems by methodically identifying the location of the problem in your code. In some circumstances however, you may encounter a particularly evasive bug. That's when you may want to use the program, Tracer.

Three types of bugs warrant the use of this program. First is the bug that causes an unhelpful full-page error report. Without guidance, if your Web page contains a lot of programming, it may be difficult to narrow down the problem. The second kind of bug results in a page crash, which gives you no error report at all, because the bug is so severe it crashes HTML/OS, and HTML/OS is unavailable to issue the error report. (See the accompanying "Automatic Crash Recovery" note.) The third kind of bug is one in the logic of your programming. Here, the ability to follow the values in variables as they change during program execution comes in handy.

Automatic Crash Recovery—*It is not easy to crash HTML/OS, but it can be done. If a crash occurs, you'll see an error report by the Web server. You won't see a full-screen message centered in the middle of a white background (that would be an HTML/OS full-screen error report).*

If this happens, HTML/OS automatically recovers. The next time you run HTML/OS, you'll experience a 10-second delay. After that, the pages will begin working again. If after the crash, you experience peculiar behavior, log out of your copy of HTML/OS and log in again.

In all three of these instances, you have little idea about the cause of the problem or where the problem occurred in your page. One way to solve such a problem is to comment out code, as explained in the "Commenting Out Code" section earlier in this chapter. Another way is to use the Tracer program.

Tracer is a trace file analyzer. Using Tracer requires you to place TRACE tags in your Web page, run the page, and then view the trace logs created by the TRACE tag with Tracer.

Tracer is also convenient when you wish to track down a logic problem. In such a case, you want to follow the values in multiple variables as HTML/OS makes its way through your instructions. Although you can display intermediate values in your code (a technique described in the "Displaying Intermediate Values" section earlier in this chapter), you can also use Tracer, which enables you to view a history or trace of the values in variables at the time the page was interpreted by HTML/OS.

The Trace Console

Tracer is included with your copy of HTML/OS. You'll find it in the Utilities menu on the HTML/OS desktop. Figure 7.3 shows Tracer's main screen. The options bar, located at the top of the screen, has links to clear the trace log (see the accompanying note, "The Trace Log"), show or hide page code, and launch an on-line help utility. The name of the trace you are currently viewing is immediately under the Options bar. In the upper-right corner, Forward and Back arrows enable you to move among the different traces within the log.

The Trace Log—*The trace log contains multiple traces. Each time you run a page with* TRACE *tags, a new trace is placed in the log. The trace log itself is designed not to exceed 100,000 bytes. If the file exceeds this limit, HTML/OS removes traces from the file to make room for new traces.*

The main screen is divided into two sections. To the left is a view of a trace. Here, using the various options provided, you can control the view of the data in the trace log file for a particular trace. To the right is the source code of the page you traced.

The Trace view, appearing on the left side of the screen, is a grid containing all or some of the information placed in a trace by a Web page containing TRACE tags. Trace entries appear as rows ordered chronologically. The top row contains the first log entry made. In general, a row in the Trace view can indicate the following problem spots:

- Reading from a variable
- Writing to a variable
- Running a TRACE tag (flag)

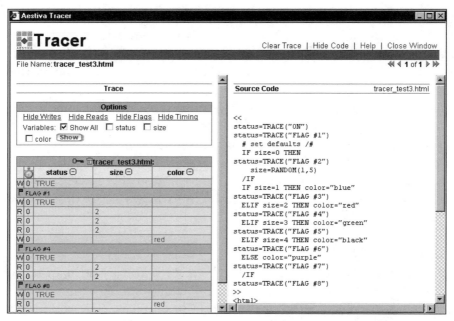

Figure 7.3: The main Tracer screen includes a Trace view with many controls.

Tracer places reads and writes to a variable in a single column for that variable. This allows you to follow the reads and writes to a single variable by reading down a column. Not all variables are listed—only those you wish to follow. To select a set of variables to follow, use the Variables option in the Options box at the top of the Trace view. Place check marks next to the variable names you want to follow and click the **Show** button.

If you wish to hide the reads or writes from Trace view, click the **Hide Reads** or **Hide Writes** links. These links toggle back and forth between Hide and Show. Tracer also provides a **Hide Flags** and **Show Flags** toggle link. Click this link to hide or show lines that display flags set by the TRACE tag.

Figure 7.3 displays a 16-line trace. Each row is preceded by a single-letter code. *W* means write. *R* means read. Rows preceded by a flag indicate a TRACE flag has been run. In the next section, you learn how to write TRACE tags to generate these kinds of logs and how to use them to debug code.

Using the *TRACE* Tag

Placing TRACE tags in different locations of a document instructs HTML/OS to write log entries to a trace log file as it runs the page. The TRACE tags are placed inside Overlays and are written as follows:

```
temp=TRACE(parameter)
```

Here *parameter* is either a reserved-word the TRACE tag understands, or a text message, also known as a flag. When you execute TRACE, it does one of two things; if the *parameter* is a text message (a flag), the text message is added to the trace log. If the *parameter* is a reserved-word, TRACE performs the operation defined for the reserved-word. The reserved-words are as follows:

Ignore—Ignores subsequent TRACE tags in document. The Ignore parameter is useful if you place a number of TRACE tags in a document but want to deactivate them without having to delete them from the document. In this event you place the line temp=TRACE("ignore") at the top of the document.

Clear—Deletes the trace log file. The Clear parameter is useful if you have too many trace entries in a log. It is usually a good idea to clear your trace at the top of the page.

On—Turns on variable tracing. The On parameter turns on the logging of reads and writes to all variables. Note that tracing still occurs if you do not turn on logging. TRACE tags containing text messages (flags) will still be logged; but log entries will not be written when variables are read and written to.

Off—Turns off variable tracing. To turn off the logging of reads and writes to variables, use the Off parameter.

Buffer—Buffers logging and starts system-time recording. Set the Buffer parameter when you want to use Tracer for an entirely different purpose— to measure how long it takes to run different tags in your program. When you set this parameter, HTML/OS stores log entries internally before writing them to the trace log file. It also logs the computer system time with every entry. You buffer log entries because otherwise, the time delays created by TRACE itself could render the time measurements useless.

Finding the Last Point of Execution

If you encounter a crash or a full-page error report, you need to know the last point of execution in your code before execution failed. To find this location, use TRACE with text messages (flags). Working your way from top to bottom, place lines like temp=TRACE("Point A"), and temp=TRACE("Point B") in your program. Run the page so it produces the same error as before. Pull up the log report in Tracer and view the trace. You will see flags like Point A, and Point B appear on different rows, preceded by a graphic flag. The last flag you see is the last point of execution reached.

As an example, consider debugging the Hello World program that follows this paragraph. We purposely placed an error in the page. Running the page produces a full-screen error like that shown in Figure 7.1. The trace of the page, as viewed in Tracer, is shown in Figure 7.4 on the left side of the screen. The following code, with TRACE tags is shown on the right.

```
<<
  # set defaults /#
  IF size=0 THEN
    size=RANDOM(1,5)
  /IF
  IF size=1 THEN color="blue"
  ELSEIF size=2 THEN color="red"
  ELIF size=3 THEN color="green"
  ELIF size=4 THEN color="black"
  ELSE color="purple"
  /IF
>>
<html>
<title>Hello World</title>

<font color=<<color>> size=<<size>> face=arial>
<b>Hello World</b></font>
<form method=post ACTION=<<Page>>>
<select name=size>
<option value=0>RANDOM
<option value=1>Tiny
<option value=2>Small
<option value=3>Medium
<option value=4>Large
<option value=5>X-Large
</select>
<input type=submit value="Go">
</form>
</html>
```

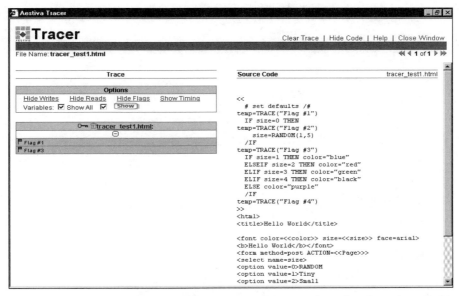

Figure 7.4: Here's a trace of a Hello World program populated with **TRACE** flags.

The last flag shown is `Flag #3`, which appears just before the `IF-THEN` statement. It's no wonder—there's a mistake immediately after this. An `ELIF` tag was mistakenly written as `ELSEIF`.

Following Changes in Variables

To follow the values of a variable as your page is executed turn on variable logging at the top of the document. To follow the contents of variables in a specific part of the page, turn on variable logging at the top of the section and turn it off at the end of the section. At the top of the section, write `temp=TRACE("on")`. At the end, write `temp=TRACE("off")`. Run the page and then, in Tracer, pull up the trace. Select the variables you wish to follow at the top of the Trace view and click the **Show** button. Looking down a variable column tells you how the variable changed as the page ran. Compare this to the code shown on the right side of the page. Using this information, check the logic of your program until you understand why your program did not run as you intended.

For example, consider debugging the same Hello World program in the previous section. Suppose you wish to see if the variable `size` changed in the first `IF-THEN` statement. Using your Web-based editor, type the `TRACE` tags shown on the right side of Figure 7.5 into the Hello World program. Run the page. Its trace appears on the left side of this figure. Looking down the `size` column, you see two entries, a read and a write. First size was 0. Then it was changed to 4.

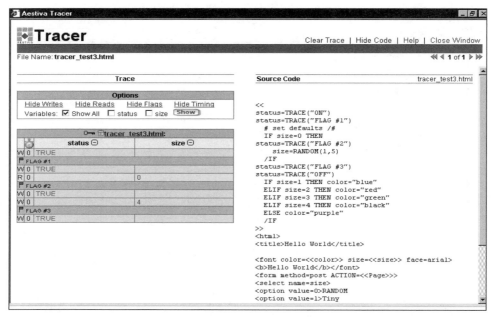

Figure 7.5: Here's a trace of a Hello World program with variable tracing.

Summary

In this chapter, you learned the most common techniques involved in debugging a Web page. As you have seen, debugging is first and foremost about locating the position of the problem in the Web page. Like they say in real estate, it's all about "location, location, location." Once you know the location of a problem, it becomes manageable.

In this chapter, you also learned that bugs should be resolved systematically. While shot-in-the-dark approaches are okay when you first encounter a bug, if your bug is not resolved in a few minutes, it is best to drop such attempts and become methodical. This technique separates the amateurs from the professionals.

Finally, with a bit of experience, you'll find debugging is like solving puzzles—it can be challenging, stimulating, and intellectually rewarding.

Exercises

The following exercises provide buggy Web applications. Using what you learned in this chapter identify and correct the bugs. Answers to all exercises are provided on this book's companion Web site as described in the book's Preface.

Exercise 1

The following code has a few bugs. Test, identify, and correct them.

```
<html>
<title>10-Line "Average" Calculator</title>
Enter number below. We'll calculate a running average.
<form method=post ACTION=dobuttons>
Number: <input type=text name=n>
<input type=submit name=mybutton value="Add To Average">
<input type=submit namr=mybutton value="Clear">
</form>
<< IF msg != "ERROR" THEN
        DISPLAY "msg" DISPLAY
    /IF
>>
</html>
<<overlay dobuttons
   IF mybvutton="Clear" THEN
      I=0 SUM=0 AVE=0 LASTNUM=0 N=0
      msg="Calculator Cleared. Start Again."
   ELSE
      I=I+1 SUM=SUM+N AVE=SUM/I LASTNUM=N N=0
        msg="Total Entries: "+I+"<br>"+
            "Total: "+SUM+"<br>"+
            "Average: "+AVE+"<br>"
/IF
>>
```

Exercise 2

The following code is also buggy. Test, identify, and correct the bugs in this application.

```
<html>
<title>25-Line RPN Calculator</title>
25-Line RPN Calculator<br><br>
Stack: <<mystack[1,1]<br>
<form method=post ACTION=calc>
<input type=text name=n size=8>
<input type=submit name=mybutton value="Enter">
<input type=submit name=mybutton value="Clear"><br>
<a href=myop name=op value=add>Add</a>
<a href=myop name=op value=sub>Subtract</a>
```

```
<a href=myop name=op value=div>Divide</a>
<a href=myop name=op value=mul>Multiply</a><br>
<a href=myop name=op value=sqr>Square</a>
<a href=myop name=op value=sqt>Square Root</a>
<a href=myop name=op value=inv>Inverse</a><br>
<a href=myop name=op value=abs>Absolute</a><br>
<a href=myop name=op value=log>Log</a><br>
<a href=myop name=op value=int>Integer</a><br>
</form>
</html>
<<overlay calc
    IF mybutton="clear" THEN stack=""
    ELSE APPEND stack TO n /APPEND
    stack=GETCOLNOTEQ(stack,1,"")
    n=""
    /IF
    GOTO PAGE
>>
<<overlay myop
    IF ISINTEGER(n)=FALSE THEN n="" GOTO PAGE /IF
    stack1=stack[1,1]
    stack2=stack[1,2]
    IF op="add" THEN stack2=stack1+stack2 stack1=""
    ELIF op="sbt" THEN stack2=stack1-stack2 stack1=""
    ELIF op="div" THEN stack2=stack1/stack2 stack1=""
    ELIF op="mul" THEN stack2=stack1*stack2 stack1=""
    ELIF op="sqr" THEN stack1=SQUARE(stack1)
    ELIF op="sqt" THEN stack1=SQRT(stack1)
    ELIF op="abs" THEN stack1=ABS(stack1)
    ELIF op="inv" THEN stack1=INVERSE(stack1)
    ELIF op="int" THEN stack1=FLOOR(stack1)
    ELIF op="log" THEN stack1=LOG10(stack1)
    /IF
    stack[1,1]=stack1 stack[1,2]=stack2
    stack=GETCOLNOTEQ(stack,1,"")
    n=""
    GOTO "PAGE"
>>
```

## CHAPTER 8

Building Text Editors

Web-based text document editors are an important component of advanced Web-based applications. They're deployed most often in the Web-based pages used to maintain a Web site. These back-end systems give staff the ability to edit Web pages, text files containing configuration settings, and page headers or footers. Text editors are also used in workflow systems where documents need to be edited and passed between different parties in an organization. You also find Web-based text editors in systems that edit templates used in e-mail auto-responders. There seems to be no end to the situations that require a Web-based text editor.

In this chapter, you start by building a six-line text editor. Then, learn how to integrate it into a back-end system and add features to it. As you go through this chapter, we recommend you use your copy of HTML/OS—experimenting with the code provided.

The Six-Line Text Editor

This text editor is called a "six-line editor" because, well, it takes only six HTML/OS instructions to build it. This Web-based editor is shown in Figure 8.1. The code for the editor is as follows:

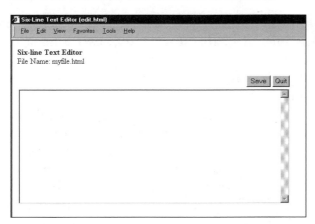

Figure 8.1: You build the six-line text editor by using six HTML/OS instructions and three HTML form components.

```
<<
ted_file="myfile.html"
COPY FILE=ted_file TO ted_text /COPY
>>
<html>
<b>Six-line Text Editor</b><br>
File Name: <<ted_file>>
<form method=post ACTION=ted_edit>
<table border=0>
<tr><td align=right>
<input type=submit name=ted_button value=Save>
<input type=submit name=ted_button value=Quit></td></tr>
<tr><td>
<textarea name=ted_text cols=65 rows=15>
</textarea>
</td></tr>
</table>
</form>
</html>
<<overlay ted_edit
IF ted_button="save" THEN
   COPY ted_text TO FILE=ted_file /COPY
   GOTO PAGE
ELSE
   GOTO "menu.html"
/IF
>>
```

The six-line editor uses one assignment (the first instruction), two COPY tags, an IF-THEN statement, and a GOTO tag. That's five instructions. Oh yes, it also displays the value of ted_file in an Overlay after the text File Name:—that's a total of six HTML/OS instructions.

The editor has three HTML form elements: a text area and two submit buttons. One button is Save; the other is Quit. When the page is launched, an Underlay at the top of the document assigns myfile.html to the variable ted_file. We use ted_file in the six-line editor instead of hard-coding the document name in each Overlay tag, because it's good programming to place those variables that might change in the future at the top of your document. That way, if you ever need to use the editor to edit other documents, you can do so by simply changing the first line. Placing definitions at the top of a document makes them easier to edit.

After this variable assignment, you COPY the contents of file ted_file into ted_text, the variable assigned to the text area. The text area, where the file is edited, is 65 columns by 15 rows. When a user clicks a button, the on-click Overlay ted_edit runs. It uses an IF-THEN statement to run different Overlay tags depending on which button the user the clicks. If the user clicks Save, the text in the box is saved to the filename stored in ted_file, which is myfile.html, and the page is redisplayed. If the user clicks Quit, the user is sent to menu.html.

You can use this six-line editor as part of a back-end system—a system designed for staff of an organization rather than public visitors of a Web site. A minimal back-end system requires the addition of a login page and a menu of staff options. For example, suppose you want to build a back-end system that gives staff the ability to edit a few files. Here's a password page you can use:

```
<html>
<title>Password Page (password.html)</title>
Staff Access - For Authorized Personnel Only
<form method=post ACTION=be_check>
Enter Password: <input type=password name=be_password size=15>
<input type=submit value="Enter">
</form>
</html>
<<overlay be_check
IF be_password = "please" THEN GOTO "menu.html" ELSE GOTO PAGE
/IF
>>
```

Here's a Web page that provides a menu of staff options:

```
<html>
<title>Staff Menu (menu.html)</title>
Staff Menu - For Authorized Personnel Only<ul>
<li> <A HREF=edit.html>Edit myfile.html</A>
<li> <A HREF=edit2.html>Edit myfile2.html</A>
<li> <A HREF=edit3.html>Edit myfile3.html</A>
</ul>
</html>
```

This back-end system is composed of an entry page (`password.html`), a staff menu (`menu.html`), and one or more editors (`edit.html`, `edit2.html`, and `edit3.html`). It's a complete system, because it includes a password-protected entry page and a menu of staff options. The entry page is accessed with a URL called a Start-link. Creating a Start-link is explained in Chapter 2, *Logging into Your Copy of HTML/OS*.

The password page used here is simply an HTML form that's linked to an on-click Overlay with an `IF-THEN` statement that tests whether the password entered by the user matches the word `please` (or any password you hard-code there). Note that putting the word *please* in the page is not a security problem. See the attached Security note in this section. The password page may be substituted with more advanced entry pages, such as those discussed in Chapter 9, *Building Login Pages*.

Security—*Placing security information in Overlays, such as a password, is not a security hazard, because Overlays are processed on the server and are not transferred to the browser. Of course, HTML is transferred across, so you don't want to place any secure information in the HTML code itself. Also, do not store HTML documents containing secure information on the public side of HTML/OS. Documents that are public are marked with a red (warning) diamond in the HTML/OS File Manager and can be moved to the private side. See Chapter 2, Logging into Your Copy of HTML/OS, for a discussion of this topic.*

The password page links to a staff menu page, which is simply an HTML document with hypertext links that launch applications for staff use. In this case, three links were put on the page; each links to a different copy of the six-line editor shown in Figure 8.1. Each of the editors should be modified so it links to a different document.

In this back-end system, the six-line editor was duplicated three times. But what if you don't want to maintain multiple copies of the editor? If you need to add features to the editor, you want to make changes in only a single file, not multiple files. You can accomplish this by making the following two changes: First, edit the staff menu page so the hypertext links point to the same six-line editor and contain *name-value* pairs that set `ted_file` to the filename that needs to be edited when the user clicks the link, as in the following example:

```
<A HREF=edit.html name=ted_file value="myfile6.html">Edit
myfile6.html</A>
```

Second, take out the first instruction of the six-line editor so it doesn't overwrite the value of `ted_file` set in the link the user clicks. Now the back-end system is composed of only three documents, and more importantly, it uses only one editor. When users click a link on the staff menu page, `ted_file` is set to the document name specified in the link and a single six-line editor runs; it is ready to edit the file set in `ted_file` defined in the link.

Advanced Options

The series of pages described in the previous section is amazing– a complete back-end system in only a dozen or so lines of code. We recommend you use your Web-based editor and type these files into some pages and try them!

Of course, there's no sense on sitting on what you've learned. Completing your first text editor will make you hungry for more features and more capabilities. A number of questions may pop into your head, such as how to give users the ability to do the following:

- Resize their text area
- Select from files in a directory
- Spell-check their work
- Revert to prior versions of a document
- Collaborate with others on a document

To allow such activities, you need advanced options. In the remainder of this chapter, you'll be working through each, one at a time, adding code to the six-line editor for each appropriate option. Each time you start with the original six-line editor at the beginning of this chapter and add the necessary code. The descriptions are independent of each other, unless mentioned otherwise. Feel free to read only those that interest you.

User-Controlled Text-Area Resizing

Perhaps the most important element of a text editor is the text area used to edit text. In the six-line editor, the size of this text area is hard-coded in the program. This can cause problems since, as a developer, you don't know the size or resolution of a user's screen. In fact, in some cases, neither does the user. The users may use different computers to access the editor. In some cases, the screen may be 800 by 600 pixels. At other times, it may be 1024 by 768. To make matters worse, different browsers render text areas differently. Who is to say which browser the user is using? Or how individuals configured their browsers. All of this makes it a good idea to give the users the ability to adjust the size of their text area.

To accomplish that, you add two inputs to the screen that allow the users to enter the number of columns and rows they want for the text area. You also add a Change button. When the user clicks Change, you check the settings and save them to a file. When entering the page, load the settings previously saved in the file. Use these settings when the text area is displayed. An editor with this new option is shown in Figure 8.2. The code is shown follows the figure.

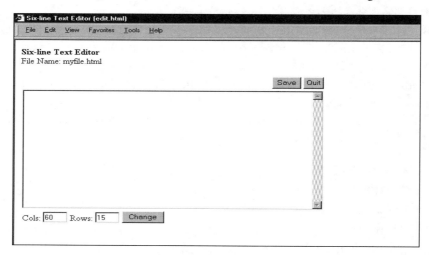

Figure 8.2: The six-line editor now has user-controlled text-area resizing.

```
<<
  ted_file="myfile.html"
  COPY FILE=ted_file TO ted_text /COPY
  COPY FILE="configs.txt" TS="," to temp /COPY
  x=temp[1] y=temp[2]
>>
<html>
<title>Six-line Text Editor (edit.html)</title>
<b>Six-line Text Editor</b><br>
File Name: <<ted_file>>
<form method=post action=ted_edit>
<table border=0>
<tr><td align=right>
<input type=submit name=ted_button value=Save>
<input type=submit name=ted_button value=Quit></td></tr>
<tr><td>
```

```
<textarea name=ted_text cols=<<x>> rows=<<y>>>
</textarea>
</td></tr>
<tr><td>
Cols: <input type=text name=x size=4>
Rows: <input type=text name=y size=4>
<input type=submit name=ted_button value=Change>
</td></tr>
</table>
</form>
</html>
<<overlay ted_edit
IF ted_button="save" THEN
   COPY ted_text TO FILE=ted_file /COPY GOTO PAGE
ELIF ted_button="change" THEN
   IF ISINTEGER(x)="FALSE" OR x < 5 OR x > 200 THEN x=60 /IF
   IF ISINTEGER(y)="FALSE" OR y < 5 OR y > 100 THEN y=15 /IF
   COPY ROW(x,y) TO FILE="configs.txt" TS="," /COPY
   GOTO PAGE
ELSE
   GOTO "menu.html"
/IF
>>
```

The code in bold is the code you add to the six-line editor to provide this resize option. Starting at the top of the code, the instruction COPY FILE="configs.txt" TS="," TO temp /COPY reads the file configs.txt into temp. The parameter TS="," indicates you are reading a comma-delimited file. The file, as you will see, contains two cells (one row with two columns). The first cell contains the number of columns for the text area. The second cell contains the height, in rows. The next line loads these into x and y. Note that temp[1] is the same as temp[1,1], and temp[2] is the same as temp[2,1], as explained in Chapter 6, *Variables, Conditionals, and Loops*.

You use the values x and y to dynamically set the number of columns and rows in the text area by replacing the column and row values in the document with the Overlays <<x>> and <<y>>, respectively.

Lower on the page, in bold, you see a new HTML table row. The HTML table row contains two input boxes and Submit button that give users the ability to configure the text area. Note these HTML elements are placed under the text area, away from the Save and Quit buttons, because smart design dictates that you separate application buttons from those the user needs for configuration.

When a user clicks Change, the on-click Overlay, `ted_edit` runs. The IF-THEN statement runs the instructions in bold. These instructions start with a test of the values in x and y. If they don't have good values, they're set to 60 and 15, respectively. Then they are saved. Note how you use the ROW tag to produce a two-column by one-row variable that is saved to a comma-delimited file with the COPY tag. This is why, at the beginning of this page, it was assumed the file `configs.txt` was two columns by one row, with the width of the text area in the first column and the height in the second column.

Overall, the resize option you added to this page, required about five new instructions and a new HTML table filled with the necessary HTML elements. The option gives the user the ability to configure the text area as needed. Unfortunately, this solution has one minor flaw. In fact, the flaw is so minor, most would not worry about it, but we shall.

The problem is we're saving the setting in a text file. Users using two different computers will need to reset their text area if they need to go back and forth between two computers. This can happen if a user, for example, edits the file from both home and work or from two different computers at work.

The solution is to save the data in a cookie rather than a file. This solution can be a bit tricky; but it's worth it, because it attaches the setting to the computer the user is on. To accomplish this, you need to replace the instructions that read and write to `configs.txt` with instructions that read and write to cookies. You use the tags COOKIEREAD and COOKIEWRITE. Your first attempt might produce the following code:

```
<<
   ted_file="myfile.html"
   COPY FILE=ted_file TO ted_text /COPY
   x=COOKIEREAD("ted_width")
   y=COOKIEREAD("ted_height")
   IF ISINTEGER(x)="FALSE" OR x < 5 OR x > 200 THEN x=60 /IF
   IF ISINTEGER(y)="FALSE" OR y < 5 OR y > 100 THEN y=15 /IF
>>
<html>
<title>Six-line Text Editor (edit.html)</title>
<b>Six-line Text Editor</b><br>
File Name: <<ted_file>>
```

```
<form method=post action=ted_edit>
<table border=0>
<tr><td align=right>
<input type=submit name=ted_button value=Save>
<input type=submit name=ted_button value=Quit></td></tr>
<tr><td>
<textarea name=ted_text cols=<<x>> rows=<<y>>>
</textarea>
</td></tr>
<tr><td>
Cols: <input type=text name=x size=4>
Rows: <input type=text name=y size=4>
<input type=submit name=ted_button value=Change>
</td></tr>
</table>
</form>
</html>
<<overlay ted_edit
IF ted_button="save" THEN
   COPY ted_text TO FILE=ted_file /COPY GOTO PAGE
ELIF ted_button="change" THEN
   IF ISINTEGER(x)="FALSE" OR x < 5 OR x > 200 THEN x=60 /IF
   IF ISINTEGER(y)="FALSE" OR y < 5 OR y > 100 THEN y=15 /IF
   stat=COOKIEWRITE("ted_width",x,ADDAYS(today,100))
   stat=COOKIEWRITE("ted_height",y, ADDAYS(today,100))
GOTO PAGE
ELSE
   GOTO "menu.html"
/IF
>>
```

The code in bold contains the new instructions that read and write to cookies. Starting at the top, the COPY tag, which read from configs.txt, was exchanged with two COOKIEREAD tags, which read from cookies. The two IF-THEN statements you added check the values from the cookie. Some people may not accept cookies, so it is reasonable to give proper values to x and y in the event they have bad values. At the bottom of the page, the COPY tag that wrote to configs.txt was exchanged with two COOKIEWRITE tags that write to cookies.

The COOKIEWRITE tags (see syntax of COOKIEREAD, COOKIEWRITE, and ADDAYS in Appendix D, *HTML/OS Tag Reference Guide*) are set to expire 100 days in the future.

The problem however with this page is that it doesn't work—at least not completely. The tags are correct; but when working with cookies, you can't save them and expect them to be readable in the page displayed immediately after the write. You need to wait until the page after that. This is just how cookies work. What this means is you don't want to read them after writing them. You can accomplish this by setting a value in a variable when you write to cookies and checking that value before reading them, so you can avoid reading them if you've just written them. The code to do this is follows. The repairs to the page are shown in bold. Now you have a user-controlled, text-area resize option that stores its data in cookies.

```
<<
   ted_file="myfile.html"
   COPY FILE=ted_file TO ted_text /COPY
   IF cookie_justwrote != "TRUE" THEN
     x=COOKIEREAD("ted_width")
     y=COOKIEREAD("ted_height")
   /IF
   cookie_justwrote="FALSE"
   IF ISINTEGER(x)="FALSE" OR x < 5 OR x > 200 THEN x=60 /IF
   IF ISINTEGER(y)="FALSE" OR y < 5 OR y > 100 THEN y=15 /IF
>>
<html>
<title>Six-line Text Editor (edit.html)</title>
<b>Six-line Text Editor</b><br>
File Name: <<ted_file>>
<form method=post action=ted_edit>
<table border=0>
<tr><td align=right>
<input type=submit name=ted_button value=Save>
<input type=submit name=ted_button value=Quit></td></tr>
<tr><td>
<textarea name=ted_text cols=<<x>> rows=<<y>>>
</textarea>
</td></tr>
```

```
<tr><td>
Cols: <input type=text name=x size=4>
Rows: <input type=text name=y size=4>
<input type=submit name=ted_button value=Change>
</td></tr>
</table>
</form>
</html>
<<overlay ted_edit
IF ted_button="save" THEN
   COPY ted_text TO FILE=ted_file /COPY
   GOTO PAGE
ELIF ted_button="change" THEN
   IF ISINTEGER(x)="FALSE" OR x < 5 OR x > 200 THEN x=60 /IF
   IF ISINTEGER(y)="FALSE" OR y < 5 OR y > 100 THEN y=15 /IF
   stat=COOKIEWRITE("ted_width",x,ADDDAYS(now,100))
   stat=COOKIEWRITE("ted_height",y,ADDDAYS(now,100))
   cookie_justwrote="TRUE"
   GOTO PAGE
ELSE
   GOTO "menu.html"
/IF
   >>
```

File Selection

The six-line editor is fine if you know in advance the name of the file to edit. But what if you need to add a way for your user to select a file? In the example code in this section, you give the user the ability to select a file from a specific file directory. To accomplish this, you will want to add a page to the editor that lists the files in that folder. Let's call this page select.html. When users first enter the editor from menu.html, you want to link them to this page instead of the editor. The link in menu.html might look as follows:

```
<A HREF=select.html>Edit Archived Documents</A>
```

In select.html, you want to list the files in some directory and generate links that look like the following:

```
<A HREF=edit.html name=ted_file VALUE=[location1]>[location2]</A><br>
```

[location1] is where the full name of the file should go and [location2] is where the text for the link should go. A link like this was created in the section titled "The Six-Line Text Editor" at the beginning of this chapter. But this time, you need to create the link dynamically. To accomplish this, you use the tag FILELIST. This tag fills ted_files with a list of files from a specified directory. It places each file in a different row. See the Appendix D *HTML/OS Tag Reference Guide* for its syntax.

You then loop across the rows of ted_files, displaying a link for each file you loop across. FOR loops are discussed in Chapter 6, *Variables, Conditionals, and Loops*. The code for the Web page follows:

```
<html>
<title>Document Selection (select.html)</title>
Select document to edit or <A HREF="menu.html">quit</A> to
menu.
<ul>
<<
user_folder="/archive"
ted_files=FILELIST(user_folder)
FOR NAME=ted_files ROWNAME=x DO
    DISPLAY
        "<A HREF=edit.html name=ted_file VALUE=" +
        user_folder + "/" + x[1] + ">" + x[1] + "</A><br>"
    /DISPLAY
/FOR
>>
</ul>
</html>
```

The DISPLAY tag inside the FOR loop displays links, one link per file. The code user_folder + "/" + x[1] replaces [Location1] and x[1] replaces [Location2]. Now you have a page that displays a list of files in a directory. Clicking a filename sets ted_file and launches edit.html. Remember to delete the line ted_file.html="myfile.html" at the top of edit.html so ted_file is not overwritten when a user clicks a link. An example select.html is shown in Figure 8.3.

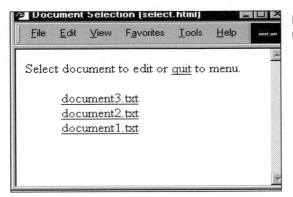

Figure 8.3: A file selection screen is a useful addition to the six-line editor.

Adding Delete and Copy Buttons

Now that you know how to edit multiple files, it only makes sense to give the user the ability to delete and copy files too. This can be done from the file selection page.

To do this, place radio buttons next to each file. Add Delete and Copy buttons to the top of the page. Put a text box to the left of the Copy button, so the user has a place to put a destination filename. When the user clicks the Delete button, you want to delete the selected file. When the user clicks the Copy button, you want to copy it to the filename specified next to the Copy button. The page is structured as follows:

```
<html>
<title>Document Selection (select.html)</title>
Select document to edit or <A HREF="menu.html">quit</A> to
menu.
<form method=post action=dostuff>
<font size=1>Destination</font><br>
<input type=text size=15 name=ted-dest>
<input type=submit name=button value=Copy>
<input type=submit name=button value=Delete><BR>
<<
user_folder="/archive"
ted_files=FILELIST(user_folder)
FOR NAME=ted_files ROWNAME=x DO
    DISPLAY
        "<input type=radio NAME=ted_selection VALUE=" + x[1] +
">" +
```

```
        "<A HREF=edit.html NAME=ted_file VALUE=" +
        user_folder + "/" + x[1] + ">" + x[1] + "</A><br>"
    /DISPLAY
/FOR
>>
</form>
</html>
<<overlay dostuff
  IF ted_selection="" THEN GOTO PAGE /IF
  IF button="Copy" THEN
     ted_dest=TRIM(ted_dest)
     IF COUNT(ted_dest,"/")>0 OR COUNT(ted_dest," ")>0 OR
        COUNT(ted_dest,"\")>0 THEN GOTO PAGE
     /IF
     COPY FILE="/archive/" + ted_selection TO FILE="/archive/"
+ ted_dest /COPY
  ELIF button="Delete" THEN
       temp=SYSRM("/archive/" + ted_selection)
  /IF
  GOTO PAGE

>>
```

When the user clicks Delete or Copy the on-click Overlay, dostuff runs. The first IF-THEN statement redisplays the page if no file has been selected.

If the user clicks Copy, the value placed in the input box, preceding the Copy button, is trimmed (duplicate spaces are deleted along with any leading or trailing spaces), and an IF-THEN statement returns to the top of the page if the name contains bad characters. If the file is fine, the selected file is copied. If the user clicks Delete, the selected file is deleted.

Adding Spell-Check

Although forms on the Web rarely include spell-check capability, if you can add such spell-check capability, why not add it? It shows a high level of sophistication on your part as a Web developer and it's a useful addition to any Web-based text editor.

To accomplish this, you need a spell-check kit. The kit described here is available in Aestiva's freeware library. It's called Spell-Kit. The kit is about 7 megabytes and unpacks to about 50 megabytes.

If you're using the preinstalled copy of HTML/OS included with this book, you will have enough room to install it. But don't install more than one copy. There's no quicker way to run out of hosting space than to install multiple copies of this application.

Download Spell-Kit to your computer, and then, using the File Manager, upload it to your copy of HTML/OS. Using the Install option in the Control Panel, install your copy. Install it in its default folder, which is /apps/spellcheck. Once it's installed, you can add spell-check to any HTML form by making a few modifications to the page. Adding spell-check capability to a page takes two steps.

First you need to add a Spell-check button to the HTML form. Second you need to add instructions in the on-click Overlay the form uses to call a Spell-Kit page. These instructions set up a number of parameters required by Spell-Kit and launch it. The parameters are explained in the online help included with Spell-Kit. The six-page text editor, properly set up with a Spell-check button, is shown in the following code. Changes appear in bold:

```
<<OF ted_file!="ERROR" THEN
ted_file="myfile.html"
COPY FILE=ted_file TO ted_text /COPY
/IF
>>
<html>
<b>Six-line Text Editor</b><br>
File Name: <<ted_file>>
<form method=post ACTION=ted_edit>
<table border=0>
<tr><td align=right>
<input type=submit name=ted_button value="Spell Check">
<input type=submit name=ted_button value=Save>
<input type=submit name=ted_button value=Quit></td></tr>
<tr><td>
<textarea name=ted_text cols=65 rows=15>
</textarea>
</td></tr>
</table>
</form>
</html>
<<overlay ted_edit
```

```
IF ted_button="save" THEN
  COPY ted_text TO FILE=ted_file /COPY GOTO PAGE
ELIF ted_button="Spell Check" THEN
  spell.return=page
  spell.form="/apps/spellcheck/template.html"
  spell.textarea.var="ted_button"
  spell.engine="/apps/spellcheck/index.html"
  GOTO spell.engine
ELSE
    GOTO "menu.html"
/IF
>>
```

When the user clicks the Spell Check button, the document /apps/spellcheck/ spell.html runs and displays a spell-check page, giving the user the ability to check and correct spelling mistakes. A spell-check page is shown in Figure 8.4.

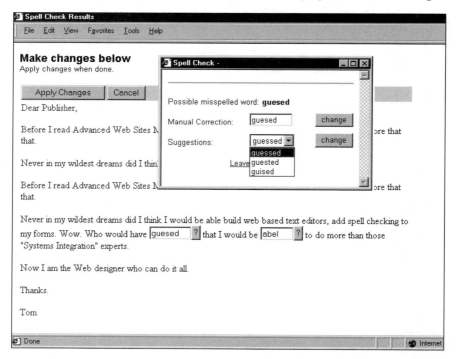

Figure 8.4: A spell-check screen is another useful addition to the six-line editor.

Version Control

The six-line editor does not automatically save a document's past versions. Of course, most editors don't either. But in certain situations, the ability to archive past versions of a document automatically is useful. Suppose you have a back-end system like the one described earlier in this chapter. The system had a menu page with links that allowed the user to edit different documents. If one of those documents were the home page of the Web site, version control on that page could come in handy.

To add version control to a document, you need to create a place for the archived files. You should also save files to the archive only in special situations, not with every change. Otherwise you'll end up with too many files. One way to do this is to add a Save To Archive button, so users can manually save documents to the archive. You will also need a Load From Archive button, so the user can revert to prior versions. See the following code:

```
<<
ted_file="myfile.html"
COPY FILE=ted_file TO ted_text /COPY
>>
<html>
<b>Six-line Text Editor with Version Control</b><br>
File Name: <<ted_file>>
<form method=post action=ted_edit>
<table border=0>
<tr><td align=right>
<input type=submit name=ted_button value=Save>
<input type=submit name=ted_button value=Quit></td></tr>
<tr><td>
<textarea name=ted_text cols=65 rows=15>
</textarea>
</td></tr>
<tr><td>
<input type=submit name=ted_button value="Save To Archive">
<input type=submit name=ted_button value="Load From Archive">
</td></tr>
</table>
</form>
</html>
```

```
<<overlay ted_edit
IF ted_button="save" THEN
   COPY ted_text TO FILE=ted_file /COPY GOTO PAGE
ELIF ted_button="Save To Archive" THEN
   [location1]
ELIF ted_button="Load From Archive" THEN
   [location2]
ELSE
   GOTO "menu.html"
/IF
>>
```

When the user clicks Save To Archive, the instructions at [location1] need to copy the file to a directory. The file would be given a unique name similar to the original. For example, the archive of myfile.html might be /archive/myfile~12345.html. The number 12345 represents the number of minutes since the beginning of the millennium. When the user clicks Load To Archive, the instructions at [location2] would go to a page that displays a list of archived files, so the user can select one and load it into the editor.

Save to Archive

Saving to the archive requires that you first calculate a new filename and copy the file to the archive. To accomplish this, you use TIMEFROM to calculate the number of minutes since the last millennium, REPLACE to do a search and replace when calculating the new archive name, and COPY to copy the document to the archive. The instructions to do this are as follows:

```
num=TIMEFROM("01/01/2000","minutes")
ted_file_archive = "/archive/" + REPLACE(ted_file, ".html",
"~"+num+".html")
COPY ted_text TO FILE=ted_file /COPY
COPY ted_text TO FILE=ted_file_archive /COPY
```

Load from Archive

At [location2], you want to go to archive.html. So you need to replace [location2] with the following code:

```
GOTO "archive.html"
```

The page `archive.html` is similar to the page `select.html` discussed in the section titled "File Selection" in this chapter. Here too, you want to display a list of files. But in this case, you want to list only those files associated with the current file (since /archive might be used to store other archived files). A revised `select.html`, one that shows only filenames beginning with the file name (without the `.html`) is shown in the following code. Modifications to the original version of `select.html` appear in bold.

```
<html>
<title>Document Selection (archive.html)</title>
Select document to load or <A HREF="edit.html">quit</A> to
editor.
<ul>
<<
user_folder="/archive"
ted_files=FILELIST(user_folder)
ted_files=GETCOLBEGIN(ted_files,1,ted_file+"~")
FOR NAME=ted_files ROWNAME=x DO
    DISPLAY
       "<A HREF=edit.html name=ted_file VALUE=" +
       user_folder + "/" + x[1] + ">" + x[1] + "</A> (" + x[3]
+ ")<br>"
    /DISPLAY
/FOR
>>
</ul>
</html>
```

A user who clicks the Load From Archive button is directed to this page. The page uses `FILELIST`, scans the directory, filling `ted_files` with a list of files. It puts the filenames it finds in column 1 and the modification dates of the files in column 3. The `GETCOLBEGIN` tag takes `ted_files` and returns only those rows where the name in column 1 begins with the filename and a tilde. That restricts `ted_files` to only those of interest. This is followed by a `FOR` loop that loops across the files in `ted_files`. It displays a hypertext link for each file. It follows each with the file creation date in parenthesis.

Explanations of the tags `FILELIST`, and `GETCOLBEGIN` can be found in Appendix D, *HTML/OS Tag Reference Guide*. For an explanation of `FOR` loops, refer to Chapter 6, *Variables, Conditionals, and Loops*.

Document Collaboration

Many staff environments require collaboration between multiple people on a single document. Often the collaboration takes the form of a workflow system. For example, a writer might be responsible for editing an HTML document for an online publication. The document is then passed to an editor for review, who then passes it to a Webmaster, who puts it online. This kind of collaboration is an example of a three-person workflow system.

Other forms of collaboration include systems in which multiple parties have simultaneous access to documents; but only one person can work on a document at a time. This is not really an example of workflow. Rather it's an example of a file editor with file locking. One algorithm you can use to ensure that a file is editable by only one staff member at a time is as follows: Whenever a user wishes to edit a document, that user must check a status file. The status file should contain the user ID of the last person who edited the document and the time of that edit. If the time in the file is too old or the status file has nothing in it, which occurs when the user releases the document, the party requesting the file can edit it. If not, the editor tells the user the document is not available. This kind of document-editing system is not discussed here but is left as an exercise.

Here we discuss the construction of a workflow system. Workflow systems can be built with databases or with files. Here we present a file-based version of workflow system. If you want to build a database-based workflow system, keep in mind that the concepts discussed here can be translated to the database-based situation. In that case, documents are stored as fields in a database, rather than as separate files, and the document's work area, is actually another field in the database, rather than a directory. Of course, this will make more sense after you learn how to build a file-based workflow system.

Let's consider a two-person workflow system consisting of a writer and a Webmaster. The technique is the same if you have three or more people. The system works like this. Each person in the workflow system has a separate work area —a private directory. A document, at any point in time, is placed in one of those directories, indicating the person to whom the document belongs. In this example, the documents available to our writer are stored in /work1. The documents available to our Webmaster are stored in /work2. Completed documents are stored in the /work3. We call /work3 our archive. To create a workflow system, you need to add file selection to the six-line editor and add buttons in the six-line editor that transfer files between the different directories. The writer will need the Send to Webmaster button. The Webmaster will need buttons Return to Writer, Send to Archive, and Load From Archive.

The text editor needs to offer different options to the writer and the Webmaster. In addition, each person using the workflow system needs to see only his or her own files. In the back-end system discussed in the beginning of this chapter, a single password was used to access the system. Typically more advanced login pages are used. Since this is not the topic of this chapter, we'll avoid this issue by simply changing the password page, so it can accept two passwords, one for the writer and one for the Webmaster. The workflow system here is comprised of a password page that links directly to a file selection page. (The menu.html page has been omitted.) The password page is as follows:

```
<html>
<title>Password Page (password.html)</title>
Staff Access - For Authorized Personnel Only
<form method=post ACTION=be_check>
Enter Password: <input type=password name=be_password size=15>
<input type=submit value="Enter">
</form>
</html>
<<overlay be_check
IF  be_password = "hemmingway" THEN
 wf_wa ="/work1" wf_user="Writer" GOTO "select.html"
ELIF be_password = "linuxdude" THEN
 wf_wa ="/work2" wf_user="Webmaster" GOTO "select.html"
/IF
GOTO PAGE
>>
```

When a user logs in, the variable wf_wa (the WorkFlow Work Area) is set to /work1 or /work2, depending on whether the user is a writer or a Webmaster; wf_user is set to the type of user, and the page select.html launches.

The page select.html is almost identical to the select.html used in the section, "File Selection," earlier this chapter. However, this time, files selected must originate in the /work1 or /work2 directories, depending on who accesses the page. The new select.html is as follows:

```
<html>
<title>Document Selection (select.html)</title>
Select document to edit.
<ul>
```

```
User: <<wf_user>><br>
File Area: <<wf_wa>><br><br>
<<
user_folder=wf_wa
ted_files=FILELIST(user_folder)
FOR FILE=ted_files ROWNAME=x DO
    DISPLAY
        "<A HREF=edit.html NAME=ted_file VALUE=" +
        user_folder + "/" + x[1] + ">" + x[1] + "</A><BR>"
    /DISPLAY
/FOR
>>
</ul>
</html>
```

The next thing to do is change edit.html so it displays the workflow buttons we mentioned previously, and program them to move files between the /work1, /work2, and /work3 work areas. You want to use a single edit.html, which eliminates the need to maintain multiple versions of the editor. You need to ensure that different buttons display depending on the value of wf_wa. The file is structured as follows:

```
<<
COPY FILE=ted_file TO ted_text /COPY
>>
<html>
<b>Workflow Editor</b><br>
User: <<wf_user>><br>
File Name: <<ted_file>>
<form method=post action=ted_edit>
<table border=0>
<tr><td align=right>
<<[Location1]>>
<input type=submit name=ted_button value=Save>
<input type=submit name=ted_button value=Quit></td></tr>
<tr><td>
<textarea name=ted_text cols=65 rows=15>
</textarea>
```

```
</td></tr>
</table>
</form>
</html>
<<overlay ted_edit
IF ted_button="save" THEN
   COPY ted_text TO FILE=ted_file /COPY GOTO PAGE
ELIF button="Send To Webmaster" THEN
   [Location2]
ELIF button="Return To Writer" THEN
   [Location3]
ELIF button="Send To Archive" THEN
   [Location4]
ELIF button="Load From Archive" THEN
   [Location5]
ELSE
   GOTO "menu.html"
/IF
>>
```

[Location1] is where you want to display the workflow buttons, which are different for the writer and the Webmaster. This requires an IF-THEN statement. You can write the following code:

```
IF wf_wa="/work1" THEN
   DISPLAY
      '<input type=submit name=ted_button value="Send To
Webmaster">'
   /DISPLAY
ELIF wf_wa="/work2" THEN
   DISPLAY
      '<input type=submit name=ted_button value="Return to
Writer">'+
      '<input type=submit name=ted_button value="Send To
Archive">'+
      '<input type=submit name=ted_button value="Load From
Archive">'+
   /DISPLAY
/IF
```

The code at locations [Location2], [Location3], and [Location4] need to move files between /work1, /work2, and /work3. At [Location2], for example, you can use the following instructions:

```
new_file=REPLACE(ted_file,"/work1","/work2")
temp=SYSMV(ted_file, new_file)
```

You use the REPLACE tag to perform a search and replace on the work areas, so a destination name can be created. Then SYSMV moves the file to the new destination. See Appendix D, *The HTML/OS Reference Guide*, for a description of SYSMV. Use same technique at [Location2] and [Location3], except that the work areas are different.

[Location5] runs when the user clicks the Load From Archive button. Here you want to launch select.html so it lists the files in /work3. To accomplish this, before launching select.html, you set a variable loadfromarchive to TRUE. Then in select.html, you set the user_folder to /work3, in the event loadfromarchive is TRUE. Then after you return to edit.html, you set loadfromarchive to FALSE . These are the changes needed to complete this two-person workflow system. The revised six-line editor, edit.html, is as follows:

```
<html>
<< loadfromarchive="FALSE">>
<b>Workflow Editor</b><br>
User: <<wf_user>><br>
File Name: <<ted_file>>
<form method=post action=ted_edit>
<table border=0>
<tr><td align=right>
<<
IF wf_wa="/work1" THEN
   DISPLAY
      '<input type=submit name=ted_button value="Send To
Webmaster">'
   /DISPLAY
ELIF wf_wa="/work2" THEN
   DISPLAY
      '<input type=submit name=ted_button value="Return to
Writer">' +
```

```
    `<input type=submit name=ted_button value="Send To
Archive">'+
    `<input type=submit name=ted_button value="Load From
Archive">'
  /DISPLAY
/IF
>>
<input type=submit name=ted_button value=Save>
<input type=submit name=ted_button value=Quit></td></tr>
<tr><td>
<textarea name=ted_text cols=65 rows=15>
</textarea>
</td></tr>
</table>
</form>
</html>
<<overlay ted_edit
IF ted_button="save" THEN
   COPY ted_text TO FILE=ted_file /COPY
ELIF button="Send To Webmaster" THEN
   new_file=REPLACE(ted_file,"/work1","/work2")
   temp=SYSMV(ted_file, new_file) GOTO PAGE
ELIF button="Return To Writer" THEN
   new_file=REPLACE(ted_file,"/work2","/work1")
   temp=SYSMV(ted_file, new_file) GOTO PAGE
ELIF button="Send To Archive" THEN
   new_file=REPLACE(ted_file,"/work2","/work3")
   temp=SYSMV(ted_file, new_file) GOTO PAGE
ELIF button="Load From Archive" THEN
  loadfromarchive="TRUE"
  GOTO "select.html"
  ELSE
   GOTO "menu.html"
/IF
>>
```

The new version of select.html is as follows:

```
<html>
<title>Document Selection (select.html)</title>
Select document to edit or <A HREF="menu.html">quit</A> to
menu.
<ul>
<<
IF loadfromarchive="TRUE" THEN
  user_folder="/work3"
ELSE
  user_folder=wf_wa
/IF
ted_files=FILELIST(user_folder)
FOR FILE=ted_files ROWNAME=x DO
    DISPLAY
        "<A HREF=edit.html NAME=ted_file VALUE=" +
        user_folder + "/" + x[1] + ">" + x[1] + "</A><BR>"
    /DISPLAY
/FOR
>>
```

Summary

In this chapter you learned how to tailor Web-based text editors to fit many needs. Unlike the legacy world, where text editors serve a general word-processing function, Web-based text editors can be customized and integrated into specific business and organizational systems.

Despite the sophistication of the systems built in this chapter, the construction of these text editors required mostly COPY, DISPLAY, and GOTO tags, IF-THEN statements, and the occasional FOR loop. Other HTML/OS tags were called upon in special situations. Specifically, COUNT, FILELIST, REPLACE, TIMEFROM, TRIM, GETCOLBEGIN, SYSMV, and SYSRM were used. Overall, a total of twelve different HTML/OS tags were used to build the text-editors used in this chapter.

If you found some of the tags used in this chapter difficult to understand, we recommend you refer to Appendix D, *The HTML/OS Reference Guide*. Log into your copy of HTML/OS and experiment with the tags by building simple pages that use them.

In the next chapter, you'll learn about building login pages. Login pages are used in membership systems, in back-end systems, such as those in this chapter, and in situations where access to a Web-application needs to be controlled.

Exercises

Even most Web developers can't build Web-based editors. But now you can! Do the following exercises to refine your skills, so this kind of development becomes second nature to you. Answers to all exercises are provided on this book's companion Web site as described in the book's Preface.

Exercise 1

Add a Reload button to the six-line editor. Hint: Reloading a page is a matter of redisplaying the page when a user clicks a Reload button.

Exercise 2

Add a Save/View button to the six-line editor. Hint: Viewing a page is a matter of going to the page. Use the GOTO tag to do this.

Exercise 3

An editor with a file selection provides the ability to select files in a directory. The file select.html in this chapter does not issue any special message when the directory is empty. Change select.html so that if it finds no files, HTML/OS displays the message "No Files Found" rather than an empty list of files. Hint: When FILELIST finds no files, it returns an empty string.

Exercise 4

This chapter includes code for resizing a text area and saving the values in a cookie. Modify this example so it works when users don't have cookies. To accomplish this, modify the page so text area heights and widths are saved and loaded from a file, in the event cookies are not readable.

Exercise 5

The select.html pages in this chapter display a single column of file names. Using HTML tables, modify select.html so it displays filenames, file sizes, and modification dates in different columns—not unlike the File Manager used in HTML/OS.

## CHAPTER 9

Building Login Pages

Whether you're interested in building a staff password page that's hidden from public view, a membership login with a Lost Your Password option, or a login page that separates wholesalers from retail customers, you'll want to read this chapter.

Off the Web, there is little flexibility in the way login pages are designed. You enter your login and password and that's it. The entire page is dedicated to logging you in. On the Web login boxes are merged with other information on the page. The page may include options to e-mail users' passwords, in case they forgot them. This is not done off the Web.

Once again, as you have seen throughout this book, Web-based computing offers greater design flexibility than legacy-style computing. In this chapter, you learn how to program login pages and how to modify them to serve a wide variety of needs.

We start out by discussing the overall security mechanism used by HTML/OS. Then we introduce a ten-line login page that reads its password information from a text file. Later you modify it to read its data from a database. Then we provide code examples and explanations about how to modify the page to perform custom tasks.

Web-Access Security

In HTML/OS you provide access to Web pages in only two ways. Either the user has a special URL to that page that you enabled in the HTML/OS Control Panel, or the user clicks a link to that page from an existing HTML/OS Web page. Building login pages is not about creating security mechanisms. It's about controlling the movement of users into the site once they're on the login page. Most often you set up a Start-link to allow users to access to the login page itself. Setting up Start-links is described in Chapter 2, *Logging into Your Copy of HTML/OS*.

Login Page Functionality

All login pages share specific commonalities. Once on a login page, the user typically reaches an HTML form containing input boxes for a login and password. When the user clicks the Submit button on the HTML form, an on-click Overlay checks the user's access information against hard-coded values such as data in a password file or a user database. If it matches that data, a GOTO tag gives the user entry to a page on the site. From there, the user has access to any page linked to that page and to any pages that page links to.

Once the user has logged in, you must set certain variables in the login page depending on what you want to accomplish when the user logs in. For example, you may want to set a user ID, load personal settings, define a user level, or set a home directory. These settings will be available for the remainder of the user session, because HTML/OS variables carry across Web pages automatically. You can use these settings to write or not write links to certain sections of the site, place the user in a specific directory tree, or limit a user's access to data in a database.

The login pages discussed in this chapter read their user data from either comma-delimited text files or user databases. As a rule, it's better to place user logins and passwords in a database table, rather than a text file. But when you have few users, it is reasonable to store the logins and passwords in a comma-delimited text file.

The Ten-Line Login Page

In the previous chapter, you saw a two-line password page that allowed access to a back-end system. Of course, that two-line password page had its limitations. For one, it requested only a password. It didn't request a login. While a password is often enough, in this chapter, login pages require a login and a password. Second, the two-line password page did not have any error reporting. If the user entered a bad login, the page was redisplayed without an error message. This ten-line login page includes error reporting and requests both logins and passwords. The login page is shown in Figure 9.1. The code is shown here:

```
<html>
<title>Login Page (login.html)</title>
<<
   IF lp_msg != "ERROR" THEN
     DISPLAY "<font color=red>" + lp_msg + "<font>" /DISPLAY
     lp_msg = "ERROR"
/IF
>>
```

```
<form method=post ACTION=lp_check>
Login ID: <input type=text size=30 name=lp_login><br>
Password: <input type=password size=30 name=lp_pass >
<input type=submit value=Login>
</form>
<< lp_login="" lp_pass ="">>
</html>
<<OVERLAY lp_check
  IF lp_login ="" OR lp_pass ="" THEN  lp_msg  = "Bad Login."
GOTO PAGE  /IF
  COPY FILE="logins.txt" TS="," TO lp_table /COPY
  temp=GETCOLEQ(lp_table,1,lp_login)
   IF temp[2,1] != lp_pass THEN
       lp_msg="Bad Login"  GOTO PAGE
  ELSE
     GOTO "staff.html"
  /IF
>>
```

You use the first Overlay in the page to display an error message, if an error exists. The IF-THEN statement checks to see whether lp_msg is ERROR. If it isn't, it displays lp_msg and sets it to ERROR. Remember, in HTML/OS, the default value of variables is ERROR, so the IF-THEN statement displays lp_msg only after it receives a value.

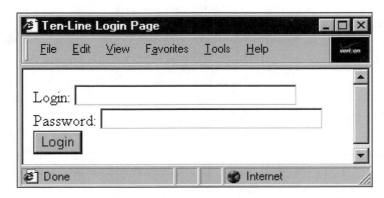

Figure 9.1: The ten-line login page uses ten HTML/OS instructions and an HTML form.

To log in, users enter a login and password and click Login, which triggers the on-click Overlay `lp_check`. The first line of the on-click Overlay determines whether the user forgot to enter a Login or a password. If so, it sets an error message and redisplays the page. Otherwise, the logins and passwords, which are stored in a comma-delimited text file, are loaded into `lp_table`. The login file has logins in column 1 and passwords in column 2. The first three lines of the file might look as follows:

```
"John","please"
"Johnny","njk100k"
"Janet","qqyw123"
```

When the file loads into `lp_table`, it becomes a variable with two columns. The `TS=","` parameter of the `COPY` tag tells HTML/OS the file is comma-delimited. The variable `lp_table` that's created is a 2-column by 3-row table that looks as follows:

John	please
Johnny	njk100k
Janet	qqyw123

To determine whether a row in `lp_table` has the proper login ID and password, use the tag `GETCOLEQ`. `GETCOLEQ` is part of a family of Overlay tags designed to pull rows out of a variable (containing multiple columns and rows) that match specific criteria. These tags return a new table with only those rows that match. In the case of `GETCOLEQ`, the criterion is that a specified column equals a specified value. For further information, see Appendix D, *HTML/OS Tag Reference Guide*.

The instruction, `temp=GETCOLEQ(lp_table,1,lp_login)`, creates `temp`. If `lp_login` is not in any of the rows of column 1, `temp` is an empty string (a one-column by one-row table with nothing in it). If it finds a match, `temp` becomes a two-column by one-row variable containing the login in the first column and the password in the second column.

The next instruction tests to see whether the password the user entered matches the second column of `temp`. If it doesn't, HTML/OS prepares and displays an error message—denying the user access to `staff.html`.

Using a Database

Our preceding login page assumes logins and passwords are stored in a text file. This is not convenient if you have many logins or if you're building a membership system in which users are automatically added and deleted. In these circumstances, it's much better to place login information in a user database.

To do this, you need to set up a user database first. Setting up a database is discussed in Chapter 4, *Your First Web Database Program*. We shall assume you have set up a database called /work/users with the fields, user_login, and user_password (among others.)

Start with the ten-line login page and delete the instructions in the on-click Overlay that read from a comma-delimited file and fill temp with rows for lp_login. Replace those instructions with a database search. The ten-line login page that reads from a database looks as follows:

```
<html>
<title>Login Page (login.html)</title>
<<
   IF lp_msg != "ERROR" THEN
      DISPLAY "<font color=red>" + lp_msg + "</font>"/DISPLAY
      lp_msg = "ERROR"
/IF
>>
<form method=post ACTION=lp_check>
Login ID: <input type=text size=30 name=lp_login><br>
Password: <input type=password size=30 name=lp_pass >
<input type=submit value="Login">
</form>
<< lp_login="" lp_pass ="">>
</html>
<<OVERLAY lp_check
   sstr='user_login="'+lp_login+'" AND
user_password="'+lp_pass+'"'

temp=DBFIND("/work/users",sstr,1,1,"user_login,user_password")
   IF temp[2,1]  != lp_pass THEN
        lp_msg="Bad Login"   GOTO PAGE
   ELSE
        GOTO "staff.html"
   /IF
>>
```

The modified lines appear in bold. The first bold line sets up a Boolean search. This topic is discussed further Chapter 12, *Building Query Pages*. The next instruction does the search. It uses DBFIND, the same Overlay tag you used in Chapter 4, *Your First Web Database Program*. When a user enters a login and password and clicks Login, a variable containing a search query is set up. Then DBFIND searches the database. If no matches are found, temp is filled with the empty string. If a record is found, temp becomes a two-column by one-row variable containing the login in the first column and the password in the second column. Notice the similarity to the original login page. After that an IF-THEN statement tests to see whether the second column of temp contains the password the user entered. If it does, the user is logged in. If not, the IF-THEN statement sets an error message and redisplays the page.

The Automatic Login

Sometimes it's a good idea to allow certain users to log in automatically by setting a cookie on a user's browser. The cookie should contain a login and password and be set by a special page, at the user's request. Automatically logging in a user is not a good idea when secure information and/or credit card information is available, but it's useful for less critical situations.

One way to log in a user automatically is to add an Underlay to the login page that determines whether a cookie has been set. If it has been set, you test the login and password. If they are set correctly, you send the user directly to staff.html. The Underlay to do this is as follows:

```
<< lp_login=COOKIEREAD("auto_login")
   lp_pass=COOKIEREAD("auto_pass")
   IF lp_login != "ERROR" THEN
     sstr='user_login="'+lp_login+'" AND
user_password="'+lp_pass+'"'

temp=DBFIND("/work/users",sstr,1,1,"user_login,user_password")
     IF temp[2,1] = lp_pass THEN
      GOTO "staff.html"
     /IF
   /IF
>>
```

To test using automatic login, you will want to set up a Web page that writes cookies. You use COOKIEWRITE to do that. See Appendix D, *HTML/OS Tag*

Reference Guide for help using the cookie tags. Here's a page that writes cookies. You can use this page to test the automatic login Underlay we just discussed:

```
<html>
<title>Test Cookie Write</title>
<<   mylogin="user001"
       mypass="12345"
      temp=COOKIEWRITE("auto_login",mylogin, ADDDAYS (NOW, 10)
      temp=COOKIEWRITE("auto_pass",mypass, ADDDAYS (NOW, 10)
>>
Login set to <<mylogin>>.<br>
Password set to <<mypass>>.<br>
Cookie written. Make sure login-password pair is in user
database.
</html>
```

Loading User-Specific Information

When a user logs into a site, you often want to set certain information about that user or perform certain functions. Depending on the login system you are building, any of the following questions might need to be answered with some special programming:

- What is the user's ID?
- Is the user a wholesaler or a retail customer?
- What is the user's access level?
- How many times has the user logged in?
- Is this user staff?
- Does the user have an outstanding balance due?
- Are messages waiting for this user?
- How should this user's Web pages be displayed?

The most common way to answer these questions is to add programming instructions to the login page preceding the GOTO "staff.html" line. Additional user information loads from the user database when you check the login and password.

For example, let's say you have a Web site that serves both retail and wholesale customers. You have a field in the users database called user_level, which can have the values W or *R*. When a user logs in, you could add this to the information you collect from the database. The on-click Overlay on the login page might look as follows:

```
<<OVERLAY lp_check
   sstr='user_login="'+lp_login+'" AND
user_password="'+lp_pass+'"'

temp=DBFIND("/work/users",sstr,1,1,"user_login,user_password,user_level")
   IF temp[2,1]  != lp_pass THEN
       lp_msg="Bad Login"   GOTO PAGE
   ELSE
       user_level=temp[3,1]
       GOTO "staff.html"
   /IF
>>
```

Changes appear in bold. As you see, the field list in DBFIND contains an additional field. The additional field is extracted from the database /work/users when the query runs. In this example, it's placed in column 3 of temp. Just before logging in, the variable user_level is set to this value.

As another example, suppose the user database has a field containing an expiration date. Suppose you want to let the user log in to the staff area only if the user's account has not expired. Here you would want to read this field and see if it is in the past. The on-click Overlay on the login page might look as follows:

```
<<OVERLAY lp_check
   sstr='user_login="'+lp_login+'" AND
user_password="'+lp_pass+'"'

temp=DBFIND("/work/users",sstr,1,1,"user_login,user_password,user_lastday")
   IF temp[2,1] != lp_pass THEN
       lp_msg="Bad Login"   GOTO PAGE
   ELIF ISPAST(temp[3,1])="TRUE" OR ISPAST(temp[3,1])="ERROR" THEN
```

```
    lp_msg="Access disabled. Account has expired."
    GOTO PAGE
ELSE
    GOTO "staff.html"
/IF >>
```

Here the field `user_lastday` is loaded from the database (in addition to the valid user login and password). The `IF-THEN` statement contains an additional test that determines whether `user_lastday` is in the past or invalid. You use the `ISPAST` tag, which returns `TRUE` for dates in the past. It returns `FALSE` for dates not in the past. It returns `ERROR` for invalid dates. In this `IF-THEN` statement, if `temp[3,1]` is not a valid date or it's in the past, an error message is set and the page redisplays, thus denying the user access to `staff.html`.

Lost Your Password?

Ever lose you password? What a bummer! If the Web site or system you are accessing has a way for you to recover your password, you're in luck. There's nothing more embarrassing than having to call the office and bother someone to recover your password.

The Lost Your Password option is a must in login systems with thousands of users. Most often, you make the link small and unobtrusive but place it in close proximity to the login and password input boxes.

Creating a Lost Your Password option requires the following:

- Users have unique e-mail addresses assigned to them
- The e-mail addresses are already on file in a users database
- You feel comfortable e-mailing the login and password to the address on file

If these conditions are satisfied, you can create a Lost Your Password option. To do this, you build a page that e-mails users a message with their login and password. A two-page set is shown here; users access the first page of the two-page set from a link next to the login form. It might look as follows:

```
<font size=1 face=arial,helvetica>
<A HREF="forgot.html">Forgot your password?</a>
</font>
```

On `forgot.html`, you place an HTML form that requests an e-mail address. When a user clicks the button on the form to request login and password

information, you check the database for that user's login information. If you find
it, you compose the e-mail message, send it out, and go to `forgot_thanks.html`
to instruct the user to pick up his or her e-mail information. If you can't find the
e-mail address, you issue an error message.

The page `forgot.html` looks as follows:

```
<html>
<title>Forgot Your Password </title>
<b>Forgot Your Password?</b>
Enter email address you have on-file with us
and we'll email you your login and password.
<<
   IF lp_msg != "ERROR" THEN
      DISPLAY "<font color=red>" + lp_msg + "<font>" /DISPLAY
      lp_msg = "ERROR"
/IF
>>
<form method=post action=lp_emailcheck>
Email Address: <input type=text size=30 name=lp_email>
<input type=submit value="E-mail Me Now">
</form>
</html>
<<OVERLAY lp_emailcheck
   sstr='user_email="'+lp_email+'"'

temp=DBFIND("/work/users",sstr,1,1,"user_email,user_login,user_p
assword")
   IF temp[1,1] != lp_email THEN
        lp_msg="E-mail Address Not Found. Try again. "  GOTO
PAGE
   ELSE
user_login = temp[2, 1]user_password = temp [3,1]
      msg='Dear Sir/Madam,' + LF +
           ' Here is your password. Please keep on file.' +
           ' Login ID: ' + user_login + LF +
           ' Password: ' + user_password + LF +
          'Thank you for using our Lost Your Password
feature.' + LF +
```

```
        '- Staff' + LF
     MAIL msg TO ADDRESS=lp_email
       SUBJECT='Recovered Login and Password'
     /MAIL
     GOTO "forgot_thanks.html"
  /IF
>>
```

The page `forgot_thanks.html` looks as follows:

```
<html>
<title>Forgot Your Password - Thanks</title>
<b>Your login and password has been emailed to you.</b><br><br>
Check your e-mail box and return to the login page to try
again.<br><br>
Happy to be of service.<br>
-Staff
</html>
```

The page `forgot.html` uses an HTML form that requests the e-mail address. When a user clicks E-mail Me Now, the on-click Overlay `lp_emailcheck` runs. `lp_emailcheck` places a message in `msg`. The MAIL tag sends the message. Then `forgot_thanks.html` is displayed.

Note how `msg` is composed. An LF appears at the end of each line. LF stands for linefeed. Unlike Web pages, each line of an e-mail message should end with this special character. The line break in Web pages is `<br>`. The line break in e-mail messages is LF.

Those Darn Line Breaks—*Line breaks are tricky little characters. First of all, you can't see them. Second, the characters you use as line breaks are different on Unix, Windows, and Macintosh systems. Here are the kinds of characters each system uses:*

- *The line break for Macintosh files is CR (the carriage-return character).*
- *The line break for Unix files is LF (the linefeed character).*
- *The line break for Windows files is CR+LF (carriage-return followed by a linefeed).*

Here are some guidelines that may help you:

- *Web pages ignore the differences in line breaks. They're translated into spaces. Don't worry about them when working with Web pages.*
- *When composing e-mail, terminate each line with LF.*
- *When working with text files, sometimes (not often, but often enough) it is best to know the kind of line breaks used. In these cases, before working with the file, replace CR+LFs to LFs and CRs to LFs. Use REPLACEALL. The tag does a search and replace, for example,*
  `mytxt=REPLACEALL(REPLACEALL(mytxt,CR+LF,LF),CR,LF).`

Using an E-mail Template

It is often a good idea to make automated e-mails customizable. The way to do that is to store the e-mail message you'll be sending out in a separate file (the template) and make the file editable with a text-editor similar to those discussed in Chapter 8. *Building Text Editors*.

To change this code so it uses a template, place the e-mail message in forgot_password.txt. Replace any variables in the message with placeholders (unique sequences of characters you can replace later with the actual variable values). In the following example, we use the placeholders [login] and [password]. The template file for the message is as follows:

```
Dear Sir/Madam,
  Here is your password. Please keep on file.
  Login ID: [login]
  Password: [password]
Thank you for using our Lost Your Password feature.
- Staff
```

You place the placeholders, [login] and [password], where the actual variables should go.

In the programming, after the file is read into a variable, the actual variables replace the placeholders. You use REPLACEALL to do this. The on-click Overlay for the template page shown previously, modified to read its message from a file and perform the necessary search-and-replace procedures, is as follows:

```
<<OVERLAY lp_emailcheck
  sstr='user_email="'+lp_email+'"'

temp=DBFIND("/work/users",sstr,1,1,"user_email,user_login,user_p
assword")
  IF temp[1,1] != lp_email THEN
      lp_msg="E-mail Address Not Found. Try again. "  GOTO
PAGE
  ELSE
user_login = temp[2,1] user_password = temp[3,1]
      COPY FILE="forgot_password.txt" TO msg /COPY
      msg=REPLACEALL(msg," [login]",user_login)
      msg=REPLACEALL(msg," [password]",user_password)
      MAIL msg TO ADDRESS=lp_email
```

```
       SUBJECT='Recovered Login and Password'
     /MAIL
     GOTO "forgot_thanks.html"
  /IF
>>
```

Changes appear in bold. The COPY tag copies `forgot_password.txt` into `msg`. Two search-and-replace actions are performed. Each time REPLACEALL looks for a placeholder and replaces it with the contents of a variable. The rest of the on-click Overlay is the same as before.

Summary

In this chapter, we've reviewed how to set up login pages. You discovered that you can tailor them in an infinite number of ways to serve just about any need; but the construction process is the same. Give the user access to a page using a Start-link or a link from another HTML/OS page. Then, on that page, add an HTML form. When the user tries to log in, check a file or database. If login is successful, set some variables, perform some tasks, and let the user into the private side of your site.

Exercises

In the following exercises, you modify the ten-line login page. In each case, start with the version of the ten-line login page that reads from a database found in the "Using a Database" section earlier in this chapter. Answers to all exercises are provided on this book's companion Web site as described in the book's Preface.

Exercise 1

Modify the ten-line login page so it sets a wholesale or retail flag when the user logs in. If the user is a wholesaler, send the user to `wholesale.html`. If not, send the user to `retail.html`. Create a Start-link for your login page.

Exercise 2

Modify the ten-line login page so it checks the users' account balances before letting them in. Hint: To do this, use a users database with a `user_balance` field. To test your page, have the login page deduct some amount from users' balances every time they log in.

## CHAPTER 10

HTML Forms Processing

It's difficult to imagine an advanced Web site without HTML forms. The most sophisticated HTML forms work in concert with other HTML forms placed on additional Web pages. You see them used in multipage questionnaires, product checkout pages, and sophisticated user input forms like the Web-based tax filing service shown in Figure 10.1.

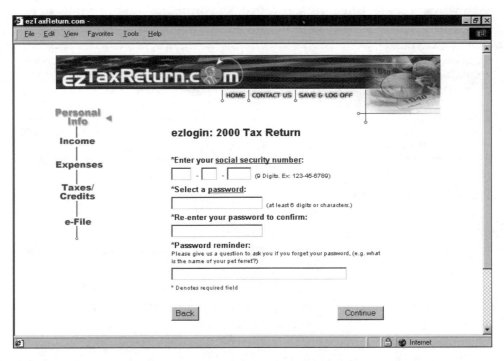

Figure 10.1: This U.S. Tax Filing Service is an application of HTML forms processing in an HTML/OS-driven Web site.

More often HTML forms are confined to a single Web page. They are used in everyday Web components such as login pages, guest books, database record editors, text editors, calculators, data-entry pages, setting pages, and almost everywhere data needs to be captured from users.

The HTML form is the primary mechanism for collecting data from users. It plays a central role in advanced Web site construction, because advanced Web sites require user interaction. Unfortunately, books on HTML cannot fully explain the capabilities of HTML forms. Without a complimentary engine such as HTML/OS, HTML tags are limited. That is why, although this book assumes you have knowledge of HTML, it does not assume you have a complete knowledge of HTML forms. This chapter fills this gap.

This chapter begins with a discussion of 10 HTML form components. You learn how each component is initialized and how each passes data to variables when the user submits an HTML form. Later in the chapter, the topic of how to validate user input is discussed. Then, at the end of this chapter, you explore the construction of a fifteen-line spreadsheet editor and a six-line upload page—two useful applications you can build with HTML form components.

Chapter Conventions—*This chapter does not organize HTML form tags by their formal names. Instead, combinations of HTML form tags, along with their defining attributes, have been isolated and called* components. *Unnecessary HTML attributes have been dropped. This chapter is a practical guide, so we avoid those HTML tags that play a minimal role in advanced cross-browser Web-site construction. Consult an official HTML reference if you need more complete description of the form tags and attributes available in HTML.*

The Components

You build almost all HTML forms using 10 main components, which you place between a set of `<form  ACTION=destination>` and `</form>` tags. The *destination* here refers to another HTML document or an on-click Overlay. See the accompanied "The HTML/OS Destination" note.

Unlike many HTML tags, HTML forms cannot be nested (placed within each other) and neither can their components. Furthermore, it is usually best to place only one HTML form on a Web page. When a user clicks a Submit button in an HTML form, only the data in the HTML form passes to the Web server. Data in other HTML forms on the page is lost. As a result, putting more than one HTML form on a page can cause confusion for users and is not advised.

The HTML/OS Destination—*Hypertext links,* GOTO *tags, and* ACTION *parameters in HTML forms require that you specify a destination. The destination may be a document name specified as full or relative path, such as* cart.html *or* /work/two.html. *If no dot appears in the destination, HTML/OS assumes the destination is an on-click Overlay. In these first two cases, the user never sees the actual document name specified since it is encoded and hidden from the user. These links are said to be inside HTML/OS. If the destination is written as a full URL, such as* https://www.securepost.com/capture.html, *the link is said to be outside HTML/OS. The users do see the URL in their browsers, and when they click it, they are sent directly to the remote location without any passing of data to the server hosting the copy of HTML/OS. The data is processed on a remote server, outside HTML/OS. This last kind of destination is not discussed here. Here only destinations that stay inside of the HTML/OS environment are discussed.*

These 10 HTML form components, which are sufficient for building an advanced Web site or a Web-based application, are shown in Figure 10.2:

- Textarea
- Select
- Text box
- Password box
- Hidden

- Radio
- Checkbox
- Upload
- Submit
- Image

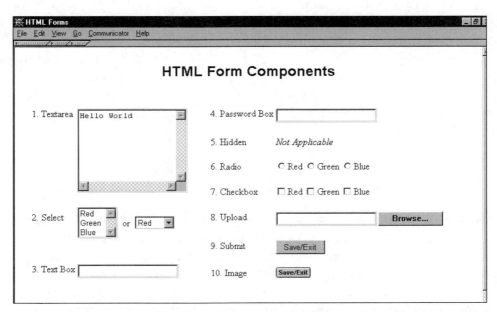

Figure 10.2: These 10 HTML form components are all you need to build an advanced Web site.

Setting up an HTML form component requires three pieces of information. First, you need to know the attributes of the HTML form tag that gives the component the look you want. For example, the single-row input box uses the attribute `size` to set the length of the input box. As another example, the input text area uses the attributes `cols` and `rows` to set the number of rows and columns of the input text area.

Second, you need to know the content of the component when it's displayed. For example, if a pull-down menu appears on the screen, you may wish to set the default selection. Or if a text box appears on the screen, you will want to determine the text in the box. In HTML/OS the HTML form components are initialized with the values in the variable names specified in the HTML form at the time of page rendering. For example, writing `<input type=text name=abc size=20>`, builds a single-row input box on the screen that's 20 characters wide. The `name=abc` in the component tells HTML/OS to initialize the box with the contents of the variable `abc`. Setting up the content of an HTML form component is about making sure the content of the variable name in the HTML form is what you wish to appear on the screen when the component is displayed.

Last, you need to know what information passes back to HTML/OS when the user submits the HTML form. Typically, this is just the variable name defined in the form. However, in the special case when multiple HTML form components, each with the same variable name, are placed in an HTML form, the submitted data is placed in different rows of the same variable. This is discussed when relevant, as each component is discussed.

A brief description, or capsule, of each HTML form component is provided here. Each includes the component's name, its syntax, a brief description of how it is initialized, and how it passes data to HTML/OS when it's submitted. An example is also provided for each component as well. Use these capsules as a convenient reference.

Using Textarea

```
<textarea cols=no_of_columns rows=no_of_rows name=name></textarea>
```

This component displays an editable text area *no_of_columns* wide and *no_of_rows* high filled with the contents of the variable *name*. One component is used per *name*. This component requires a closing `</textarea>` tag. When submitted, the content of the text area is placed in the variable *name*. When writing the tag you don't need anything between the `<textarea>` and `</textarea>` tags. Placing text between them overrides the contents of the text area with that text.

Example:

```
<textarea cols=65 rows=15 name=mydata></textarea>
```

Using Select

```
<select name=name size=no_items>
<option value=v1>item1<option value=v2>item2<option value=v3>...
</select>
```

This component displays a pull-down menu. It uses the two HTML tags `select` and `option`. One set of components is used per *name*. The first item in the pull-down menu on the screen is *item1*. The second is *item2* and so on. The pull-down menu will show *no_items* items at a time. A scroll bar will appear on the screen if the total number of menu items exceeds the size specified. A menu item will be highlighted on the screen if its value matches the contents of the variable *name*. When submitted, the value associated with the item selected (*v1*, *v2*, *v3*, etc.) is saved to the variable *name*.

Example:
```
<select name=gender><option=M>Male<option=F>Female</select>
```

Placing the word *multiple* in the `<select>` header enables select boxes to accept more than one selection. Menu items with values that match a row in the specified *name* are highlighted on the screen. When submitted, the values associated with the items selected are placed in the specified *name*, one per row.

Example:
```
<select name=addons size=2 multiple>
   <option value=1>Onions<option value=2>Extra Fries<option
value=3>Coke
   </select>
```

If `addons` is a one-column, two-row variable containing a 1 in one cell and a 3 in the other, the menu items *Onions* and *Coke* will be highlighted. If the user selects both *Extra Fries* and *Coke*, `addons` will become a one-column, two-row variable containing a 2 in one cell and a 3 in the other.

Using Text Box

```
<input type=text name=name size=no_cols>
```

This component displays a single-row input box, *no_cols* characters wide. Most often only one component is used per *name* specified. The box is initialized by HTML/OS with the contents of the variable *name*. When submitted, the values the user entered in the box are placed in the specified *name*.

When more than one input box has the same *name*, the boxes load with different rows of the specified name. When submitted, the values in each box are placed in the specified *name*, one per row.

Example:
```
<input type=text name=mytext size=60>
```

Using Password Box

```
<input type=password name=name size=no_cols>
```

This component is similar to the text box (type=text). Here too a single-row text box, *no_cols* characters wide, is displayed. Use one component per *name* and then initialize the box with the contents of the variable *name*. But here, characters in the box are displayed as stars (*). Here too, when the user submits the HTML form, the values entered in the box are placed in the specified *name*.

Example:
```
<input type=password name=mypassword size=30>
```

Using Hidden

```
<input type=password name=name>
```

This component is an invisible HTML form component. You initialize the box with the contents of the variable *name*. But it is not visible. You use one component per *name*. When the user submits the HTML form, the value stored in the input box is placed in the specified *name*.

Example:
```
<input type=hidden name=myrecord>
```

Using Radio

```
<input type=radio name=name value=v1>
<input type=radio name=name value=v2>
<input type=radio name=name value=v3>
```

This component is a radio button. Unlike all the previous HTML form components, here the component is repeated. Typically one component is specified for each possible value of the same variable name. A radio button will appear selected on the screen if its value matches the contents of the variable *name*. Radio buttons function so that the user can select only one button at a time (for a given variable name). When the user submits the HTML form, the value in the component (*v1*, *v2, or v3*) that he or she selected is saved to the variable *name*.

Example:
```
<input type=radio name=color value=red>Red<br>
<input type=radio name=color value=black>Black<br>
<input type=radio name=color value=green>Green<br>
```

Using Checkbox

```
<input type=checkbox name=name value=v1>
<input type=checkbox name=name value=v2>
<input type=checkbox name=name value=v3>
```

This component is a check box button. It is similar to the Radio component in that the component is repeated for each possible value of the same variable name. Unlike the Radio component, the user can select multiple check boxes for a given variable name. A check box will appear clicked on the screen if its value matches the contents of any of the rows in column one of the variable *name*. When the user submits the HTML form, the values in the selected components (*v1*, *v2, or v3*) are saved to different rows of the variable *name*. This component behaves similarly to the Select component (with the `Multiple` flag) discussed earlier in the "Using Select" section.

Example:
```
<input type=text name=extra value="SK150">Carrying Case<br>
<input type=text name=extra value="SK567">Extended Warranty<br>
```

Using Upload

```
<input type=file size=no_cols name=filename>
```

This component is a special file upload button. It looks like a text box with an extra Browse button used for browsing the user's computer for a file. To use an Upload component, you need to add `enctype="multipart/form-data"` to the HTML form header. An upload page is presented at the end of this chapter. This component does not give you the ability to set the default contents of the Upload box. When the user submits the HTML form, the file is uploaded and the name of the file in the Upload box is saved to the variable *filename*. The actual file is placed in the `/upload` directory with the name *filename*.

Example:
```
<input type=file size=50 name=myfile>
```

Using Submit

```
<input type=submit name=name value=value>
```

This component is a submit button. When the user clicks it, the data in all components in the HTML form are submitted. The submit button itself displays as the *value* specified. When the user submits the HTML form, this *value* is placed in the specified *name*.

Example:
```
<input type=submit name=mybutton value="Continue">
```

Using Image

```
<input type=image border=width name=name src=image_name>
```

This component is another kind of submit button. Here too, when a user clicks the button, the data in all HTML form components are submitted. The submit button itself is the *image_name* specified in the component. The image will have a border, *width* pixels wide. Unlike other submit buttons, when the user submits the HTML form, a *value* is not placed in the specified *name*. Instead the value TRUE or FALSE is placed in the *name*. Your code can use this value to detect which button is clicked.

When a user clicks an Image button, HTML/OS captures the pixel coordinates where the button was clicked and places those values in `name.x` and `name.y` where *name* is the variable specified in the component.

Data Validation

Data validation involves checking whether the information placed in a component makes sense. For example, you need to check a box asking for an e-mail address to ensure the data the user places in the box is a valid e-mail address. In some cases, the input is required. At other times, it is not. In addition, data validation involves presenting the information in a helpful way to users so they are less likely to make mistakes. When users type entries, they often introduce errors. That's why it's better to provide pull-down menus, radio buttons, or check boxes, if you can use them, to capture user input.

In many situations, however, users have no choice but to type their entries. In this section, you look at the code necessary to detect user errors, and to alert them of their mistakes as well as ensure that the data users enter in HTML forms is validated.

Avoid Browser-Side Data Validation—*Browser-side data validation involves adding JavaScript functions to HTML forms. The functions are activated before the HTML form is submitted, alerting the user of invalid data. These JavaScripts however have problems. First, some browsers will crash or complain when they run JavaScripts. Second, technically speaking, JavaScript does not protect your site from bad data, because JavaScript can be turned off or bypassed. These reliability problems are unsolvable. Browser-side data validation should be avoided.*

Writing the Code

You add data validation to HTML forms in the same manner regardless of the HTML form you are working with. When the user submits the HTML form, an on-click Overlay runs. At the top of this Overlay, you add IF-THEN statements to check the data entered in the form. If an error is found an error message is set and the page is redisplayed. If no problems are found, the instructions already in the on-click Overlay run. The HTML form is typically structured as follows:

```
<html>
<title>Sample HTML Form</title>
<form ACTION=process_me>
<<[Location1]>>
html form components go here
</form>
<<OVERLAY process_me
[Location2]
other instructions go here
>>
```

[Location1] is where you place the error message. The code you place at [Location1] displays the error message if it exists. For example, the following code can be used:

```
IF fp_error != "ERROR" THEN
  DISPLAY fp_error /DISPLAY
/IF
fp_error="ERROR"
```

When this Overlay first runs, fp_error is ERROR so the Overlay does nothing. If, on the other hand, a value is placed in fp_error, the contents of fp_error are placed in the document, alerting the users of the error they made.

[Location2] is where you place the data validation instructions. For example, an HTML form that requests the e-mail address my_var, might have an on-click Overlay with the following instructions:

```
fp_error=""
IF COUNT(my_var, "@")!=1 OR
    LENGTH(my_var)<7 OR
    COUNT(my_var," ")>0 OR
    COUNT(my_var,".")=0 THEN
    fp_error=fp_error + "Bad E-mail Address.<br>"
/IF
IF fp_error != "" THEN
    fp_error="<font color=red>Error: "+fp_error+"<br>Please Try
Again.</font>"
    GOTO PAGE
/IF
```

First, fp_error is initialized to the empty string. Then an IF-THEN statement runs. You would use this particular IF-THEN statement to validate an e-mail entry. If the entry doesn't have a single at sign (@), if it doesn't contain a dot, if it has a space, or if it's less than seven characters in length, the e-mail address is invalid. You can place additional IF-THEN statements after this one if you need to validate data entered into other input boxes.

After that an IF-THEN statement sees whether fp_error is still the empty string. If it is not an empty string, an error occurred. In this case, fp_error is beautified a bit and the page is redisplayed. If fp_error is still an empty string, no validation error has been detected so instructions you place after the code can run.

The Thirty-Line Guest Book

As an example, consider the task of building a guest book with data validation. Names users enter in the guest book are appended to a comma-delimited file.

Here you place an input form in an HTML form, requesting a user's full name, e-mail address, and phone number. You validate all three inputs. If successful, you append the user data to a comma-delimited text file and redisplay the page with a *Thank You* message. If not, you redisplay the page with an error message. The page requires about 30 lines of HTML/OS instructions and 4 HTML form components. You use the seven HTML/OS tags IF-THEN, DISPLAY, COUNT, TRIM, LENGTH, REPLACEALL, and GOTO. For details on these tags see Appendix D, *HTML/OS Tag Reference Guide*. Here's the code:

```
<html>
<title>Guest Book Page</title>
<b>Guest Book</b><br>
Enter personal information below so we can update you from time
to time.
<form ACTION=process_it>
<<IF fp_error != "ERROR" THEN
    DISPLAY fp_error /DISPLAY
  /IF
  fp_error="ERROR"
>>
Full Name: <input type=text size=60 name=guest_fullname><br>
E-mail Address: <input type=text size=60 name=guest_email><br>
Day time Phone: <input type=text size=60 name=guest_phone><br>
<input type=submit value="Add To Guest Book">
</form>
</html>
<<OVERLAY process_it
    fp_error=""
    my_var=guest_fullname
    IF COUNT(TRIM(guest_fullname)," ")=0 OR
LENGTH(guest_fullname)<4 THEN
        fp_error=fp_error + "Enter Full Name.<br>"
    /IF
    my_var=guest_email
    IF COUNT(my_var, "@")!=1 OR
      COUNT(my_var," ")>0 OR
      LENGTH(my_var)<7 OR
      COUNT(my_var,".")=0 THEN
      fp_error=fp_error + "Bad E-mail Address.<br>"
    /IF
    my_var=guest_phone
    my_var=REPLACEALL(my_var,")", "")
    my_var=REPLACEALL(my_var,"(", "")
    my_var=REPLACEALL(my_var,"-", "")
    my_var=REPLACEALL(my_var," ", "")
    IF ISINTEGER(LEFT(my_var,7))="FALSE" OR LENGTH(my_var)<7
```

```
THEN
        fp_error=fp_error + "Bad Phone Number.<br>"
    ELIF ISINTEGER(LEFT(my_var,7))="TRUE" AND LENGTH(my_var)<10
THEN
        fp_error=fp_error + "No Area Code in Phone Number.<br>"
    /IF
    IF fp_error != "" THEN
        fp_error="<table border=0 width=700><tr><td
bgcolor=red>"+
                "<font face=arial,helvetica size=2
color=white>"+
                "Error: "+fp_error+"Please Try
Again.</font></td>"+
                "</tr></table>"
    GOTO PAGE
    ELSE
        fp_error="ERROR"
    /IF
    APPEND ROW(guest_fullname,guest_email,guest_phone) TO
        FILE="myguests.txt" TS="," /APPEND
    guest_fullname=""
    guest_email=""
    guest_phone=""
    fp_error="<table border=0 width=700><tr><td
bgcolor=green>"+
                "<font face=arial,helvetica size=4 color=white>"+
                "Thank You.</font></td></tr></table>"
    GOTO PAGE
  >>
```

[Location1] and [Location2] in the earlier code in the "Writing the Code" section are replaced with instructions appearing in bold. [Location1] displays fp_error if fp_error contains a value other than ERROR. [Location2] runs three validation statements, appends a row of data to the file myguests.txt, clears the variables used in the guest book, sets fp_error to a *Thank You* message, and redisplays the page.

In the previous example, you validated an e-mail address. You also need to validate other kinds of data. Furthermore, sometimes you require the data and sometimes you do not.

As a rule, data that's not required should still be validated. If the data is not required, use the same instructions to test the data's validity; but also accept an empty string as a valid input. Here are instructions for validating e-mail, integers, a single word, a phone number, a full name, a zip code, a credit card number, and a currency. In each case, the variable you're testing is called `str` and the variable `req` is preset to `Y` in the event the input is required. In each example, if an error is detected, an error message is placed in the variable `fp_error`.

```
# validating e-mail /#
IF req !="Y" AND str != "" THEN
   IF (COUNT(str,"@")!=1 OR LOCATE(str,".")=0 OR
     LOCATE(str," ")!=0 OR LENGTH(str)<7) THEN
       fp_error="Invalid e-mail.<br>" /RETURN
   /IF
/IF
# validating integers /#
IF req !="Y" AND str != "" THEN
   IF ISINTEGER(str)!="TRUE" THEN
       fp_error="Invalid number.<br>" /RETURN
   /IF
/IF
# validating single word /#
IF req !="Y" AND str != "" THEN
   IF LOCATE(TRIM(str)," ") != 0 THEN
     fp_error="Invalid word.<br>"
   /IF
/IF
# validating phone number /#
IF req !="Y" AND str != "" THEN
    str=REPLACEALL(str,")", "")
    str=REPLACEALL(str,"(", "")
    str=REPLACEALL(str,"-", "")
    str=REPLACEALL(str," ", "")
    IF ISINTEGER(LEFT(str,7))= "FALSE" OR LENGTH(str)<7 THEN
      fp_error="Invalid phone number.<br>"
```

```
      ELIF ISINTEGER(LEFT(str,10))= "FALSE" OR LENGTH(str)<10
THEN
        fp_error="Invalid phone number. No area code?<br>"
      /IF
/IF
# validating full name /#
IF req !="Y" AND str != "" THEN
  IF (COUNT(TRIM(guest_fullname)," ")=0 OR
    LENGTH(guest_fullname)<4) THEN
        fp_error="Invalid full name.<br>"
  /IF
/IF
# validating U.S. zipcode /#
IF req !="Y" AND str != "" THEN
  IF (LENGTH(str)<5 OR
    ISINTEGER(LEFT(str,5))="FALSE" OR
    ISINTEGER(REPLACEALL(str,"-",""))="FALSE") THEN
        fp_error="Invalid zip code.<br>"
    /IF
/IF
# validating credit card /#
IF req !="Y" AND str != "" THEN
  str=REPLACEALL(REPLACEALL(REPLACEALL(str,"-","")," 
","",""),",","")
  IF ISMOD10(str)= "FALSE" THEN
      fp_error="Invalid credit card number."
  /IF
/IF
# validating currency /#
IF req !="Y" AND str != "" THEN
    str=TRIM(REPLACEALL(REPLACEALL(str,",",""),"$",""))
    IF str != FORMAT(str,"normal",2) THEN
      fp_error="Invalid Data Type"
    /IF
/IF
```

You can use these instructions in your code to validate various kinds of data. You can also use them to build a VALIDATE tag using HTML/OS functions. An exercise at the end of this chapter, for those readers familiar with the concept of defining functions, is provided.

The Fifteen-Line Spreadsheet Editor

Suppose you want to give users the ability to edit the contents of a table of information. For example, a site may include a table of products currently on sale—information that needs to be edited by staff. As another example, you may need to provide a screen for filling out the x-y coordinates of a chart. In both these cases, a spreadsheet editor is necessary for editing a delimited text file containing the table of information. A sample spreadsheet editor is shown in Figure 10.3.

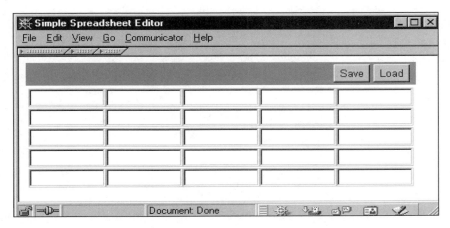

Figure 10.3: This spreadsheet editor gives users the ability to edit two-dimensional data.

To build the editor, you must place multiple input boxes on the screen in a two-dimensional grid. Each input box must have its own name so it can be initialized and pass data back to HTML/OS. You accomplish this by specifying the exact cell in the specified name for each component. For example, to build a grid with two columns and two rows, you can write the following code:

```
<input type=text name=my_var[1,1] size=5>
<input type=text name=my_var[2,1] size=5><br>
<input type=text name=my_var[1,2] size=5>
<input type=text name=my_var[2,2] size=5>
```

When HTML/OS renders these four components, it initializes them with the values in the cells specified. When a user submits the HTML form containing these components, the values the user enters in the text boxes replace the values in these cells.

To build a spreadsheet editor, you can type multiple components, as shown previously, into a Web page. However, this method lacks flexibility. You may want to make the editor adjust to the full size of a table that has been read from a file. You may want the editor to be adjustable by the user. You cannot provide these options if you simply type the components into a document. Instead, you should place the components dynamically in the page. An editor built this way follows:

```
<<
    csv_file="edit_csv.txt"     # data file name /#
    csv_x=5                     # width /#
    csv_y=5                     # height /#
    COPY FILE=csv_file TS="," TO csv_array /COPY
>>
<html>
<title>Simple Spreadsheet Editor</title>
<form method=post action=do_csv>
<center>
<table border=1 cellpadding=3 cellspacing=0>
<tr><td align=right bgcolor=#777777>
<input type=submit name=mybutton value="Save">
<input type=submit name=mybutton value="Load">
</td></tr>
<tr><td>
<table border=0 cellpadding=0 cellspacing=0>
<<
y=1
WHILE y <= csv_y DO
  DISPLAY "<tr>" /DISPLAY
  x=1
  WHILE x <= csv_x DO
    DISPLAY "<td><input type=text size=10 "+
            "name=csv_array["+x+","+y+"]></td>"
    /DISPLAY
```

```
   x=x+1
  /WHILE
  DISPLAY "</tr>" /DISPLAY
  y=y+1
/WHILE
>>
</form>
</table>
</td></tr></table>
</html>
<<OVERLAY do_csv
IF mybutton="Save" THEN
    COPY csv_array TO FILE=csv_file TS="," /COPY
ELIF mybutton="Load" THEN
    COPY FILE=csv_file TS="," TO csv_array /COPY
/IF
GOTO PAGE
>>
```

The Underlay on the page initializes the settings for the page and loads the table of information from a delimited text file. Inside the page, an Inlay uses a WHILE loop to display the HTML form components. Note that the HTML form includes two submit buttons; one to save and one to load the file. Also see how the *name* in the input box is composed. The code `name=csv_array[" + x + "," + y + "]></td>"` builds the name used in the component. It is important to remember that the column and row numbers need to be dynamically generated since they are different for each component.

This spreadsheet editor was built with the four HTML/OS tags COPY, IF-THEN, WHILE, and DISPLAY. It required fifteen HTML/OS instructions and two submit buttons. More advanced spreadsheet editors are available in the Clip library in the **Aestiva** Web site's User Center at http://www.aestiva.com/support/.

The Six-Line Upload Page

The ability to upload a file is a feature that's needed in many Web-based systems. Whether you want to build a page that uploads comma-delimited files, spreadsheets, documents, or images, you first need to know how to build an upload page.

The Upload component described in the beginning of this chapter is the component you use to build this page. First you place the Upload component in your HTML form. Then you add a special attribute to the HTML form header so it accepts file uploads (you see that shortly). When the user submits the HTML form, the file that's uploaded is saved to a file. The file needs to be unique for each user, because multiple uploads may be occurring simultaneously. The file is then moved to its desired destination name.

Here's an upload page that uses six HTML/OS instructions, an Upload component, and a submit button. The page allows users to upload a company logo, `mylogo.gif`:

```
<html>
<title>Six-Line Upload Page</title>
<b>Upload Company Logo</b>
<form enctype="multipart/form-data" ACTION=upload_me><br>
<font size=1>FILE</font><br>
<input type=file name=file<<usernum>> size=20>
<input type=submit value="Upload Company Logo Now">
</form>
</html>
<<OVERLAY upload_me
        temp=GETCOLEQ(FILELIST("/upload"),1, "file"+usernum)
        IF temp[1]= "file"+usernum AND temp[2] > 500 THEN
            temp=SYSMV("/upload/file"+usernum, "mylogo.gif")
            GOTO "upload_succeeded.html"
        ELSE
            GOTO "upload_failed.html"
        /IF
>>
```

The HTML form header includes the `enctype="multipart/form-data"` attribute, which you need to include whenever you use Upload components in HTML pages. Technically speaking the attribute tells the HTML browser how to encode the uploaded file. Without it file uploads fail.

The Upload component saves uploaded files in the /upload folder with the name specified in the *name-value* pair in the tag. Here the *name-value* pair is `name=file<<usernum>>`. USERNUM is an Overlay tag that contains the user's session number. As a result, this Upload component always places the uploaded data in a unique file for that user. This way of specifying the name is necessary to allow two users to upload a file at the same time without overwriting each other.

When a user submits the HTML form, the contents of the file on the browser computer is uploaded and saved to `/upload/file356`, for example (for a user with a USERNUM of 356), and then the on-click Overlay `upload_me` runs.

The first instruction in the on-click Overlay lists the files in the `/upload folder`, extracting from the file list only the row that matches the filename of the uploaded file. You use the FILELIST and GETCOLEQ tags to accomplish this. The tags are *nested*, meaning you place one inside the other. To understand how nested tags work, always start from the inside and work out. The inner-most HTML/OS tag is FILELIST, which produces a multicolumn variable. Column 1 contains filenames. Column 2 contains file sizes. This table is used as the first parameter of GETCOLEQ, an HTML/OS tag that extracts from a table only those rows in which a particular column (in this case column 1) matches a specified value (in this case the file name). See Appendix D, *HTML/OS Tag Reference Guide* for a detailed description of these tags.

The matching row is placed in the variable `temp`. When a user successfully uploads a file, the first cell of `temp` contains the filename, and the second cell contains the number of bytes uploaded. As a precaution, both of these cells are checked before moving the uploaded file to its intended destination—`mylogo.gif`.

Summary

In this chapter, you reviewed the 10 HTML form components used in advanced Web-site construction. Interestingly enough, although these 10 components are powerful, as a user of the Web, you are already familiar with them. They are the building blocks of all Web sites. No matter how advanced you get, these components stay the same.

You also learned some data-validation techniques and reviewed two applications: a fifteen-line spreadsheet editor and a five-line upload page. We recommend you copy the code in this chapter into your copy of HTML/OS and modify the code until you are comfortable using all 10 HTML form components.

Exercises

The following exercises require heavy use of HTML forms and a thorough understanding of HTML/OS fundamentals. Some of the exercises are fairly involved. Complete these exercises to reinforce what you've learned in this chapter and in Part II, *Programming Basics*. Answers to all exercises are provided on this book's companion Web site as described in the book's Preface.

Exercise 1

Build a calculator that can add, subtract, divide, and multiply two numbers. Build it using the following sets of HTML components:

- Build the calculator using two text boxes with a pull-down menu (with the operators add, subtract, multiply, and divide) placed between the two and followed by a Calculate button. Show the calculation result when the page is redisplayed.
- Build the same calculator using only pull-down menus. Replace each text box with five pull-down menus each containing the numbers 0 through 9.
- Build the calculator using a long text area with buttons underneath it. Make it resemble a calculator touch pad on your keyboard. In other words, the buttons should include a three-by-three grid of numbers between 1 and 9. Then to the right of these, place the buttons 0, 00, and Enter. Above these, place the four operators Add, Subtract, Multiply, and Divide.

Exercise 2

Build a set of instructions that validate a date. Hint: Use the ISDATE tag, which is described in Appendix D, *HTML/OS Tag Reference Guide*.

Exercise 3

Build a VALIDATE tag that takes three parameters; the data being validated, a data-type code (such as email, word, creditcard, etc.), and a req flag that is set to y if the field is required. Use the instructions provided earlier in this chapter to build the function. Use the FUNCTION tag to do this. It is described in Appendix D, *HTML/OS Tag Reference Guide*.

Exercise 4

The spreadsheet editor presented in "The Fifteen-Line Spreadsheet Editor" section of this chapter reads values organized in a two-dimensional grid. Replace the text boxes with check boxes, and add a Clear button and a Next Generation button to create the classic Game of Life. Hint: The Game of Life is played on a two-dimensional grid. Each cell is either alive/on or dead/off. The new state of each cell (The Next Generation) is determined by its old state and the sum of the alive cells among its surrounding eight nearest neighboring cells. The rules are as follows: A cell in the next generation is alive if a living cell is surrounded by either 2 or 3 alive cells or if a dead cell flips into the alive state by being surrounded by exactly 3 living cells. Otherwise it dies. These special rules were invented by the mathematician J.H. Conway. In the actual game the grid is infinite. In this case, you can use a 15-by-15 set of cells.

Exercise 5

Build a color selector bar—a bar with 16 colors on it. When the user clicks a color the selected color displays on the screen. Hint: First create an image bar, 160 pixels wide with one color for every 10 pixels. Then note that Image components can tell you the pixel location on the image clicked when the user submits the image. Use this to determine the color selection.

PART III
Database Programming

CHAPTER 11

The Web Database

This chapter introduces you to the Web database architecture used by HTML/OS. You learn about the kinds of database fields available to you, how to pass data to and from databases, how to merge data from a database into a Web page, and how to build an eight-line database record editor. By the end of the chapter you'll have a basic understanding of how to work with database records. The chapter starts with a brief discussion of how the Web database used by HTML/OS differs from conventional database architectures.

The main thing to note about the HTML/OS database architecture is that it's very reliable and easy to use since it is not built from multiple products and components designed prior to the advent of the Web. The architecture purposefully lacks the complexities of legacy systems.

Web Versus Legacy Databases

Before diving into how HTML/OS databases work, it is important to note that the Web databases used by HTML/OS have architectural features distinct from legacy databases—databases engineered prior to the advent of the Web. The differences are widespread, spanning how data is displayed, maintained, accessed, and stored. If you are unfamiliar with legacy database architectures, that's okay. But you may find this section's discussion helpful to more fully appreciate the advantages of HTML/OS databases.

First and foremost, legacy databases run as stand-alone products without the Web. These products were originally designed for delivering information to standard computer screens, so the products are often poor or incapable of rendering Web pages. Most leave the task of Web page rendering to integration tools, also known as middleware products.

These legacy databases connect with middleware products via database servers used to serve database information to other programs. On the Web however, you already have servers that can serve database information—the same Web servers that serve Web pages. The HTML/OS database architecture takes advantage of this. With HTML/OS, database servers and middleware products are not needed. For you this means no database server to set up and maintain. This also increases site reliability since, if the database server fails, the Web site fails.

Second, the Web database used by HTML/OS provides a seamless connection between data in databases and Web pages. Single instructions are used to move data back and forth among Web pages, HTML form components, and database tables. Legacy databases hooked up to the Web do not do this. They must channel data through database gateway languages such as SQL (structured query language). In HTML/OS there is no such limitation.

Last, the HTML/OS database is Web-based. Administration, programming, and data maintenance is done through a browser. Legacy databases, at best, are partially administered through a browser. Changes to HTML/OS databases can be performed from the nearest computer hooked up to the Web.

The HTML/OS Database Architecture

Although HTML/OS databases have many differences with legacy databases, their primary purpose, the storage of large amounts of well-organized information, is the same. Like other databases, the HTML/OS database organizes information in tables subdivided into multiple records, which themselves are subdivided into one or more fields.

In HTML/OS, when setting up a database, you decide on the database tables and fields needed for your project and create them with a point-and-click application called dbConsole. There are no schemas to set up, as discussed in the accompanying note, "No Schemas to Define."

No Schemas to Define—*In HTML/OS a database and a table are the same. In legacy systems a database has multiple tables, each related to the next with schemas—sets of definitions that link fields together. In HTML/OS these schemas are not needed. This makes it easier at a later date to change or add fields to your tables to accommodate design changes or add new features. Note that although the HTML/OS database is relational, these relations do not need to be set up in advance. Instead, they are set up within Overlay tags. This topic is discussed in Chapter 12,* Building Query Pages.

The Database Table

The HTML/OS database table is composed of data and indexes (cross-referencing data used to speed up access to data) stored in multiple files, each placed in the same directory. These files share the same name except for their extensions. Data is placed in files with the extension db. Index information is placed in files with the extension idx. The name of a database is the name of these files without their extension. For example, the database `/work/customers` uses the files `/work/customers.db` and `/work/customers.idx`.

Like HTML files, databases can be specified by full path or relative to the current directory. A Web page in the `/work` directory, for example, can reference the `/work/customers` database as `/work/customers` or simply `customers`.

Each record in a database is composed of multiple fields. The first field of all HTML/OS records is called `RECORD`. It contains a unique number, called the *record ID*, which is determined automatically when a record is created. All other fields are definable. The naming convention used to name fields is the same as that used for variables, as explained in Chapter 6, *Variables, Conditionals, and Loops*.

Field Types

Each field can store one type of information. The requirement that fields store only one kind of information is used as a convenience to the HTML/OS engine. Without predefined field types, computer searches run slower. The field types used by HTML/OS, along with their 3-letter codes, are; String or `STR`, Integer or `INT`, Floating Point or `FLT`, Currency or `DOL` and Date or Time or `DAT`.

Strings

String is computer talk for text. In HTML/OS, strings can be 1 to 100,000 characters in length, like cells in HTML/OS variables. They can contain text, HTML, names of images and binary files, logical values (`TRUE` or `FALSE`), or entire text documents.

Integers

These are whole numbers, negative or positive. They can be between 1 and 11 characters, like integers in variables. Note that credit card numbers and social security numbers are not integers. They are too long and often contain other characters such as spaces and hyphens. Use `STR` for those situations.

Floating Points

Floating point is computer talk for fraction. These are numbers, positive or negative, up to 11 characters in length, inclusive of a decimal point. They have the same limits placed on fractions used in HTML/OS variables.

Currencies

Currencies are fractions with two digits after the decimal point. Currencies are limited to 999,999,999 in whatever currency you are using.

Date and Time

Date and Time fields can contain dates, times, or a combination of dates and times. These fields must obey the same rules that dates and times obey when stored as variables. See the "Using Different Kinds of Variables" section of Chapter 6, *Variables, Conditionals, and Loops* for specific rules and limits.

Working with Databases

Using HTML/OS databases *usually* requires two steps. First you set up the databases you need in dbConsole. See the accompanying "On-the-fly Database Construction" note regarding the use of the word "usually."

Second, once the databases are set up, you read and write to them using Overlay tags placed in your document. The Overlay tags transfer data between databases and HTML/OS variables. These Overlay tags, called DB tags for short, begin with the characters DB. They have names like DBADD, DBDELETE, and DBEDIT.

You learn how to use these tags in the section "Using DB Tags," later in this chapter. Here you look at the options provided to you by dbConsole.

On-the-fly Database Construction—*Database setup is "usually" performed within the dbConsole application. But it doesn't have to be. You can use Overlay tags. In circumstances where you want your application to set up databases or provide database maintenance functionality, Overlay tags such as* DBCREATE, DBPURGE, DBIMPORT *can be used. Most often however, you want to use dbConsole since it is point-and-click. See the knowledge base on the Aestiva Web site at* http://www.aestiva.com/support/ *for information about building databases on the fly.*

Using dbConsole

You first encountered dbConsole in Chapter 4, *Your First Web Database Program*. There you used dbConsole to build a database and populate it. Here you look at the other options available to you. To run this application, click the **dbConsole** icon on your HTML/OS desktop. Click **Open** to select a database. You should see a screen like that shown in Figure 11.1. An Options menu appears on the left side of the screen. You use the first option, Open, to select a database table. See the attached note, "Open Means Selected."

Once a database has been selected, you can use the options Edit, Purge, Index, Change, Import, Export, Copy, Delete, and Info. You can use Open and Create used selecting a database. These options are discussed separately in the sections that follow.

Edit

Click **Edit** to pull up the first record of your selected database table. The name of that database is shown at the top of the right pane of dbConsole's window. You use

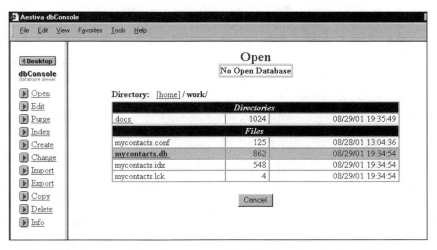

Figure 11.1: The database selection screen highlights databases making them easy to recognize.

Edit to edit records in the database manually. Options to add, delete, and modify the contents of fields in the record are provided. An Autosave option is also provided. When you place a check mark next Autosave, dbConsole automatically saves the current record as you move forward and back among the records.

***Open Means Selected**—The term "open" in dbConsole is used to indicate the selection of database tables. It does not mean "open" in the computer networking sense. Web databases do not keep connections to databases open or persistent as you work with them, since the Web pages that access databases are themselves not persistent. Web databases have open connections to them only in the split second they are accessed.*

Purge

Click **Purge** to expunge the database of deleted records—records that you have internally marked as deleted (see the "Copy and Delete" section later in this chapter) but still occupy space in the database. Purge rewrites the database files, eliminating these empty spaces in the table. Purging eliminates empty space and makes databases smaller, faster, and more manageable. Once a database has been purged, the deleted records become unrecoverable. Until then, you can recover deleted records with the DBSEARCHX and DBGETX tags. These tags are not described in this book but are described in the **Aestiva** knowledge base at http://www.aestiva.com/support/.

Index

Use this option to rebuild cross-referencing files used by HTML/OS to access the database. Indexing is advised if you have more than a two thousand records that have not been indexed. Indexing improves the performance of database searches and record retrieval.

In HTML/OS you can build these cross-referencing files or indexes in steps. This ability to index incrementally is provided so large databases, otherwise requiring a lot of time to index (more time than the browser has available to it before it times out), can be indexed in stages. Click **Index**, set your index increment, and click the **Index** button. The index increment is the number of records to be indexed per step. A database smaller than 100 megabytes can be indexed in a single step. For databases with record sizes of about 2 kilobytes, an increment value of 50,000 is recommended. Repeat until no remaining records need to be indexed.

Create

This option builds a new database table. When a database is selected the structure of the currently selected database is used as a starting point. When no database is selected, an empty form is provided. Click **Create** to view an input form used for defining the fields in a table. Each row of the form has a place for you to specify a field name, a field type, whether the field should be indexed, and a field length. Click the **Add Fields** button above the input form to enlarge your input form to accommodate additional fields. A Create screen is shown in Figure 11.2. As you specify the fields in your database keep in mind the following:

- Field names are specified like variable names. The names cannot begin with a number and must contain only numbers, letters, and underscores, but no special characters such as a space or a dollar sign.

- When specifying a field type make sure you do not confuse integers with strings. Credit card numbers, Social Security numbers, and large IDs are strings. Logical values such as TRUE and FALSE are also stored in the database as STR. If you plan on referencing images, sound or video files, or any binary files, place the names of those files in a STR field and the files in a directory of your liking. Note that the entries for the field do not need to contain the full URL to the image or binary file. It does not need to contain the full path to the file either. Just the name of the file is needed. The path to the file can be specified later in the HTML document.

- Leave indexing set to Y so you can search your fields. Setting a field index to N disables the index for that field. That will save some hard disk space but these days, hard disk space is not a premium.
- If you specify a field type of STR, it can be 1 to 100,000 characters in length. If you specify a field type of INT, FLT or DOL, specify a length of 1 to 11. Anything more is a waste. If you specify a field type of DAT, specify a field length of 16 to leave room for both dates and times.

Once you have defined the fields you want for your database, enter a name for the database, and click **Create Database**. After creating a database, you can select it with **Open**, import data into it, manually add data to it with **Edit**, and access it with Overlay tags you place in HTML documents.

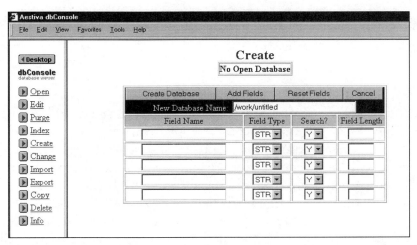

Figure 11.2: You can expand the database Create screen to accommodate additional fields by clicking the Add Fields button.

Change

Use the Change option to change the fields defined for a database that has already been created and populated with data. Figure 11.3 shows a Change database screen. It includes options to add, delete, and change fields.

To change a field, select it and click **Change**. Then make the changes you want, return to make changes to any other fields you want, and click **Save Changes** when done. The database structure will be changed, preserving the data in the database. Note that reductions in field sizes are not advised unless you are sure none of your fields exceeds the newer smaller field size. Otherwise data may be truncated, which means that some of the data may be lost.

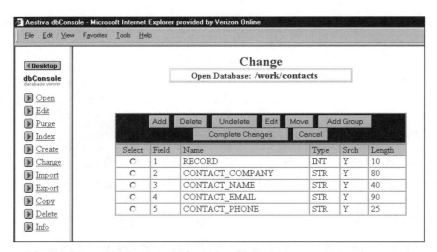

Figure 11.3: The Change database screen includes an Add Group option for adding group fields.

Group Fields

The Change database section also includes a button called **Add Group**, which gives you the ability to add a special type of field, called a group field, to the record definition. Any number of group fields may be added. Group fields are virtual fields built from one or more regular fields—like those defined on your Create screen. When a group field is searched, HTML/OS searches through a special index defined for all the fields belonging to it.

Group fields have another property too; they are word-indexed. This means that all words within the fields defined for the group field are internally cross-referenced. Multiword searches of group fields are much faster than searching within standard fields. The indexes used with standard fields are not indexed by each word in the field. Group fields are discussed in greater detail in Chapter 12, *Building Query Pages*. The Group field is useful when building high-speed searches where, for example, users enter one or more words in a single Find box on a Web page.

Import

Use this option to load many records at one time from a text file into a database. Suppose, for example, you have data in a legacy database or spreadsheet you wish to load into your Web database. Your first step is to export the data from the other database or spreadsheet into a delimited text file. You use the Save As or Export option of your other database or spreadsheet program to do this. Save the file as a tab-delimited, CSV, or comma-delimited file. Almost all database and spreadsheet programs have an option to export data as some kind of delimited text file.

Once your data has been exported as a file, upload it using the File Manager to your HTML/OS site. Now you're ready to import it.

Click **Import** on your dbConsole menu and select your delimited text file. You will see a screen like that shown in Figure 11.4.

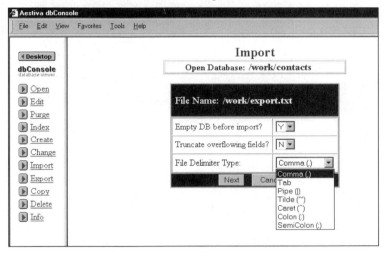

Figure 11.4: The Import option in dbConsole allows you load various kinds of delimited files into HTML/OS databases.

Select the delimiter of your file and click **Continue**. The Import option will read in the first line of the file and list it on the left side of the page as shown in Figure 11.5. To the right of each column entry is a pull-down menu allowing you to select the field the column of the delimited text file should be loaded into. To ignore a column of text in the file, set the pull-down menu to **Skip**. When done, click **Import** and all the records in the file will be loaded into the database. After importing your data you will want to check it. Click **Edit** to browse the imported records to ensure data has been placed in their proper fields.

Export

The Export option exports a database to a comma-delimited text file. Use this option if you need to transfer data from an HTML/OS database to a legacy database or spreadsheet.

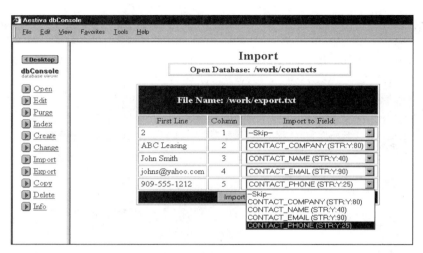

Figure 11.5: When importing from a delimited file, for every column in the file, you specify the field in the database it should fill.

Copy and Delete

The Copy and Delete options allow you to copy or delete a database table. These options copy or delete all the files associated with the specified database. These files include db and may include idx if the database is indexed. Note that databases can also be moved and deleted with the HTML/OS File Manager.

Info

Click **Info** to view the structure of your database along with general information about the database. This is a good screen to print for a handy reference of the fields in your database. See Figure 11.6.

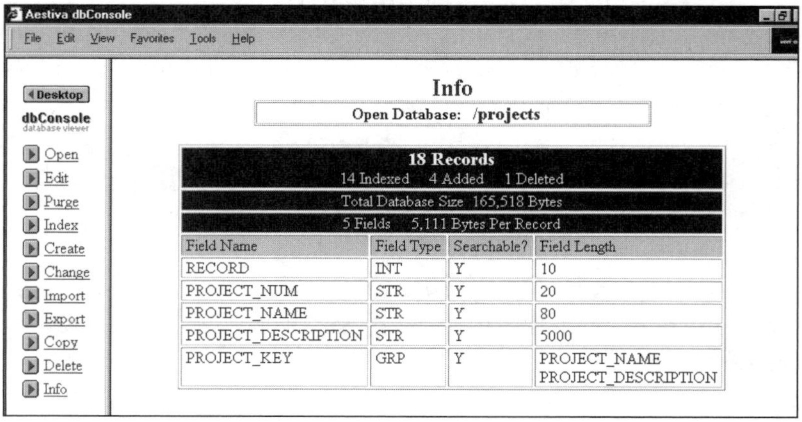

Figure 11.6: The Info screen in dbConsole provides a snapshot of your database.

Using DB Tags

Once you've created a database and added some records to it, or perhaps loaded it with data imported from another database, you are ready to add Overlay tags to your document to access it.

DB tags, the Overlay tags that work with databases, are available for performing, among other tasks, basic operations such as reading, editing, or adding records to a database. They are discussed here. More advanced tags for indexing, purging, and copying databases are also available but not discussed here.

DB tags are described in Appendix D, *HTML/OS Tag Reference Guide* and the **Aestiva** knowledge base at http://www.aestiva.com/support/.

The Eight-Line Database Editor

Let's look at an eight-line database editor that lists records in a guest book database and allows users to specify a record to edit, delete, or copy to a new record. We introduce this Web page to illustrate the basic DB tags; DBGETREC, DBEDIT, DBADD, and DBDELETE. The eight-line database editor is shown in Figure 11.7.

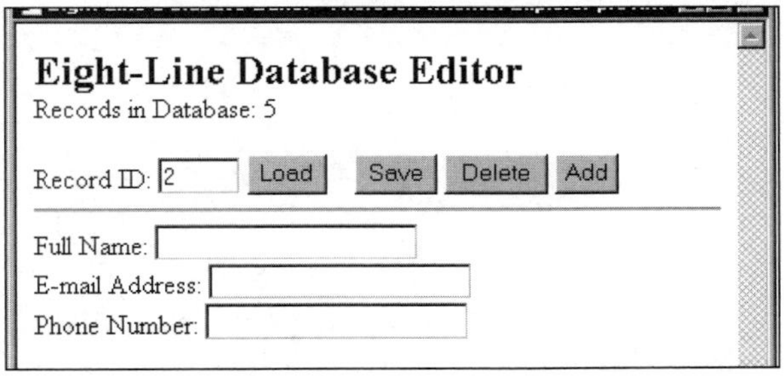

Figure 11.7: This eight-line database editor is great at editing small databases.

The code for the database editor in Figure 11.7 is as follows:

```
<html>
<title>Eight-Line Database Editor</title>
<font size=5><b>8-Line Database Editor</b></font><br>
Records in Database:
<< myrecords=DBFIND("tinydb","",1,100,"record")
   DISPLAY COLTOLIST(myrecords,1," ") /DISPLAY
>>
<form method=post action=dbopts>
Record ID: <input type=text name=record size=10>
<input type=submit name=mybutton
value="Load">   
<input type=submit name=mybutton value="Save">
<input type=submit name=mybutton value="Delete">
```

```
<input type=submit name=mybutton value="Add"><hr>
Full Name: <input type=text name=f1><br>
E-mail Address: <input type=text name=f2><br>
Phone Number: <input type=text name=f3><br>
</form>
</html>
<<OVERLAY dbopts
IF mybutton="Load" THEN
  temp=DBGETREC("tinydb",record)
ELIF mybutton="Save" THEN
  temp=DBEDIT("tinydb",record)
ELIF mybutton="Delete" THEN
  temp=DBDELETE("tinydb",record)
ELIF mybutton="Add" THEN
  temp=DBADD("tinydb",record)
/IF
GOTO PAGE
>>
```

The eight-line database editor uses the tinydb database with the fields f1, f2, and f3. The editor first lists the records in the database. This is followed by a row that contains an input box to enter a record number followed by Load, Save, Add, and Delete buttons. Below that row are three input boxes for entering a full name, e-mail address, and phone number.

The first Overlay in the eight-line database editor reads the database tinydb and places a column of record numbers in the variable myrecords. The DBFIND tag, as you may recall, is the same Overlay tag used and described in Chapter 4, *Your First Web Database Program.*

This instruction is followed by one that displays the value returned by COLTOLIST(myrecords,1," "). The COLTOLIST tag converts a column of numbers in a variable to a list, with each list entry separated by a special character known as a delimiter. The first parameter of COLTOLIST is the variable from which a column is extracted. The second is the column number, and the third parameter is the delimiter. Here column 1 was specified and the delimiter is a space.

The tag specified here, for example, would convert a variable with the word Larry in column 1, row 1 and larry@3stooges.com in column 1, row 2 and 415-555-1234 in column 1, row 3, into the text Larry larry@3stooges.com 415-555-1234. Here COLTOLIST is used to convert the column of records returned by the database search into a list of record numbers, each separated from the next with a space.

Below this instruction is an HTML form linked to the on-click Overlay dbopts. When a user clicks any of the buttons in the HTML form, the on-click Overlay dbopts runs. The dbopts Overlay contains an IF-THEN statement. The Overlay that runs depends on which button the user presses.

In HTML/OS, only a single DB tag is required to perform most database operations, because most DB tags work with all the fields in a record at one time.

If the user clicks the Save or Add button, the tags DBEDIT or DBADD run. These tags fill the fields of a database record using the values in variables named the same as the fields used by the database. For example, suppose you run the following instructions:

```
f1="Larry" f2="larrry@3stoogest.com" f3="415-555-1234"
temp=DBADD("tinydb")
```

This creates a new record in the database tinydb, with the values Larry, larry@3stooges.com, and 415-555-1234 in the fields f1, f2, and f3 respectively. The DBADD tag, after adding the record to the database, places the value TRUE in column 1, row 1 of temp, and the value OK in column 1, row 2. It also places the record ID of the record added in column 2, row 1 of temp. temp is the value returned by the DBADD tag.

Note that the DBADD and DBEDIT tags, like other tags in HTML/OS, return a value, which is why you write temp=DBADD and not just DBADD. The value returned is called a status result. The value abides by an HTML/OS convention used for all status results (assuming the Overlay tag returns a status result). A TRUE or a FALSE is placed in column 1, row 1. In column 1, row 2, the word OK is placed, or in the event the tag encounters a problem, an English-like error message. (Supplemental data is sometimes placed in other cells of a status result, depending on the particular Overlay tag.) Status results are described for each Overlay tag, if created, in Appendix D, *HTML/OS Tag Reference Guide.*

In the eight-line database editor, options to delete and load data are also provided. Clicking **Delete** runs the DBDELETE tag. This tag deletes a specified record from the database and returns a status result.

When a user clicks the **Load** button, the DBGETREC tag runs. This tag loads data from a record into variables. You might say it does the opposite of DBEDIT. Whereas DBEDIT loads data from variables into a record, DBGETREC takes data from a specified record and loads it into variables. For example, the reverse of the two-line DBADD instruction previously described would be:

```
temp=DBGETREC("tinydb",record)
```

`record` is the record ID of a record you wish to load. The DBGETREC tag takes the values in the fields of the specified record and loads them into variables of the same name. As you may recall from Chapter 10, *HTML Form Processing*, once a variable is loaded it appears in the HTML form automatically. In the eight-line database editor, the DBGETREC instruction is followed with a GOTO PAGE and no other instructions. That's all that is needed to load the data from the record into the form on the page. Once the page is reloaded it will display the data from the record since HTML forms display the values in the variable environment.

Whenever the eight-line database editor page is reloaded, the current set of records in the database displays, the HTML form displays with the current values of the fields in the database record, and the user is provided, once again, with options to edit a database record.

Summary

In this chapter you obtained a basic understanding of Web databases. You've seen that working with databases requires one tag per operation and that all the fields in a record are typically read or written once.

The eight-line database editor used in this chapter, while serving to explain the Overlay tags DBADD, DBDELETE, DBEDIT, and DBGETREC, had three obvious limitations:

- While the editor was suited to editing a small number of records, it is not suited to larger databases. Here we display all the record numbers on the screen. You would not want to do that when you have many records.
- Only record numbers were displayed on the screen. A good record editor would list additional information for each record, and to load a record, you would simply click an item in the list.
- The editor allows the user to edit any record. You do not want to do that if you wish to limit the records the user is able to edit.

These issues and more are left for Chapter 14, *Building Database Editors*. There you'll learn how to build more sophisticated database record editing systems.

Next, in Chapter 12, *Building Query Pages*, you explore how to retrieve, not one or all of the records in a database, but a selection of records. You move on to learning the details and variations of how one queries and extracts information from databases.

Exercises

The following exercises give you a feel for working with the basic DB tags described in this chapter. You are asked to take the eight-line database editor and modify it in a number of ways. Answers to the exercises here are provided on this book's companion Web site as described in the book's Preface.

Exercise 1

The eight-line editor used in this chapter does not display messages as records are edited, added, or deleted. Add messages to the application, so when a database operation is performed, its success or failure is reported at the top of the page.

Exercise 2

Convert the eight-line editor into a guest book page. To do so, eliminate all buttons on the page except the Add button. Rename the button to *Save To Guest Book*. And, when the record is added, display a *Thank-you* message at the top of the page.

Exercise 3

Take the guest book you constructed in the previous exercise and add data validation to it so the user is not able to add a record to the database if a valid e-mail address has not been entered or if the e-mail address entered already exists. To accomplish this, use the same e-mail validation methods used in Chapter 10, *HTML Form Processing*. To see whether a user is already in the database, use DBFIND.

CHAPTER 12

Building Query Pages

Most database searches start with a user entering values in one or more text boxes in an HTML form, clicking a Find button, and getting a listing of results. In this chapter you learn how to build these kinds of pages. You start with a page consisting of a single input. Then you explore, in general, how queries are constructed and how to set up and use group fields—special fields that accept multiword queries. Later you explore search pages with multiple input boxes, and at the end of this chapter you learn how to build query pages that search more than one database.

Later, in Chapter 13, *Building Database Reports*, you learn how the queries are displayed, sorted, or broken up so search result pages can be printed. Here, you focus on the construction of queries, using a simple report page to display your search results. The page, /work/report.html, displays results using a LAYOUT tag, the same tag used and described in Chapter 4, *Your First Web Database Program*. The page /work/report.html is as follows:

```
<html>
<title>Two-Line Database Report</title>
Search Results:<ul>
<table border=1>
<< DISPLAY
        LAYOUT(myresults,"<tr>",
            "<td>",[1],"</td>",
            "<td>",[2],"</td>",
            "<td>",[3],"</td>",
            "</tr>")
    /DISPLAY
>>
</table>
</ul>
</html>
```

This page displays the first three columns of the variable `myresults`, the variable we shall load with search results throughout this chapter. Unless stated otherwise, we shall also assume the database `/work/contacts` with the five fields `record` (the first field of all HTML/OS databases), `contact_company`, `contact_name`, `contact_phone`, and `contact_email`.

The Four-Line Query Page

You start by looking at a simple search page consisting of a text box and a Find button. The code for the page is as follows:

```
<html>
<title>Four-Line Query Page</title>
<form method=post ACTION=findit>
Enter Search: <input type=text name=mysearch size=10>
<input type=submit value="Find" ></form>
</html>
<<overlay findit
      mysearch=CUTALL(mysearch, '"')
      myquery= 'contact_company ~ ' + '"' + mysearch + '"'
      myresults=DBFIND("/work/contacts",myquery,1,50,
            "contact_company,contact_name, contact_phone")
      GOTO "/work/results.html"
  >>
```

When a user enters a value in the HTML form and clicks Find the on-click Overlay `findit` runs. There, `mysearch`, the variable submitted by the form, is stripped of any double-quotes using the CUTALL tag. Then a special instruction called a *query string*, is created and saved to the variable `myquery`. This special instruction is one of the parameters of the DBFIND tag—telling the tag which records to retrieve from the database and place in `myresults`. After DBFIND runs, the user is directed to the page `/work/results`, where the variable `myresults` is displayed. The bold instructions of this on-click Overlay set up the query string used in the DBFIND tag. The two instructions convert the input typed into the HTML form by a user into a query string the DBFIND tag can understand.

Creating query pages is really about placing an HTML form with one or more inputs on a page and then, after the HTML form is submitted, converting the values entered by the user into a query string. In the next section you dive into the specifics of how these query strings are composed.

The Query String

When an HTML form is submitted a set of variables entered by a user is available for your use. To convert these variables to a query string, you first need to know how query strings are formatted.

In HTML/OS these query strings, also known as Boolean expressions, are built from one or more statements, the smallest of which is composed of three parts: a field name, an operator, and a value. The statement, contact_name ~ "Bill", is such an example. The field name is contact_name. The operator is a tilde (~), which means *begins with*. The value is Bill.

Multiple statements can be combined with the words AND or OR. You use AND to find the overlap between two search results. You use OR to combine two search results. You can also precede these statements with the word NOT, indicating all records other than the search results. For example, let's say you have the statement RECORD > 5 and another statement RECORD < 10. Writing (RECORD > 5 AND RECORD < 10) gives you the overlap of these two statements—all numbers greater than 5 but less than 10. Writing (RECORD > 5 OR RECORD < 10) gives you all possible records. Writing NOT(RECORD > 5) gives you all records less than or equal to 5. It's the same as writing RECORD <= 5.

In general, it is a good idea to surround pairs of statements combined with the AND or OR words with parentheses, so the whole pair of statements can be thought of as a single statement and combined with others, using the NOT, AND, or OR tags. Parentheses eliminate ambiguity. When DBFIND encounters a set of parentheses, it calculates the searches in the inner parentheses first. As an example, consider the following query string:

```
(RECORD > 5 AND RECORD < 10) OR (RECORD > 15)
```

The use of parentheses tells DBFIND how to combine the individual statements. In this query string DBFIND will take the first set of statements in parenthesis and combine it with the last statement, RECORD > 15. The result is all records between 5 and 10 plus records greater than 15.

Using Quote Marks

The query string contact_name ~ "Bill" has quote marks around the value Bill. The query string RECORD > 5 does not. So when should you use quote marks? The rule is that you can always use quote marks around a value; but they are optional when the value is a number The query string RECORD > 5 can be written as RECORD > "5" as well.

Quote marks are needed since values in query strings often contain spaces. Without the quote marks, queries will fail when they encounter values with spaces, because DBFIND will get confused as to where values begin and end.

In the four-line query page, you used the CUTALL tag to extract the quote mark from the query. Then a query was composed with double quotes around the value. This was done so, regardless of the user input, the DBFIND tag would properly interpret the query string.

The best advice is to use quote marks whenever you're in doubt, because as long as you use them correctly, they never cause problems—and in fact often avoid subtle problems that otherwise may creep into your code.

Field Operators

When building query strings, each value is compared against a field using a special operator consisting of one or two characters. This operator will depend on the kind of field being compared against. The Integer (INT), Floating Point (FLT), Currency (DOL), and Date and Time (DAT) fields use the same sets of operators. String (STR) uses a different set of operators. Note also that comparisons on strings are case insensitive. For example, *Bill* will match *bill* or *biLL* in a string search. The operators available to each are as follows:

Operators for Integers, Floating Points, Currencies, and Date and Time

      <   Less than

      <=   Less than or equal

      >   Greater than

      >=   Great than or equal

      <>   Not equal (Same as !=)

      =   Equal

Operators for Strings

      =   Equal

      ~   Begins with

      ~~   Contains

These operators give you flexibility in setting up queries on a database. The two bold lines of the four-line query page described in the "Four-Line Query Page" section at the beginning of this chapter search only the contact_name field. But what if you want the search to include other fields? There are two ways to accomplish this. First, you can set up a group field that includes the fields you want to search and have your query string search that field instead of contact_name. Group fields are described in the next section of this chapter. Or you can compose a more complex query. For example, the two bold lines of the four-line query page could be substituted with the following lines:

```
mysearch=CUTALL(mysearch, '"')
myquery= '(contact_company ~ ' + '"' + mysearch + '") OR' +
         '(contact_name    ~ ' + '"' + mysearch + '") OR' +
         '(contact_phone   ~ ' + '"' + mysearch + '") OR' +
         '(contact_email   ~ ' + '"' + mysearch + '")
```

Note the mixed use of quote marks. Since you want to place a double quote before and after the value in `mysearch`, you need to paste these together carefully, keeping in mind double quotes need to be surrounded by single quotes.

Also note that the use of the tilde (~) operator. This operator, which means *begins with*, finds all records where the specified field begins with the value specified. The operator tilde-tilde (~~), which means *contained in*, finds all records where the specified field contains the value specified. See the accompanying "Using the Tilde-Tilde Operator" note.

***Using the Tilde-Tilde Operator**—Searches using the tilde-tilde (~~) operator are slower than other searches, because* DBFIND *needs to locate a specific pattern within a field and is not able to take advantage of its internal cross-referencing (indices). While most queries take about one-fiftieth of a second, the tilde-tilde search can take much longer. In databases containing more than 10,000 records, for example, the search can take many seconds. Unless your database is small, it is better to set up group fields than use a tilde-tilde search.*

Using Group Fields

In the previous section query strings contained standard fields defined as Integers, Floating Points, Currencies, Date and Time, and Strings. Query strings can also search group fields. You set up group fields in dbConsole. They are virtual fields composed of one or more string (STR) fields. Like searches on strings, searches of group fields are case insensitive.

Let's set up a group field for the contact database discussed at the start of this chapter and in Chapter 4, *Your First Web Database Program*. To do this, access your HTML/OS desktop and click the dbConsole icon.

1. Then click **Open** and select the database /mycontacts.
2. Click **Change**.
3. Click **Add Group** to add a group field to the database. You should see a screen like that shown in Figure 12.1.

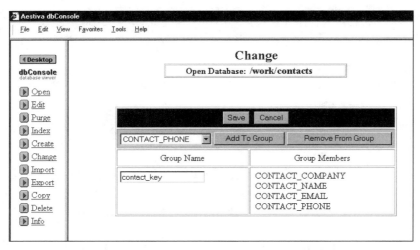

Figure 12.1: Use the Change section in dbConsole to add group fields to databases.

Suppose you want searches to span the fields `contact_company`, `contact_name`, `contact_email`, and `contact_phone`.

1. Enter the field name `contact_key` in the Group Name text box.
2. Select a field from the pull-down menu, and click **Add To Group** repeatedly until the Group Members list contains all of the fields you want in the group.
3. Click **Save** when done.
4. Then click **Complete Changes**.

Now `/work/contacts` has a group field called `contact_key`.

The code to search a group field is like the code used to search other kinds of fields except that the operators that work with group fields differ, because group fields are word-indexed, meaning each field is searched according to the words in the field, not just the field as a whole.

If a user enters multiple words into a search, DBFIND, when searching group fields, checks those words against all the words in fields that are members of the group field. When searching string (STR) fields, DBFIND looks at the entire field as one value. For example, a search for *Blue Box* searches fields with the word *Blue* followed with a space, followed by *Box*. If the search is done on a group field, the words *Blue* and *Box* are considered two different searches. Each word is matched against the words in the fields belonging to the group field.

Searches of group fields are done in one of two ways. On one hand, you may want any of the words in the search to match any of the words in the fields belonging to the member fields. On the other hand, you may want all of the words in the search to match at least one word in the fields belonging to the member fields. The first kind of search is called an OR search. The second is called an AND search. In computer science the AND is sometimes represented by the ampersand (&) character and the OR is sometimes represented by the pipe (|) character. Following this convention, the operators used with group fields are followed by one of these two characters. They are as follows:

Operators for Group Fields

=| Equal (on any word specified, same as =)

~| Begins with (on any word in any field, same as ~)

=&   Equal (on all words specified)

~&   Begins with (on all words specified)

When setting up general searches on a Web site tilde-OR and tilde-AND searches are used most often. Tilde-OR searches are typically used for smaller databases and tilde-AND searches for larger databases. You will need to experiment with your database to see which works better for you.

To improve the search used in the four-line query page, you search a group field instead of the `contact_company` field. Instead of writing the following

```
myquery= 'contact_company ~ ' + '"' + mysearch + '"'
```

you write

```
myquery= 'contact_key ~| ' + '"' + mysearch + '"'
```

Now users entering multiple words will get matches to all of their words. And all the fields defined for `contact_key` will be searched instead of only the `contact_name` field. The new and improved four-line query page, with changes in bold, is as follows:

```
<html>
<title>Four-Line Query Page</title>
<form method=post ACTION=findit>
Enter Search: <input type=text name=mysearch size=10>
<input type=submit value="Find" ></form>
</html>
<<overlay findit
    mysearch=CUTALL(mysearch, '"')
    myquery= 'contact_key ~| ' + '"' + mysearch + '"'
    myresults=DBFIND("/work/contacts",myquery,1,50,
        "contact_company,contact_name, contact_phone")
    GOTO "/work/results.html"
  >>
```

Working with Multiple Inputs

In the four-line query page the user is presented with only a single input box. On many query pages, however, you will want to present the user with multiple query selections. Searches of automotive, real-estate, and dating databases are a few cases that require multiple search criteria.

Like all query pages, query pages with multiple user selections are about converting the variables set in the HTML form presented to the user into a query string. It's just that the query is more complex.

In general, HTML forms contain the following kinds of query requests:

Free text—Inputs asking the user to type in one or more words
Selection—Inputs asking the user select from a list of possible choices
Check all that apply—Inputs asking the user to place a check mark in zero or more boxes
Query pairs—Inputs asking the user to specify a pair of inputs such as a begin and end date

For example, an automotive database may contain a search for a car make, model, year, and whether the user wants a new or used car. The car make, model and year can be selected from a list of possible values. Multiple-selection queries involving pull-down menus or radio buttons are used. A real-estate property search may query the user for a price range, a geographic area, and ask that users check off a list of desired amenities such as skylights, fireplace, and a Jacuzzi tub. The price range is a kind of *query pair* requiring the use of two pull-down menus or text boxes, one for minimum price and the other for maximum price. The geographic area may be a Zip code typed into a box. That would be a *free text* query. The desired amenities would be a check-all-that-apply type of query. Checkboxes are used there.

To build the HTML form that requests the queries, you use the components discussed in Chapter 10, *HTML Forms Processing*. When the user submits the HTML form, you validate the data; also described in Chapter 10. If the query is valid, you build your query string. This last step is what we describe here.

In general, when building a complex query, you start by building each individual query. Then, when you are done, you paste them together. Consider, for example, a hypothetical Web page for a singles dating club. The HTML form used on the page is as follows:

```
<form method=post ACTION=matefinder>
Find a Mate:<ul>
I'm looking for a <select name=gender><option
```

```
value=M>Male<option value=F>Female</select><ul>
Age must be between <input type=text name=min_age size=5>
and <input type=text name=max_age size=5><br>
He/she may be
<input type=checkbox name=height[1,1] value=short>short,
<input type=checkbox name=height[1,2] value=ave>average,
<input type=checkbox name=height[1,3] value=tall>tall<br>
</ul>
<input type=submit value="List Eligible Mates">
</form>
```

When the HTML form is submitted the four variables; `gender`, `min_age`, `max_age`, `height[1,1]`, `height[1,2]`, and `height[1,3]` are set. To create a query string, you compose three statements. You build the first with the variable `gender`. Code the second query statement by using `min_age` and `max_age`. In the last, you use the values in the variable `height`. Once this is done, paste together the three statements with ANDs to create the final query string.

Let's assume the dating database is called `/work/singles` and contains the fields `s_gender`, `s_age`, and `s_height`. Let's also assume the `s_gender` fields always contains the letter `M` or `F`; `s_age` always contains an integer, and `s_height` always contains the word `tall`, `ave`, or `short`.

The first query statement is written as follows:

```
q1='s_gender =  "' + gender + '"'
```

The second is written as follows:

```
q2='(s_age >= ' + min_age + ' AND s_age <= ' + max_age + ')'
```

The last query statement needs to build a statement from all of the height selections. To do this, we can use these IF-THEN statements as follows:

```
q3=""
IF height[1,1] != "" THEN q3=q3 + OR
s_height="'+height[1,1]+'"' /IF
IF height[1,2] != "" THEN q3=q3 + 'OR s_height="'+height[1,2]
+'"' /IF
IF height[1,3] != "" THEN q3=q3 + 'OR s_height="'+height[1,3]
+'"' /IF
IF q3 != "" THEN q3 = " AND " + REPLACE(q3,"(OR","(") /IF
```

Combine these with the following instruction:

```
myquery=" (" + q1 + " AND (" + q2 + "AND" + q3 + "))"
```

The result is the query string needed by DBFIND to perform the search. Note that this query was built by first creating the smaller queries q1, q2, and q3. They were pasted together at the end. The composition of q1 and q2 is straightforward. The composition of q3 is tricky. There, the statement q3=q3 + "OR field ="+value+")" was used to build q3 by successively combining q3 with new statements every time a nonempty selection was found. Note that the technique can be used whether you have three items that need to be checked off, or ten items. Here we used three IF-THEN statements; but alternatively, you could use a loop (as an exercise at the end of this chapter demonstrates). In any event, the problem with the statements is that q3 starts out an empty string, so you get an extra OR in the first statement created. For example, if a user were to select short and average the value of q3 immediately following the third IF-THEN statement would be

```
((OR s_height="short")AND s_height="average")
```

To correct the extra AND, you follow the IF-THEN statement with an instruction that replaces the four character sequence (AND with the (character. That gives you the correct q3 query statement.

In general, using the techniques discussed here, you can build complex queries that span many fields. The field names and selections may change, but the concepts are the same.

On-the-Fly Joins

The query pages thus far have searched a single database. Sometimes however, querying a single database is not enough. Multidatabase searches are required when multiple results need to be simultaneously extracted from more than one database. A real-estate database report that lists the names of listing agents for each property, although the names of the listing agents are stored in a database different than the property database, is such an example. This situation requires on-the-fly joins of multiple databases. The concept of on-the-fly joins is explained in this section.

A multidatabase search should not be confused with the concept of drill-down. A drill-down search occurs when an initial search yields a result that should lead to further information (by the user clicking hyperlinks to that information, for example), some of which may be stored in other databases. A listing of real-estate properties with hypertext links of sales people's names is an example. Although multiple databases are accessed, they are not accessed at one time. On-the-fly joins are not needed.

Most often on-the-fly joins are needed when you wish to augment the search results from one database with data stored in another table. First you perform a search on a database. Then you combine the search result obtained from the first database with a search of a second database.

In HTML/OS you perform searches across multiple databases by searching each database, one after the other, taking the result of one search and feeding it into the next search, until all databases have been searched. The first search uses the DBFIND tag. Successive searches use the DBFINDJ tag.

For example, suppose you have a database called /work/orders containing, among others, the fields order_company, order_amount, and order_date. If you want all the orders between two dates, date1 and date2, you need to search the /work/orders database. The query string and search might look as follows:

```
myquery='order_date <= "' + date1 + '" AND order_date > "' +
date2 + '"'
myresults=DBFIND("/work/orders",myquery,
            1,50,"order_company,order_amount,order_date")
```

The DBFIND tag, using this query string, fills myresults with fields from /work/orders. If you recall from Chapter 4, *Your First Web Database Program*, DBFIND has five parameters. The first is the database name. The second is the query string. The third and fourth parameters specify the range of search results to return, and the last parameter is the list of fields in the specified database to return.

The /work/orders database, however, doesn't include contact names and phone numbers. That data is stored in /work/contacts. To extend the search with data from the /work/contacts database you use the DBFINDJ tag. See Appendix D, *HTML/OS Tag Reference Guide* for further information. The *J* stands for *Join*. The following code is added after the instruction containing the DBFIND tag:

```
myresults=DBFINDJ("/work/contacts","",1,50,
   "contact_name,contact_phone",myresults,1,"contact_company")
```

The DBFINDJ tag has the same parameters as DBFIND plus three additional: the search result of the prior search, the column number in the search result that matches a field in this next database and the name of that field. These three parameters define a join of the first search result table (myresults) with a database (/work/contacts). In general, when DBFINDJ does its search, it starts with a table of results from a prior search and builds a new table using that, extending that table horizontally. The variable myresults starts out with the three columns. The table returned by DBFINDJ is five columns, the last two being the contact name and phone. An as example, suppose the result of DBFIND was as follows:

```
ABC Rentals        1550.00      04/02/2001
Babott Insurance   2370.50      07/20/2001
ABC Rentals        3025.75      07/28/2001
Delphi Leasing     1900.00      12/17/2001
```

The DBFINDJ tag would match each row of this result with records in /work/contacts having the same company name. If it finds a match, a contact name and phone are added to columns four and five. If no match is found the columns are left blank. If duplicate matches are found, the row is duplicated, and columns 4 and 5 are filled with contact names and phone numbers.

Let's say, for example, /work/contacts contained the following five records:

```
Record #1:  ABC Rentals     John Smith    415-555-1234 jabcrental.com
Record #2:  Babott Insur    Max Marcs     619-515-1234 maxm@yahoo.com
Record #3:  Bella Music     Bella Brown   714-555-1212 bbrown@exite.com
Record #4:  Brass Tax       Jacki Prince  212-555-1234 sales@btax.com
Record #5:  Delphi Leasing  Janet Adams   303-555-1234 leasing@delphileasing.net
```

The join of this database with myresults, the three-column value returned by DBFIND, yield the following five-column result:

```
ABC Rentals      1550.00    04/02/2001   John Smith    415-555-1234
Babott Insur     2370.50    07/20/2001   Max Marcs     619-555-1234
ABC Rentals      3025.75    07/28/2001   John Smith    415-5551234
Delphi Leasing   1900.00    12/17/2001   Janet Adams   303-555-1234
```

The DBFIND search yielded a three-column result. This table was extended to five columns with a DBFINDJ tag, drawing two fields from a second database. If more information needs to be added to the result, you can use additional DBFINDJ tags.

Summary

In this chapter you obtained a basic understanding of how to build query pages. You learned that all search pages, whether simple or complex, are about taking the variables submitted in an HTML form and using them to build Boolean query strings.

Next, in Chapter 13, *Building Database Reports*, you learn what to do with these search results and how to format them on a Web page. The next chapter, along with this one, gives you the ability to build a wide variety of database search and result pages—an important component of advanced Web sites and Web-based applications.

Exercises

In the following exercises you extend and build additional query pages using what you learned in this chapter. Answers to these exercises are provided on this book's companion Web site as described in the book's Preface.

Exercise 1

Expand the four-line query page to accept both *equals* and *begins with* searches. Do this by adding a radio button to the page allowing users to select the kind of search they want. Then add the necessary IF-THEN statement to the on-click Overlay to set the correct operator to use in the query string.

Exercise 2

In the "Working with Multiple Inputs" section of this chapter, you built an on-click Overlay that processed a complex query for searching a singles dating database. In the on-click Overlay you used a series of IF-THEN statements to build query q3. Replace this section of code with code that uses a FOR loop across the variable height so additional selections may be added to the HTML form without having to rewrite code in the on-click Overlay.

Exercise 3

Group searches are typically used to search words within a description; but they can also be used to search lists contained within a single field. As an example, a database for real-estate properties often needs a place to store property attributes. In real estate the possible attributes of a house may exceed 50. Instead of adding a field for each attribute, it makes more sense to have a single Attributes field containing a list of attribute codes. Using this approach, build a sample real-estate database and a query page that allows a user to select one or more property attributes (high ceilings, dishwasher, dryer, fireplace, ocean view, etc.)

Exercise 4

The on-the-fly joins discussed in this chapter did not contain a query in the DBFINDJ, because they were used to extend the results of an existing search result. In some situations however a search string is needed as input to the DBFINDJ tag. For example, consider the case of an orders database and an itemsordered database. Every time an order is placed a record is added to the orders database, which may contain a customer type (wholesale or retail, for example). At the same time records are added to the itemsordered database; one new record for each item ordered. The record contains a product ID and selling price. Knowing this, build a sample two-database system and a query page that allows a user to query the database for wholesale or retail orders above or below specific price amounts.

## CHAPTER 13

Building Database Reports

A database report is worth a thousand fields. Building highly functional, easy-to-read database reports is time well spent. What's more, custom Web-based reports offer more functionality than conventional database reports. Web-based reports can be dynamic. Click a column and the report can redraw itself—sorted by that column. Click an entry and the report can give you detail on an item. In this chapter you learn how to build these kinds of reports.

In the last chapter, you built query pages that converted one or more user inputs into a query string that was then fed into a DBFIND tag to produce a search result. In this chapter, you look at the variety of ways the search result produced by DBFIND can be customized and presented on the page.

You start with a simple seven-line database report and add features to it, one by one. Changes are described and explained. By the end of the chapter, you'll know how to build multipage, printable, sortable, multipurpose reports.

Seven-Line Database Report

In Chapter 12, *Building Query Pages*, you built query strings used by DBFIND tags. Users were directed to the page /work/report.html where search results were displayed. The page was a two-line database report that took the variable myresults and displayed it using a LAYOUT tag.

In this chapter you wish to do more on the report page. Instead of assuming users access the report page after composing a query and performing a search, here you assume the user has composed a query string but has not done the search. You let the report page do the search. The page has seven HTML/OS instructions, which is why it is called a seven-line database report. It uses a DBFIND tag to search the database, a FOR loop, three DISPLAY tags for displaying three columns from myresults, and two more DISPLAY tags for displaying beginning and ending HTML table row tags (<tr> and </tr>). You place the report within an HTML table to ensure columns line up. The page is as follows:

```
<html>
<title>Seven-line Database Report </title>
<< myresults=DBFIND("/work/contacts",myquery,1,100,
        "contact_company,contact_name,contact_phone")
>>
<table border=1 cellspacing=0 cellpadding=2>
<tr><td bgcolor=#000088 colspan=4 align=center>
<b>My Report</b></td></tr>
<tr>
<td>Column One</td>
<td>Column Two</td>
<td>Column Three</td>
</tr>
<<
FOR NAME=myresults ROWNAME=myrow DO
      DISPLAY "<tr>" /DISPLAY
      DISPLAY "<td>"+myrow[1]+"</td>" /DISPLAY
      DISPLAY "<td>"+myrow[2]+"</td>" /DISPLAY
      DISPLAY "<td>"+myrow[3]+"</td>" /DISPLAY
      DISPLAY "</tr>" /DISPLAY
/FOR
>>
</table>
</html>
```

Unlike the two-line report described in Chapter 12, *Building Query Pages*, this report uses a FOR loop to display rows from myresults, one at a time. The LAYOUT tag is switched to a FOR loop to gain control over the lines displayed. The added control is not necessary at this point; but later, as you add sophisticated features to the report, it will be. As an example, suppose you want to change the seven-line report to one that displays every other row in the report in light green to emulate green bar computer paper. To do so you add an IF-THEN statement inside the FOR loop that toggles the contents of a variable back and forth between lightgreen and white. The code is shown here with changes marked in bold.

```
<html>
<title>Seven-line Green Bar Report </title>
<< myresults=DBFIND("/work/contacts",myquery,1,100,
        "contact_company,contact_name,contact_phone")
>>
<table border=1 cellspacing=0 cellpadding=2>
<tr><td bgcolor=#000088 colspan=3 align=center>
<b>My Report</b></td></tr>
<tr>
<td>Column One</td>
<td>Column Two</td>
<td>Column Three</td>
</tr>
<<
FOR NAME=myresults ROWNAME=myrow DO
IF x="white" THEN x="lightgreen" ELSE x="white" /IF
     DISPLAY "<tr>" /DISPLAY
     DISPLAY "<td><font color="+x+">"+myrow[1]+"</font></td>"
/DISPLAY
     DISPLAY "<td><font color="+x+">"+myrow[2]+"</font></td>"
/DISPLAY
     DISPLAY "<td><font color="+x+">"+myrow[3]+"</font></td>"
/DISPLAY
 DISPLAY "</tr>" /DISPLAY
/FOR
>>
</table>
</html>
```

Using the FOR loop gives you the flexibility to perform different tasks as different rows are displayed. This is not possible with the LAYOUT tag. In this green bar report, an HTML font tag is placed around each cell of myrow. The color in the font tag is set to the variable x and given values that toggle between lightgreen and white.

Adding Page Up and Page Down

The seven-line database report of the previous section displayed the variable myresults. The DBFIND tag returned the first 100 rows. In some circumstances however, you will want to display more rows. Of course, you can increase the parameter used in DBFIND; but that is not always enough. You may not want the user to scroll up and down the page. You may prefer providing links to page up and down through the results.

At least two modifications to the prior report are needed for this. First, the two parameters in DBFIND that define the range of search results to return need to be changed to variables. Second, page up and page down links need to be added to the page. When a user clicks a page up or page down link, you need Overlay tags to modify the variables used in the DBFIND tag that define the range of search results to return.

A third, optional modification is to display for the user the range of search results on the page and the total number of search results available. That data can be extracted from the TAGRESULTS variable that's set when the DBFIND tag runs. We do that here as well. Here's a page with these modifications.

```
<html>
<title>Database Report With Page Up and Page Down</title>
<< pagesize=20
   IF ISINTEGER(i)="FALSE" THEN i=1 /IF
   j=i+pagesize-1
   myresults=DBFIND("/work/contacts",myquery,i,j,
       "contact_company,contact_name,contact_phone")
      j=TAGRESULTS[4,1]
      t=TAGRESULTS[5,1]
>>
<table border=1 cellspacing=0 cellpadding=2>
<tr><td bgcolor=#000088><b>My Report</b></td>
<td align=right colspan=2>Results <<i>> to <<j>> of <<t>></td></tr>
<tr><td colspan=2><a href=pgup>Page Up</a></td>
<td align=right><a href=pgdn>Page Down</a></td></tr>
<tr>
<td>Column One</td>
<td>Column Two</td>
<td>Column Three</td>
</tr>
<<
FOR NAME=myresults ROWNAME=myrow DO
     DISPLAY "<tr>" /DISPLAY
     DISPLAY "<td>"+myrow[1]+"</td>" /DISPLAY
```

```
        DISPLAY "<td>"+myrow[2]+"</td>" /DISPLAY
        DISPLAY "<td>"+myrow[3]+"</td>" /DISPLAY
        DISPLAY "</tr>" /DISPLAY
/FOR
>>
</table>
</html>
<<overlay pgdn
    i=i+pagesize IF i > t THEN i=i-pagesize /IF GOTO PAGE
  >>
  <<overlay pgup
    i=i-pagesize IF i < 1 THEN i=1 /IF GOTO PAGE
>>
```

Changes are shown in bold. In the first Overlay you start by setting the pagesize variable. Then, you set the two parameters in DBFIND that set the range of results to return to i and j. To ensure i and j are initialized, you place an IF-THEN statement prior to the search. Just below the DBFIND instruction, values for j and t are assigned using cells in the TAGRESULTS variable filled by DBFIND. Note that although j is set before running the DBFIND tag, it is also set after the DBFIND tag runs. This is necessary since j does not always equal i+pagesize—at least not on the last set of search results a user might view. The contents of TAGRESULTS are described in the description of DBFIND in Appendix D, *HTML/OS Tag Reference Guide*.

Below this Overlay, an HTML table filled with search results is displayed. The first row displays the range of results on the page. The row below this contains Page Up and Page Down links. The first runs the pgup on-click Overlay and the other runs the pgdn on-click Overlay. When a user clicks these links, the i and j variables are adjusted causing a page up and page down when the page is redisplayed.

Building Printable Reports

Printable reports are formatted so they split nicely across different pages of a printout. Printable reports also have page numbers and headers on each page. In many ways, printable report pages are constructed like the report pages with page up and page down discussed in the previous section, except that the pages in the report are displayed all at once on the same Web page and split only when printed.

The challenge when building printable reports is fitting the lines to the printed page. Since the number of lines that fit on a page can vary from browser to browser, and since the HTML language does not include a page-break tag, you need to improvise. The trick comes from knowing that browsers, when they print Web pages, try to fit HTML tables on a single printed page. If you split the report into distinct HTML tables, each large enough to fill the page, but not too large so that it carries over to the next printed page, then you will get one HTML table on each printed page. You use that fact when building printable reports.

To convert the seven-line database report to a printable format, you need to make two modifications. First, groups of rows in the search result need to be split among different HTML tables. Second, at the top of each of these HTML tables you need to add a title line with a page number and a total number of pages. The page to do this is as follows:

```
<html>
<title>Printable Database Report</title>
<< myresults=DBFIND("/work/contacts",myquery,1,1000,
        "contact_company,contact_name,contact_phone")
    t=TAGRESULTS[5,1]
    rowsperpage=40
    page_no=1
    page_last=ROUNDUP(t/rowsperpage)
    i=1
    FOR NAME=myresults ROWNAME=myrow DO
      IF i=1 THEN
        IF i+rowsperpage > t THEN j=t ELSE j=i+rowsperpage /IF
        DISPLAY
        '<table border=1 cellspacing=0 cellpadding=2>'+
        '<tr><td align=right colspan=3>'+
        'Page '+page_no+' of '+page_last+'</td></tr>'+
        '<tr>'+
        '<td>Column One</td>'+
        '<td>Column Two</td>'+
        '<td>Column Three</td>'+
        '</tr>'
        /DISPLAY
      /IF
      DISPLAY "<tr>" /DISPLAY
```

```
      DISPLAY "<td>"+myrow[1]+"</td>" /DISPLAY
      DISPLAY "<td>"+myrow[2]+"</td>" /DISPLAY
      DISPLAY "<td>"+myrow[3]+"</td>" /DISPLAY
      DISPLAY "</tr>" /DISPLAY
      IF i=rowsperpage THEN
        DISPLAY "</table>" /DISPLAY
        i=0
        page_no=page_no+1
      /IF
      i=i+1
/FOR
>>
</table>
</html>
```

Changes are shown in bold. First you set a `rowsperpage` variable to 40. This value should be adjusted for your printer. Then `page_no` is initialized and you calculate `total_pages` by using the `ROUNDUP` tag. This tag rounds up fractions to their next largest integer. The remaining modifications are made in the `FOR` loop. At the top of each page, when `i` is equal to 1, a header is displayed. The header opens an HTML table and then displays an HTML table row that displays `page_no` and `page_last`, the current and last page (or table, since one HTML table is printed per page). When `i` is equal to the `rowsperpage`, the end HTML table tag is displayed. After every row the variable `i` is incremented, but reset to 1 at the end of each HTML table. This gives you the desired effect—a Web page with multiple HTML tables, each with `rowsperpage` rows (except on the last page) and each with its own header. When the page is printed, each HTML table will appear on a different printed page giving you the affect you want.

Building Reports with Sortable Columns

Reports with sortable columns give users maximum flexibility in how they view their reports. Ideally, you want users to click the top of any column to redisplay their report sorted by the column they clicked. If they click again, the report should be redisplayed again, this time in a reverse sort.

A subtlety to this is that clicking a column doesn't always mean you should change the order in which the column is sorted. When changing the sort column, you want to sort by the last way that column was sorted.

Adding sortable columns to a report requires three modifications. First you add links to the top of each column for users to click; then you add a variable that stores how each column is sorted along with the code needed to change the sort when a user clicks the links, and last, you replace the DBFIND tag with DBFINDSORT. The DBFINDSORT tag is similar to DBFIND except it has two additional parameters for returning search results sorted by a specific column and sort order (reverse or default). The code for a database report page with sortable columns is as follows:

```
<html>
<title>Database Report with Sortable Columns</title>
<<
  IF ISINTEGER(resort_col)="FALSE" THEN

sort_fields=ROW("contact_company","contact_name","contact_phone"
)
    sort_types=ROW("Y","Y","Y")
    sort_col=1
    sort_col_last=1
  /IF
  IF resort_col != "ERROR" THEN
    sort_col=resort_col
    resort_col="ERROR"
    IF sort_col=sort_col_last THEN
      IF sort_types[sort_col]="Y" THEN
        sort_types[sort_col]="N"
        ELSE sort_types[sort_col]="y"
      /IF
    /IF
  /IF
  sort_col_last=sort_col
  myresults=DBFINDSORT("/work/contacts",myquery,1,100,
        sort_fields[sort_col],sort_types[sort_col],
        "contact_company,contact_name,contact_phone")
>>
<table border=1 cellspacing=0 cellpadding=2>
<tr><td bgcolor=#000088 colspan=4 align=center>
<b>My Report</b></td></tr>
<tr>
<td><a href=<<page>> NAME=resort_col value=1>Column
```

```
One</a></td>
<td><a href=<<page>> NAME=resort_col value=2>Column
Two</a></td>
<td><a href=<<page>> NAME=resort_col value=3>Column
Three</a></td>
</tr>
<<
FOR NAME=myresults ROWNAME=myrow DO
     DISPLAY "<tr>" /DISPLAY
     DISPLAY "<td>"+myrow[1]+"</td>" /DISPLAY
     DISPLAY "<td>"+myrow[2]+"</td>" /DISPLAY
     DISPLAY "<td>"+myrow[3]+"</td>" /DISPLAY
     DISPLAY "</tr>" /DISPLAY
/FOR
>>
</table>
</html>
```

The first IF-THEN statement in the page initializes variables. The code inside it runs only the first time the page runs—when sort_col has not yet been initialized. It initializes sort_fields, a three-column by one-row variable containing the field names displayed in each column. Then it sets sort_types, a three-column by one-row variable that stores the sort order of each column. After that sort_col, a variable containing the current sorted column, and sort_col_last, a value for the last sorted column, are set to 1.

The next IF-THEN statement responds to clicks of a column link. It makes sure sort_col is modified only if a column is clicked, in other words, only when resort_col has an integer value. Once a click has been detected, the value of sort_col is set to resort_col and resort_col is changed back to a noninteger value. Inside this IF-THEN statement, the cell in sort_types for the clicked column number is toggled if the column that was clicked changes. Otherwise the cells in sort_types are left alone.

Finally, in the HTML table header, the column headers are changed to links that set the resort_col variable when clicked and return to redisplay the page.

Linking Reports to Detail Pages

Database reports on the Web can easily be linked to additional detail information or related reports. You do this by changing entries in the report to hypertext links. When a user clicks an item, a variable is set, and the user is sent to a detail page or another report page.

Suppose for example you have a report that displays the sales orders for the day. Each line of the report includes an order ID, an amount for the order, and the salesperson responsible for the order. The report can be extended. The order ID can be converted into a link that, when clicked, directs the user to a detail page for the order. Or the name of the salesperson can be converted into a link that, when clicked, directs the user to a page that displays the orders over the last month for that salesperson.

In general any item in a report can be converted into a link—providing an additional user selection. Click the item and more detail is provided. The kind of detail provided is up to you.

In the seven-line database report, column 1 contains the name of a company. As an example, you can convert the company name into a link. When a user clicks the link, the user is directed to a page that accesses a company database and displays information on the company. To do this, take the following line:

```
DISPLAY "<td>"+myrow[1]+"</td>" /DISPLAY
```

and replace it with:

```
DISPLAY '<td><a href=detail.html '+
        'NAME=cname value="'+myrow[1]+'">' +
        myrow[1]+"</a></td>"
/DISPLAY
```

This converts the entries in the first row into hypertext links. The other two columns of links do not change.

You write the detail page (assuming a company database with the fields `company_name`, `company_country`, `company_state`, and `company_startdate`) as follows:

```
<HTML>
<title>Company Detail Page></title>
<< temp=DBGET('companydb",'company_name="'cname+'"',1)>>
Company Detail:<ul>
Name: <<company_name>><br>
Country: <<company_country>><br>
State: <<company_state>><br>
Start Date: <<company_startdate>><br>
</ul>
</html>
```

Summary

In this chapter you obtained a basic understanding of how to build database report pages. The green bar report showed you that reports can be displayed with horizontal guides to make the report easier to read. You learned that despite the lack of printing controls in the HTML tag language, printable reports are possible. You also learned how to build reports with sortable columns—a fantastic way to empower users of your reports. Finally, at the end of the chapter you learned that you can link database reports to other reports and detail information—giving you an endless number of ways to define database reports.

Together with Chapter 12, *Building Query Pages*, this chapter gives you the ability to build complete reporting systems as well as those parts of Web-based systems requiring you to select a set of records from a database and present them to the user.

The concepts learned in these two chapters apply to more than reports. Document databases are accessed via lists of items selected from a database. Although not reports, query pages and report pages are needed. Indeed, these two chapters give you the background necessary to build a wide variety of systems involving database record selection and presentation.

Next, in Chapter 14, *Building Database Editors*, you learn how to build pages for editing database records. That chapter moves you beyond the eight-line database record editor discussed in Chapter 11, *The Web Database*, and using what you learned in the these last two chapters, gives you powerful solutions useful in advanced Web development.

Exercises

In the exercises here you combine and extend the database report features discussed in this chapter. Answers to these exercises are provided on this book's companion Web site as described in the book's Preface.

Exercise 1

In this chapter a page up and page down report was described. Alter the report so the page up option is not displayed on the first page and the page down option is not displayed on the last page of the report.

Exercise 2

The printable report used in this chapter used a hard-coded value for the number of rows per page. Make the page size adjustable using two hypertext links. When the links are clicked, have the rows per page setting increase and decrease respectively. Store the rows per page setting in a cookie and read it at the top of the page—giving you a printable report with a user-adjustable page size.

Exercise 3

Modify the report page with page up and page down so it uses page numbers rather than page up and page down links. To do this display links for each page in the report, placing in each a *name-value* pair that sets the value of the variable i (the first row of that page) when clicked.

Exercise 4

Build a database report page that has both sortable columns and a page up and page down feature.

Exercise 5

Build a report that also serves as a query system. This can be done with databases containing repeated data. For example, consider a product-order database that stores product names, salespeople assigned to the order, a product category, and an order date. Clicking a salesperson should limit the report to that salesperson. Clicking a product name should limit the report to that product. Clicking a category should limit the report to products in that category. At the top of the report, provide a query box that limits the report to a specific date range and, when clicked, also resets the report.

## CHAPTER 14

Building Database Editors

In Chapter 11, *The Web Database* you first encountered a database editor. The eight-line database editor allowed users and staff to add, edit, or delete records in a database. The simple editor however, was suited only to situations involving a single user and a small database. In this chapter you build general-purpose database editors worthy of the most advanced Web sites. The database editors you learn to build here can be adapted to a wide variety of development situations including the construction of user and membership databases, personal settings databases, real-estate, automotive, and support databases, knowledge bases, image and video databases, accounting and finance systems, and manufacturing and inventory databases. Indeed, database editors are useful everywhere a database needs to be edited.

Technically, the database editors discussed in this chapter resemble those discussed in Chapter 8, *Building Text Editors*, only here data is stored in database structures rather than text files, and instead of editing a single document or element, you edit one or more elements. The other difference is that here, when you search for an item to edit, you search a database. In text editors, when you search for an item to edit, you search for a file in a directory.

In this chapter you build all of the components that make up a database-record editing system. Your starting point is a fifteen-line editor. You add features to it, build a Find page that works along with it, and at the end of the chapter, you learn how to expand the editor to work with multiple related databases.

Accessing Your Database Editor

Most often your database editor will be password protected. To access it you need a login page. The login page can be identical to the database login page discussed in the section "Using A Database" in Chapter 9, *Building Login Pages*. No need to reinvent the wheel, you can use that one or any other login page discussed in that chapter. Just make sure you know the variable that contains the user's login ID. In that one it's `lp_login`.

If the database you wish to edit includes records that can only be edited by specific users, make sure the login ID is placed in some field of each record. If your restrictions are more general, based on groups of users for example, you will want to place a group code in each record and find the group code of the user who logged in. Most often the user's group code is stored in the login database. In these cases, when the user logs in, you retrieve the user's group code.

Once a user has logged in, you direct the user to a menu of options. The page might look as follows:

```
<html>
<title>Staff Menu (dbmenu.html)</title>
Staff Menu - For Authorized Personnel Only<ul>
<li> <A HREF=editdb.html>Edit My Database </a>
<li> <A HREF=opts.html>Other Options</a>
<li> <A HREF=opts2.html>Still Other Options </a>
</ul>
</html>
```

Nothing much here. Just a few hypertext links. But then, that's all you need. The first hypertext link goes to `editdb.html`, your database-record editor.

The Fifteen-Line Database Editor

Consider the fifteen-line database editor shown in Figure 14.1. We assume a database with six fields: `record`, `record_user`, `record_title`, `f1`, `f2`, and `f3`. The `record_user` field is used to store the login ID of the owner of the record. The `record_title` field stores the record title. And the other fields can store whatever you want. When the database editor is first accessed, an empty record is displayed. Save, Copy, Delete, and Find buttons are provided. The buttons are fully functional except Find, which is a link to a page you build later in this chapter.

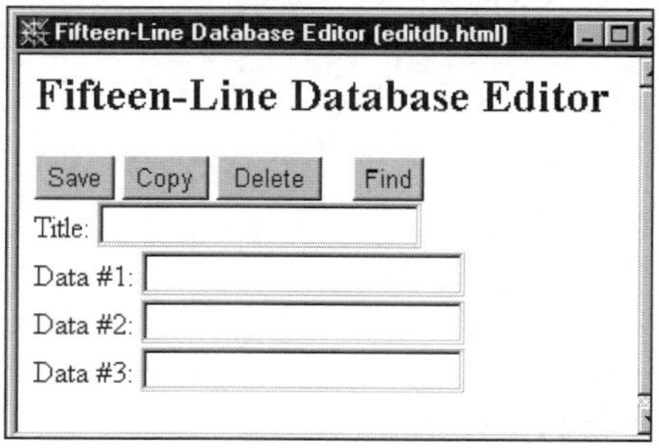

This editor blocks writes to records unless they belong to the user. This is an important consideration when building database editors, since databases often store information for multiple parties requiring access to only their data. The code for this editor is as follows:

Figure 14.1: The fifteen-line database editor works with user-assigned records.

```
<html>
<title>Fifteen-Line Database Editor (editdb.html)</title>
<font size=5><b>Fifteen-Line Database Editor</b></font><br>
<form method=post action=de_opts>
<input type=hidden name=record>
<input type=submit name=de_button value="Save">
<input type=submit name=de_button value="Copy">
<input type=submit name=de_button
value="Delete">   
<input type=submit name=de_button value="Find"><br>
Title: <input type=text name=record_title><br>
Data #1: <input type=text name=f1><br>
Data #2: <input type=text name=f2><br>
Data #3: <input type=text name=f3><br>
</form>
</html>
<<OVERLAY de_opts
de_query= `record="'+record+'"'+
            'AND record_user="'+lp_login+'"'
IF de_button="Save" THEN
  de_temp=DBFIND("bigdb",de_query,1,1,"record")
  IF de_temp=record THEN
    de_temp=DBEDIT("bigdb",record)
  /IF
ELIF de_button="Copy" THEN
  record_title=record_title+"(New)"
  record_user=lp_login
  de_temp=DBADD("bigdb",record)
  record=temp[2,1]
ELIF de_button="Delete" THEN
  de_temp=DBFIND("bigdb",de_query,1,1,"record")
  IF de_temp=record THEN
    de_temp=DBDELETE("bigdb",record)
  /IF
ELIF de_button="Find" THEN
  GOTO "finddb.html"
/IF
GOTO PAGE
>>
```

Like the eight-line editor presented at the end of Chapter 11, *The Web Database*, the fifteen-line database editor uses few Overlay tags. The editor is built with `IF-THEN`, `DBFIND`, `DBADD`, `DBEDIT`, `DBDELETE`, and `GOTO` tags. The HTML form consists of nine components consisting of four submit buttons, four text boxes, and a hidden input component.

The hidden HTML form component is used to guarantee the editor works even if the page was arrived at using a browser's Back button. See the accompanied "Back Button Protection" note.

Back Button Protection—*The Back button of HTML browsers allows users to access pages in their browser's history. This can create situations in which the data stored on the server is different than that displayed on the screen, which can cause problems if you are not careful. For example, suppose you are editing one record and then, later on, start editing another. By clicking the Back button of your browser you can recover the first edit screen. Submitting the page resubmits the data in that page to HTML/OS, which thinks you are on the second page. The remedy to this is to place in the HTML form a hidden input that stores the record ID. That way, even if the page is submitted, the record is resubmitted so your application knows which record to work with.*

When a user clicks a fifteen-line editor button the on-click Overlay `de_opts` runs. If the user clicks the Save button, you do a security check using the `DBFIND` tag. You check to see whether the record you are about to write is *owned* by that user, in other words, whether the `record_user` field is equal to the user's login ID. The check ensures that you write to records only when the user owns them. If the check is successful, `de_temp` will be equal to the record ID. If unsuccessful, `de_query` will be equal to the empty string. The record is saved only if the test is successful. Note that `de_query` is composed by writing the following code:

```
de_query= 'record="'+record+'"'+
          'AND record_user="'+lp_login+'"'
```

The `'AND record_user="'+lp_login+'"'` part of the query restricts access to only records belonging to the user. In general, security on a database is set up this way. See the accompanied note, Adding Group-Based Security.

Adding Group-Based Security—*Group-based security is when only those users belonging to a specific group can read or write to a record. To convert this page to one that uses group-based security, place a group code in the field* `record_user`. *Determine the group code for users when they log in, and in* de_query, *replace the* lp_login *variable with the variable for the group code.*

When the user clicks the Copy button, you create a new record using the data in the HTML form. This is the user's new record option. Here we call it Copy. You can name it whatever you want. No security check needs to be done here; but you do need to make sure the user's login ID is saved to `record_user` so future accesses are protected.

When the user clicks the Delete button, you want to delete the record. As with the Save button, you do a security check before changing the record. You use the same technique you used in the Save option which deletes the record only if the user owns it.

Adding User Feedback

The fifteen-line editor can be improved by adding user feedback to it. You do this by displaying a message at the top of the page after a user clicks a button, providing feedback to actions taken. This is a highly recommended modification, since without this feedback users may become uncomfortable regarding the success or failure of the actions they take. The editor with user feedback is as follows:

```
<html>
<title>Database Editor With Feedback</title>
<font size=5><b>Database Editor With Feedback</b></font><br>
<< IF de_msg != "ERROR" THEN
     DISPLAY "<br>"+de_msg /DISPLAY
  /IF
  de_msg="ERROR"
>>
<form method=post action=de_opts>
<input type=hidden name=record>
<input type=submit name=de_button value="Save">
<input type=submit name=de_button value="Copy">
<input type=submit name=de_button
value="Delete">   
<input type=submit name=de_button value="Find">
Title: <input type=text name=record_title><br>
Data #1: <input type=text name=f1><br>
Data #2: <input type=text name=f2><br>
Data #3: <input type=text name=f3><br>
</form>
```

```
</html>
<<OVERLAY de_opts
de_query='record_user="'+lp_login+'" AND record="'+record+'"'
IF de_button="Save" THEN
   de_temp=DBFIND("bigdb",de_query,1,1,"record")
   IF de_temp=record THEN
      de_temp=DBEDIT("bigdb",record)
      de_msg="Record saved."
   ELSE
      de_msg="<font color=red>Cannot save. Use Copy
button.</font>"
   /IF
ELIF de_button="Copy" THEN
   record_title=record_title+" (New)"
   record_user=lp_login
   de_temp=DBADD("bigdb",record)
   record=temp[2,1]
   de_msg="Record added."
ELIF de_button="Delete" THEN
   de_temp=DBFIND("bigdb",de_query,1,1,"record")
   IF de_temp=record THEN
      de_temp=DBDELETE("bigdb",record)
      de_msg="Record deleted."
   ELSE
      de_msg="<font color=red>Cannot delete.</font>"
   /IF
ELIF de_button="Find" THEN
   GOTO "finddb.html"
/IF
GOTO PAGE
>>
```

The first Overlay on the page displays the message. The other modifications, all shown in bold, set values for de_msg. Note that IF-THEN statements are extended with ELSE tags to ensure all situations are captured.

The modified code shown here does a good job at providing feedback to the user. However, it can be improved even further. The Save and Copy buttons do not validate the data. Are any of the fields required? Should they be of a specific data type? These issues have not been addressed in the code. Such code will depend on the type of data you wish to validate. To add data validation to this page, apply the code provided in Chapter 10, *HTML Forms Processing*.

The Six-Line Find Page

The Find button in the fifteen-line database editor directs the user to the Find page, `finddb.html`. This page needs to give the user the ability to select a record, load the record, and direct the user back to the editor.

The design of this page will vary depending on the nature of your application. The Find page of a real-estate database may include a search by MLS number. The Find page of a classifieds system may simply be a list of the ads placed, showing the user which ads are active and which are not. The Find page for an ordering system may show the user the last fifty orders placed.

When the number of records belonging to a user is high, you provide the user a search option. If the number of records per user is limited, it is best to list the titles of those records on the screen. Here's the code for a Find page that does that:

```
<<
de_query='record_user="' + lp_login + '"'
de_choices=DBFIND("bigdb",de_query,1,100,"record,record_title")
>>
<html>
<title>Six-Line Find Page</title>
<b>Select Record to Edit:</b><br>
<a href=editdb.html>Back to Editor</a><ul>
<<
FOR NAME=de_choices ROWNAME=x DO
   DISPLAY
      "<a href=selectit name=record value=" + x[1] + ">" + x[2]
+"</a>" + "<br>"
   /DISPLAY
/FOR
>>
</html>
<<overlay selectit
    de_temp=DBGETREC("bigdb",record)
    GOTO "editdb.html"
>>
```

At the top of the page you use DBFIND to fill de_choices with the first 100 records belonging to the user. Then in the page, using a FOR loop, you display the titles of each. When the user clicks a title, record is set, and the Overlay selectit runs. There, the record loads, and the user returns to editdb.html to edit the record.

Other Features

The database record editor described here can be modified and expanded in a variety of ways. Three common changes involve switching a text box for a text area, replacing the text boxes with pull-down menus or other HTML components, and adding an image upload option to the Edit page.

Adding a Text Area

You can apply all of the advanced editor options discussed in Chapter 8, *Building Text Editors*, here. The HTML form element consisted of a text area. So, if you replace one or more of the elements of the HTML form used here with a text area you can use the features discussed in that chapter. For example, you can add text area resizing to it. You can set a cookie to the size of the text area. You can add spell-check too. Refer to Chapter 8 for details.

Varying the HTML Form

Furthermore, using what you learned in Chapter 10, *HTML Forms Processing*, you can replace the text box components with other HTML form components. For example, suppose the field f2 was restricted to the values A, B, and C. Then you would want to replace the following line:

```
Data #1: <input type=text name=f2><br>
```
with the HTML form component:
```
Data #1: <select name=f2>
<option value=A>A
<option value=B>B
<option value=C>C
</select>
```

Depending on the nature of the application, you may want to use any number of HTML form components. Refer to Chapter 10 for descriptions of each HTML form component.

Adding File Upload

As another example, suppose the field f2 contained the name of an image. You might want to display the image next to the input box and place an Upload hypertext link next to that. When a user clicks the link, you would direct the user to a more sophisticated version of the six-line upload page presented in Chapter 10. The page would look as follows:

```
<html>
<title>Ten-line Image Upload Page</title>
<b>Ten-line Upload Page</b>
<form enctype="multipart/form-data" ACTION=upload_me><br>
<font size=1>FILE</font><br>
<input type=file name=file<<usernum>> size=20>
<input type=submit value="Upload Image Now">
</form>
</html>
<<OVERLAY upload_me
        upfile="file"+usernum
        de_ext=LOWER(RIGHT(@upfile,4))
        IF de_ext != ".gif" AND de_ext != ".jpg" THEN
            de_msg="Unsupported image type" GOTO "editdb.html"
        /IF
        temp=GETCOLEQ(FILELIST("/upload"),1, "file"+usernum)
        IF temp[1]= "file"+usernum AND temp[2] > 500 THEN
            f2=record+de_ext
            temp=SYSMV("/upload/file"+usernum, "/myimages/"+f2)
            de_msg="Upload Successful."
        ELSE
            de_msg="Upload Failed."
        /IF
        GOTO "editdb.html"
>>
```

Like the six-line upload page described in the "Upload File" section of Chapter 10, here too, the file needs to be captured. But here you have provided a name for the upload file. It is *record*.jpg or *record*.gif depending on the type of image uploaded.

You also add file-type validation here, accepting only images with .gif and .jpg extensions in their names. To determine the kind of image file uploaded, you capture the last four characters of the filename on the browser computer. Use the two following lines:

```
upfile="file"+usernum
de_ext=LOWER(RIGHT(@upfile,4))
```

The first of these two lines places the variable name used in the HTML form's file component into the `upfile` variable. The name of the variable itself varies so this is tricky. When a file is uploaded, the filename of the uploaded file (on the browser computer) is placed in that variable name set in the HTML form upload component. For example, if the uploaded file is `C:\myscanner\ABCD.GIF` and the user session is 45, the contents of the variable `file45` would be `C:\myscanner\ABCD.GIF`.

Then, the first of these two lines would place `file45` in `upfile`. The second line would place in `de_ext` the lower-case value of the last four characters of `C:\myscanner\ABCD.GIF` (the value stored in the variable name stored in `upfile`). In HTML/OS, preceding the name of a variable with the @ character tells HTML/OS to use the contents of the variable specified in the variable instead of the contents of the variable itself.

After these two lines run, an `IF-THEN` statement validates the file type. If the file type is okay, the file moves to its proper destination in the `/myimages` directory, `f2` is set, and the user is returned to the `editdb.html` page.

Working with Multiple Databases

The database editors discussed in this chapter have until now worked with a single database. In some circumstances this is not enough. Sometimes a database will be related to secondary detail information that needs to be edited along with the database. That information might also reside in a database. The first database is called the *primary* database. The second is called the *secondary* database.

Product orders, for example, are organized this way. When orders are placed, each is assigned an order number and stored in a primary *order* database. The items in each order are stored in a secondary *items* database. Each record in the *items* database includes the order number, so it can be related to an order record. An order placed for three items requires a record in an *order* database and three records in an *items* database.

You also need a multidatabase system when working with multiple-choice quizzes. You can use a three-database system. You place each quiz in a *quiz* database. You store the questions used in a quiz in a *questions* database. You store the possible answers to each question in an *answers* database.

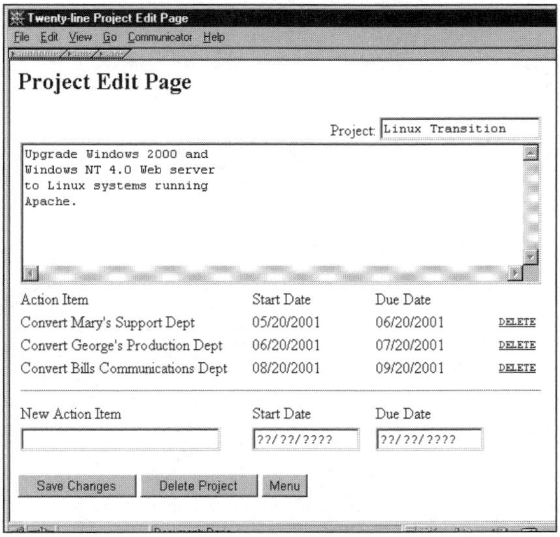

As another example, consider a project database consisting of projects and action items. Assume each project has zero or more action items associated with it. This needs two databases: one containing project descriptions and the other containing action items, start dates, and due dates. It is best to edit these two databases at the same time–using the same database edit page. Such a page is shown in Figure 14.2.

The page allows the user to enter a project description and a list of action items. Each action item has a title line, a start date, and a due date. Text boxes to add a new action item are also provided.

Figure 14.2: The project database edit page works with two databases.

To build this page, you make some assumptions about the databases being used. You call the primary database `projects` and give it the fields `record`, `project_num`, `project_name`, and `project_description`. The secondary database, you call `todos` with the fields `record`, `project_num`, `todo_line`, `todo_startdate`, and `todo_duedate`. Using these assumptions, the code for the page is as follows:

```
<html>
<title>Twenty-line Project Edit Page</title>
<b>Project Edit Page</b>
<form ACTION=project_opts>
<input type=hidden name=record>
<input type=hidden name=project_num>
<table border=0><tr><td align=right colspan=4>
Project: <input type=text name=project_name length=50><br>
<textarea name=project_description cols=65
rows=7></textarea></td></tr>
<tr><td>Action Item</td><td>Start Date</td><td>Due
Date</td></tr>
<< temp=DBFIND("todos",'project_num="' + project_num +
'"',1,100,
```

```
      "todo_line,todo_startdate,todo_duedate,record")
    IF temp[1,1] != "" THEN
      FOR NAME=temp ROWNAME=x DO
        trashlink='<font size=1>'+
          '<a href=rmx name=x value='+x[4]+'>DELETE</a></font>'
        DISPLAY '<tr><td>'+x[1]+'</td><td>'+x[2]+'</td>'+
                '<td>'+x[3]+'</td><td>'+trashlink+'</td></tr>'
        /DISPLAY
      /FOR
    /IF
>>
<tr><td colspan=4><hr size=1></td></tr>
<tr><td>New Action Item</td>
<td>Start Date</td><td>Due Date</td></tr>
<tr>
<td><input type=text name=new_todo size=25></td>
<td><input type=text name=new_startdate size=15></td>
<td><input type=text name=new_duedate size=15></td>
</tr></table><br>
<input type=submit name=mybutton value="Save Changes">
<input type=submit name=mybutton value="Delete Project">
<input type=submit name=mybutton value="Menu">
</form>
</html>
<<overlay project_opts
  IF mybutton="Menu" THEN GOTO "project_finder.html"
  ELIF mybutton="Delete Project" THEN
     temp=DBDELETE("projects",record)
     temp=DBREMOVE("todos","project_num="+project_num)
     GOTO "project_finder.html"
  /IF
  # Save Changes /#

temp=DBFIND("projects","project_num="+project_num,1,1,"record")
  IF temp[1,1]=record THEN
    # edit record /#
    temp=DBEDIT("projects",record)
```

```
    ELSE
      # create new record /#

project_num=DBFINDSORT("projects","",1,1,"project_num","y","project
_num")+1
      IF ISINTEGER(project_num)="FALSE" THEN project_num=1 /IF
      temp=DBADD("projects")
    /IF
    IF new_todo != "" THEN
      todo_line=new_todo
      todo_startdate=new_startdate
      todo_duedate=new_duedate
      new_todo=""
      temp=DBADD("todos")
    /IF
    GOTO PAGE
>>
<<overlay rmx
      temp=DBDELETE("todos",x)
      GOTO PAGE
>>
```

The page includes the elements you find in a standard edit page plus three additional features: a listing of related line items from the secondary database, a delete option next to each item, and at the bottom of the page, an option to add a new line item.

The listing of related items uses a DBFIND tag to find the related items and a FOR loop to list them on the page. The list of items is placed in an IF-THEN statement to ensure the list is displayed only when items are found. Also note that a Delete link is placed at the end of each row. The link, when clicked, runs the Overlay rmx, which uses a DBDELETE tag to remove the item before redisplaying the page.

The bottom of the HTML form includes Save Changes, Delete Project, and Menu buttons.

When a user clicks the Save Changes button, the DBFIND tag sees whether the project submitted exists in the projects database. If it does, the record is updated with DBEDIT. If it does not, a new projects record is created. This requires the creation of a new project number. It does this by taking the largest project number in the projects database (using DBFINDSORT) and incrementing it.

The line below the DBFINDSORT line sets project_num to 1 in the event DBFINDSORT yields a bad result—a situation that occurs when the project database is empty.

When a user clicks the Delete Project button the following two lines run:

```
temp=DBDELETE("projects",record)
temp=DBREMOVE("todos","project_num="+project_num)
```

The first deletes the current record in the projects database. The second uses a DBREMOVE tag, an Overlay tag for deleting multiple records concurrently similar to DBDELETE except that its parameter is a query string rather than a record number. See Appendix D, *HTML/OS Tag Reference Guide,* for a description.

When a user clicks the Menu button the user is directed to the project_finder.html page. The page is a fictitious query page left as an exercise at the end of this chapter.

Summary

In this chapter you learned about database editors, an important component of sophisticated database-driven Web sites and Web-based applications. You learned how to add user or group security to database records and how to combine multiple databases in a single page. The concepts learned here, along with those in the previous chapters of Part III, *Database Programming*, combine to give you awesome Web development capabilities.

In the next chapter you learn about database networking, a topic based on the concept of a Web network—a feature built into the HTML/OS engine that allows you to access databases and files residing at remote locations across the Web.

Exercises

In the following exercises you build database edit pages using what you learned in this chapter and the previous three chapters. Answers to these exercises are provided on this book's companion Web site as described in the book's Preface.

Exercise 1

The database editor described in the "Fifteen-line Database Editor" section of this chapter has an HTML form with three text boxes. Change one of the text boxes to a text area. Make the text area adjustable using what you learned in Chapter 8, *Building Text Editors*.

Exercise 2

Expand the six-line find page described in this chapter to include a search box that limits the display of results. Also provide a Clear button, that when clicked, goes to an on-click Overlay that resets the search. Place the search box at the top of the page, just above the report. Use what you learned in Chapter 12, *Building Query Pages*, to complete this exercise.

Exercise 3

Using what you learned in Chapter 13, *Building Database Reports*, add page up and page down links to the find page you built in Exercise 2.

Exercise 4

The project database described in the "Working with Multiple Databases" section of this chapter does not include user security. It is designed for a single user. Using the same technique used in the "Fifteen-line Database Editor" section of this chapter for extending the page so it can work with multiple users.

Exercise 5

Using what you learned in Chapter 9, *Building Login Pages*, build a login page for the project database application described in the "Working with Multiple Databases " section of this chapter and connect the page to the page you created in Exercise 4. Then, using what you learned in Chapter 12, *Building Query Pages,* build a `project_finder.html` page for it. You now have a complete multiuser, Web-based project-management application.

## CHAPTER 15

Database Networking

Web-based database networking is about accessing databases that reside at one location on the Web with Web-based programs located at other locations. Surprisingly, although the Web excels at networking, performing these tasks has not been straightforward within HTML documents and Web-based applications. In 1998, to make network access easier, Aestiva invented the Web network—a network that sits on top of the Web. The database networking used in HTML/OS takes advantage of this technology.

In this chapter you first look at the basics of Web networking and learn why it is such a powerful tool for developing advanced Web sites and Web-based applications. Then you learn how to set up a Web network. Later you learn how to define different levels of access, how to read and write to network databases, and you review development topics of interest to developers of Web sites that use networked databases.

The Web Network

The World Wide Web is the ultimate network. Its success stems from its underlying TCP/IP network protocol. In recognition of this, Aestiva developed a network architecture that takes advantage of the TCP/IP network. To ensure that it takes advantage of the TCP/IP network, the HTML/OS Web network architecture uses a direct interface to the underlying TCP/IP network of the Web. It uses no intermediate protocols. As a result, it shares many amazing features of the TCP/IP architecture, while adding a few of its own—the most striking of which, is that it's easy to use.

An HTML/OS Web network comprises of two or more copies of HTML/OS placed at different Web locations. Each copy of HTML/OS has a node name in much the same way computers off the Web have network drive names. Give each copy of HTML/OS a name such as A, B, C, or D. Once that is done and the network connections are set up, databases in your network can access the Web network by preceding them with their node name. If you are on Node B and want to access the /work/projects database on Node A you write A:/work/projects.

The Web network works for files too. If you are on Node A and want to access the file /hello.html on Node B, you write B:/hello.html. The Web network also works for HTML documents. Need to link a Web page on the A computer to B:/hello.html? Then write your hypertext link as follows:

```
<A HREF=B:/hello.html>Welcome Message From The President</a>
```

The HTML/OS Web network frees you from the intricacies of TCP/IP internals—allowing you to add sophisticated networking within the programs you build. The HTML/OS Web network has the following features:

World-wide—Different copies of HTML/OS in a Web network can reside across the world.

Hardware-irrelevant—Copies of HTML/OS can run on Macintosh, Windows, Unix, or Linux systems. The network can be heterogeneous, consisting of files and databases residing on different kinds of hardware.

Distributed—If a server running a copy of HTML/OS fails, others on the Web network will continue to operate as long as they don't need to access the failed server. There is no central point of failure.

Scalable—If a single server can't support the traffic going to it, access can be spread across multiple computers by spreading the HTML documents across multiple servers.

Tolerant—If a network connection fails, when it resumes, so too will the copies in the Web network dependent on that connection.

Easy-to-program—You access files and databases by preceding file or database names with their location in the Web network.

Easy Setup—Network setup is point-and-click, using the Control Panel that comes with each copy of HTML/OS.

The HTML/OS Web network architecture shares the cross-platform, scalability, and stability features of the Web. But unlike TCP/IP network programming, Web networking is accessible without special programming. Instead you simply follow file and database naming conventions whereby database names are preceded with node names. In the next few sections you learn what a network node is and how Web networks are set up.

The Network Node

The Web network in HTML/OS consists of two or more copies of HTML/OS. Each copy is called a node. Nodes can reside at different physical locations. Most often these nodes reside on the public Web, however Web networks can also be set up on Web servers placed within private intranets. They can even span equipment placed on both sides of a firewall (spanning an intranet and the Web) See the accompanying "Working on Both Sides of the Firewall" note if your network spans both the Web and an intranet.

When any two nodes in a Web network communicate with each other, they do so based on the settings in the two nodes. Each node determines which other nodes can access its files and databases. A node cannot access another node unless that node gives it access. Security is the responsibility of each node in the network. This is known as a peering architecture. To set up a Web network, you must set up each HTML/OS copy in the Web network. To set up a node, you use the Network and Security menu options in the HTML/OS Control Panel.

Working on Both Sides of the Firewall—The Web network used in HTML/OS has the ability to span both sides of a firewall. A firewall is a network gateway that blocks users on the public Internet from accessing sites within a private intranet while still allowing users in the intranet to access the Web. Note that HTML/OS does not adversely affect the firewall. The firewall still blocks access from the Web to copies of HTML/OS within the intranet, but copies of HTML/OS within the intranet will be able to read and write to databases and files located on copies of HTML/OS across the firewall, on the Web.

Network Setup

Consider setting up a Web network consisting of three copies of HTML/OS. To set up the network, you need to know the name of each node, the URL to each copy of HTML/OS, and (for security reasons) the first part or the entire IP address of each node. In this section assume the following for each copy of HTML/OS:

Node 1	Network Identity: A
	IP Address: `128.50.123.2`
	URL: http://www.d1.com/cgi/htmlos
Node 2	Network Identity: B
	IP Address: `128.50.50.135`
	URL: http://www.d2.com/cgi-bin/htmlos.cgi
Node 3	Network Identity: C
	IP Address: `128.50.?.?`
	URL: http://www.d3.com/scripts/htmlos.exe

Setting up a network involves two steps. First you need to define connections between the nodes. In Node 1 you define connections to Node 2 and Node 3.

In Node 2 you define connections to Nodes 1 and 3, and in Node 3 you define connections to Nodes 1 and 2. Second, in each of the nodes, you need to enable access to the other nodes. The following sections give you details for setting up the nodes.

Setting Up Node 1

To set up Node 1, access that copy of HTML/OS and follow these steps:

1. Select the Control Panel from the desktop menu bar.
2. Click **Network** in the Control Panel to expand the left menu so you can see your Network options. Next you set up the copy of HTML/OS. The name of the node is called the node identity.
3. Click **Identity** and enter A for the node name.
4. Click the **Save Settings** button when done. Now the node identity is set for this copy of HTML/OS. The node identity precedes file and database names specified in HTML documents at other nodes to access files and databases on this node. For example, to access the file /hello.html from another copy of HTML/OS you can write A:/hello.html. Note that files and databases are specified with their full path, starting with a required slash (/).
5. Next set up access to nodes B and C. Click **Configuration** on the left Control Panel menu. You'll see a screen like that shown in Figure 15.1. This screen allows you to specify multiple nodes. Each node line requires the name of the node, the URL to the node and the IP address of the remote node.

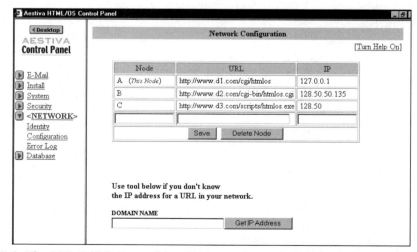

Figure 15.1: The HTML/OS Control Panel Network Configuration screen contains the nodes you peer with.

The name of the node is the node identity of the particular node. Node identities can be single characters or multiple characters (no spaces). In general, it is best to keep node names short since they precede file and database names. Nobody likes to type long names! Single character names are preferred. Or you can use short descriptive names like web, host1, or s25. The URL to the node is the URL you would enter in the Location text box of your browser to access the remote node. The last part of the URL, which is typically htmlos, htmlos.cgi, or htmlos.exe, is the name of the HTML/OS engine on the remote server. This URL is the URL to the login page of the remote server less the /login.html part.

The IP address is a security setting. When incoming network requests from a remote nodes are received, this IP address is checked to ensure the remote node is what it says it is. If the IP address is omitted, no check is done. If a partial IP address is provided, the beginning of the incoming IP address must match the setting. If a remote node comes from a location where IP addresses are set dynamically, use the first two or three parts of that IP address—the part of the IP address that does not change dynamically. An example is provided in a moment. Continue with the following steps to network Nodes 2 and 3:

6. So to network with Node 2 type B in the Node box, http://www.d2.com/cgi-bin/htmlos.cgi in the URL box, and 128.50.50.135 in the IP box and click **Save**.

7. For Node 3 type C in the Node box, http://www.d3.com/scripts/htmlos.exe, in the URL box and 128.50 in the IP box; then click **Save** again.

Now you have links set up to both of these nodes. Note that only the first two parts of the IP address are specified since the rest of the IP address is unknown. This is what happens when the remote server has a dynamically generated IP address. If you are unsure of the IP address needed, use the Get IP Address tool at the bottom of the page. See the accompanying "The IP Address Tool" note.

The IP Address Tool—*The bottom of the Configuration screen includes a Get IP Address button. Use this if you do not know the IP address of a remote domain. Enter the domain used in the URL in the URL box and click **Get IP Address**. This will give you the IP address of that domain. Note that this IP address is the IP address as seen by that server. Actually, the IP address needed in this configuration is the IP address detected from a remote request, which sometimes is different than the one reported here. If this happens and you're not concerned about security breaches within your organization, chop off the last section of the IP address and use that. When the two IP addresses differ, they usually differ only in the last part of the IP address. Dropping this last part of the IP address is a quick and easy way to enable the connection without having to hunt down the exact IP address seen in the reverse direction.*

Setting Up Node 2

Setting up the second node in our example is similar to setting up the first. Access this copy of HTML/OS, pull up its Control Panel, and follow these steps:

1. Click **Identity** and enter B for the node name. Click the **Save Settings** button when done. Now the node identity is set for this copy of HTML/OS.
2. Then click **Configuration**. You need to set up connections for Nodes 1 and 3.
3. To set up Node 1, type A in the Node box, http://www.d1.com/cgi/htmlos in the URL box, and 128.50.123.2 in the IP box; then click **Save**.
4. To set up Node 3 type C in the Node box, http://www.d3.com/scripts/htmlos.exe in the URL box, 128.50 in the IP box, and click **Save**.

Setting Up Node 3

To set up the third node in our example access this copy of HTML/OS, pull up its Control Panel, and follow these steps:

1. Click **Identity** and enter C for the node name and click **Save Settings**.
2. Then click **Configuration** on the left menu to set up connections for Nodes 2 and 3.
3. Type A in the Node box, http://www.d1.com/cgi/htmlos in the URL box, 128.50.123.2 in the IP box, and click **Save**.
4. Enter B in the Node box, http://www.d2.com/cgi-bin/htmlos.cgi in the URL box, 128.50.50.135 in the IP box, and click **Save** again.

Enabling Network Access

Once you set up your connections, you need to enable them, which involves using a network security setting. In the Control Panel of any of your three copies follow these steps:

1. Click **Security** to view the security options.
2. Then click **Network Allow**. You will see a list of remote nodes as shown in Figure 15.2. Next to each is a pull-down menu containing the two options: Limited Access and Full-Access.
3. Set these to **Full-Access**.
4. Click **Save Settings** when done.

Repeat for the other two nodes. Now the nodes are fully networked together. Later, in the "Controlling Network Access" section of this chapter, you learn how to provide only limited network access between nodes, but for now, and in situations where staff with access to one node already has access to the others, this setting is fine.

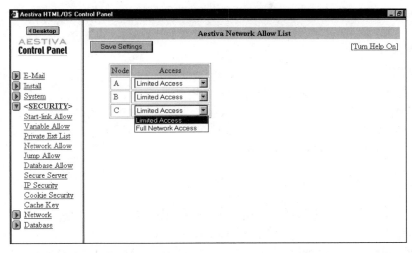

Figure 15.2: To give a node full network access to your node set their node to Full-Access in the Network Allow List page of the HTML/OS Control Panel.

Testing the Network Setup

After setting up the network nodes and enabling access you will want to test the connectivity. Here's a page you can use to test the networking. This will test the ability of HTML/OS, on a specific node, to access your other nodes. The code for the page is as follows:

```
<html>
<title>Six-Line Network Test Page</title>
Network Test:<ul>
<form method=post ACTION=testnetwork>
Enter Remote Node Name: <input type=text name=remote_node><br>
<input type=submit value="Test Access to Node">
</form>
<< IF mytest != "ERROR" THEN
       DISPLAY  mytest  /DISPLAY
       mytest="ERROR"
     /IF
>>
</html>
<<overlay testnetwork
```

```
remote_file= remote_node+":/junk.txt"
COPY "12345" TO FILE=remote_file /COPY
mytest="Writing 12345 to "+remote_file:
"+TAGRESULTS[1,2]+"<br>"
COPY FILE=remote_file TO temp /COPY
mytest=mytest+
    "Reading "+remote_file: "+TAGRESULTS[1,2]+"<br>"+
    "Got the value: "+temp+"<br>"
GOTO PAGE
>>
```

Copy this file to each node in the network. Run the page to test network access. The page asks the user for a node identity. Enter a remote node name and click **Test Access To Node**. The page tries to write the characters 12345 to a file on the remote server. It then tries to read the file it wrote. As it does this it saves the status messages returned by the Overlay tags that write and read from the remote server. These status messages are displayed for you at the bottom of the page after each test.

If network access is okay then you'll see a message like the following:

```
Writing 12345 to B: OK
Reading B: OK
```

If you do not get this, you have not successfully accessed the network. Use the error messages displayed to fix network configuration problems, if any.

Using the Network Error Log—If after using the testing page in the previous section of this chapter you are still unable to establish a network connection, use the network error log in the Control Panel. The log is written to when incoming or outgoing network accesses fail. To access the log open the Control Panel. Click **Network** *to access your Network options and then click* **Error Log**. *Error lines in the report can include valuable information. For example, if a remote access was denied by HTML/OS because the IP address of the originating request didn't match the IP address setting in the Network-Configuration section of the Control Panel, then it will be indicated here along with the IP address of the originating request.*

Controlling Network Access

In the prior sections you set up a three-node Web network with full network access. This allows any node in the network to access files and databases in any other node. Often however you do not want unrestricted access between nodes. Full-access to a remote node does just that: It gives users of the remote node full access to your system. With full access, even if they do not know the password of the node, they can get it by networking to the server. To limit access run the Control Panel and follow these steps:

1. Click **Security**; then click **Network allow**.
2. Change the node to **Limited Access** and click **Save Settings**.
3. Then click **Database allow**. You'll see a screen like that shown in Figure 15.3.

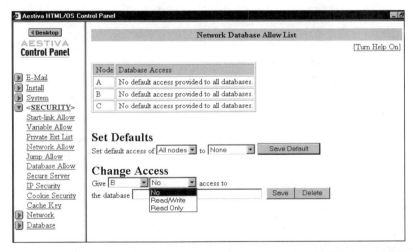

Figure 15.3: The Network Database Allow List page of the HTML/OS Control Panel is where you place limitations on other nodes accessing your databases.

The top of the page displays the current access security of each node defined in the Network Configuration page. To change the settings, use the options provided at the bottom of the page. You can set two kinds of access: database-specific and database nonspecific, known here as the default.

Default Access

Use the Set Defaults section of the page to set up access security to databases, in general. You may, for example, not mind it if specific nodes or all nodes have Read-Only or even Read/Write access to your databases. Note that you can apply these to all nodes or only specific nodes, and if a specific node needs to be denied access to your databases, you can set this as well.

As an example, suppose you wish to give Node C read access to all of your databases. To do that select **C**, select **Read Only**, and click **Save**.

Database-Specific Access

Use the Change Access section of the page to set up access security for specific databases. The default settings discussed in the previous section have secondary priority to these database-specific security settings. If for example by default all nodes have access to all databases but you add a node specific restriction, then the node specific restriction will have priority over the default settings.

Extending the example in the previous section, suppose you still want Node C to have read access to your databases, however you want to give Node C write access to the /work/postings database, and deny Node C access to the /mypasswords database as follows:

1. Use the Change Access section of the page.
2. Select **C**, and then select **Read/Write**.
3. Type /work/postings in the database text box, and click **Save**.
4. Then select C again.
5. Select **No** access, type /mypasswords into the text box, and click **Save**. The access rights for Node C will be described at the top of the page. It will read as follows:

```
Default read-only access provided to all databases.
No access to: /mypasswords
Read/Write access to: /work/postings
```

Serving Network Databases

Often, when setting up a network, you do not have access to any copies of HTML/OS other than your own. At the same time, you wish to give access to a database residing on your copy of HTML/OS without jeopardizing the security of your copy.

If this is what you want to do, then you want to be a Database Service Provider (DSP), a fancy way of saying you want to serve one or more databases to customers in a controlled and secure fashion. This section shows you how.

First, you set up your copy of HTML/OS as a DSP. To do that, give your node an identity such as DSP. Then collect the node names and IP addresses of your first customers wishing to access your database. If they do not have node names, you can select some for them. To set up customers you do not need their URLs. Note also that you do not need to set up customer nodes; you simply need to forward customers your network parameters and their new node name, if necessary. Once you are set up, issue a DSP confirmation e-mail to your customers that looks something like this:

Dear Marketing Department Web Designer,

Access to DSP databases has been configured. Please place the following network parameters in the Network section of the Control Panel in your copy of HTML/OS:

1) Set your Node Identity to: M1

2) Set up our DSP node in your Configuration:
Node: DSP
URL: http://dsp.ourdomain.com/cgi-bin/htmlos.cgi
IP: 128.356.65

3) You have been authorized for the following:
Database: Access
dsp:/sales/orders: Read Only
dsp:/sales/incoming: Read/Write

Thank you and best regards.

Jan Jackson
DSP Administrator

To set up the access level shown in this sample e-mail, do the following:
1. Access the Control Panel in your copy of HTML/OS.
2. Click **Network** and then click **Configuration**.
3. Type M1 for the Node, leave the URL blank, enter their IP address, and click **Save**.
4. Then on the left menu bar, click **Security** and **Network Allow**.
5. On the Network Allow page, change the access setting for the node M1 to **Limited-Access**, and click **Save Settings**.
6. Then on the left menu bar, under Security, click **Database Allow**. You'll see a screen that displays the network access parameters for the nodes in your system.
7. Make sure the Default Settings for All Nodes is set to **None**.
8. In the Change Access section, you can select a node, access level and enter a database name. First select **M1**, **Read Only**, type **/sales/orders** and click **Save**.
9. Finally select **M1**, select **Read/Write**, type **/sales/incoming**, and click **Save**. Now M1 is set up. Repeat for other customers, keeping everything the same except the customer node name.

Accessing Network Databases

You access databases located at remote nodes much the same way as you access regular databases. For example, consider the seven-line database report provided in Chapter 13, *Building Database Reports*. If the database used in the report resides on Node B, you could write the report as follows:

```
<html>
<title>Seven-line Network Database Report </title>
<< myresults=DBFIND("B:/work/contacts",myquery,1,100,
       "contact_company,contact_name,contact_phone")
>>
<table border=1 cellspacing=0 cellpadding=2>
<tr><td bgcolor=#000088 colspan=4 align=center>
<b>My Report</b></td></tr>
<tr>
<td>Column One</td>
<td>Column Two</td>
<td>Column Three</td>
</tr>
<<
FOR NAME=myresults ROWNAME=myrow DO
     DISPLAY "<tr>" /DISPLAY
     DISPLAY "<td>"+myrow[1]+"</td>" /DISPLAY
     DISPLAY "<td>"+myrow[2]+"</td>" /DISPLAY
     DISPLAY "<td>"+myrow[3]+"</td>" /DISPLAY
     DISPLAY "</tr>" /DISPLAY
/FOR
>>
</table>
</html>
```

The only change in the report that's necessary is the need to precede the database name with the name of the remote node (indicated in bold). The problem with this however, is that it does not address a fact of life in systems that work with networks—that the system administrator of Node B may one day change the network name from B to something else. If all you have is this one page, renaming will not be a problem. But what if you have many pages and many references to Node B?

One way around this is to build a network node assignment file. If a node name changes, you simply make a single change in a single file. In your programs, you use your own node variables, which are set in this file. As an example, suppose you have three different nodes you read or write to. In your file you can write:

```
node_dsp="A:"
node_finance="B:"
node_hr="C:"
```

Rewriting the seven-line database to take advantage of this file, you now have the following code:

```
<html>
<title>Eight-line Network Database Report</title>
<< EXPAND FILE="/nodes.txt" /EXPAND

myresults=DBFIND(node_finance+"/work/contacts",myquery,1,100,
        "contact_company,contact_name,contact_phone")
>>
<table border=1 cellspacing=0 cellpadding=2>
<tr><td bgcolor=#000088 colspan=4 align=center>
<b>My Report</b></td></tr>
<tr>
<td>Column One</td>
<td>Column Two</td>
<td>Column Three</td>
</tr>
<<
FOR NAME=myresults ROWNAME=myrow DO
     DISPLAY "<tr>" /DISPLAY
     DISPLAY "<td>"+myrow[1]+"</td>" /DISPLAY
     DISPLAY "<td>"+myrow[2]+"</td>" /DISPLAY
     DISPLAY "<td>"+myrow[3]+"</td>" /DISPLAY
     DISPLAY "</tr>" /DISPLAY
/FOR
>>
</table>
</html>
```

Changes are shown in bold. At the top of the file, the `nodes.txt` file is expanded. The `EXPAND` tag runs the instructions in the page as though the code had been written at the location where the file was expanded. The file defines the variable `node_finance`, which is used in the subsequent `DBFIND` tag to set the node name of the database. Further information on `DBFIND` and `EXPAND` is available in Appendix D, *HTML/OS Tag Reference Guide*.

Writing to Network Databases

As you see here, network databases are easy to access. In general the DB tags used to access network databases are the same as those used locally. In a few DB tags however, you need to specify additional parameters. This need to respecify occurs with the `DBADD` and `DBEDIT` tags, the two most common tags for writing to databases. With these tags, you must also specify the names of the fields you are adding or editing.

As an example, consider the eight-line database editor discussed toward the end of Chapter 11, *The Web Database*. A network-friendly version of the editor follows:

```
<html>
<title>10-Line Network Database Editor</title>
<b>10-Line Network Database Editor</b><br><br>
Records in Network Database:
<< EXPAND FILE="/nodes.txt" /EXPAND
   myrecords=DBFIND(node_finance+"/tinydb","",1,100,"record")
   DISPLAY COLTOLIST(myrecords,1," ") /DISPLAY
>>
<form method=post action=dbopts>
Record ID: <input type=text name=record size=10>
<input type=submit name=mybutton value="Load">  
<input type=submit name=mybutton value="Save">
<input type=submit name=mybutton value="Delete">
<input type=submit name=mybutton value="Add">
Full Name: <input type=text name=f1><br>
E-mail Address: <input type=text name=f2><br>
Phone Number: <input type=text name=f3><br>
</form>
</html>
<<OVERLAY dbopts
```

```
fieldlist="f1,f2,f3"
IF mybutton="Load" THEN
  temp=DBGETREC(node_finance+"/tinydb",record)
ELIF mybutton="Save" THEN
  temp=DBEDIT(node_finance+"/tinydb",record,fieldlist)
ELIF mybutton="Delete" THEN
  temp=DBDELETE(node_finance+"/tinydb",record)
ELIF mybutton="Add" THEN
  temp=DBADD(node_finance+"/tinydb",fieldlist)
/IF
GOTO PAGE
>>
```

Changes are shown in bold. Like the eight-line network database report of the previous section, you expand node names by expanding the /nodes.txt file. You tack the node_finance variable onto the beginning of all database names throughout the code, and in the DBADD and DBEDIT tags, you define a fieldlist parameter, and finally at the top of the Overlay you add dbopts. Now the database editor edits a remote database located on node_finance node, defined at the top of this "Accessing Network Databases" section, as the B Node, rather than one that is local.

Network Failure Recovery

When writing to databases on the same physical equipment as the copy of HTML/OS, you rarely need to concern yourself with network or equipment failure. After all, if the equipment fails so too does your program. Backup recovery systems are usually the remedy in cases when the equipment hosting your copy of HTML/OS fails.

When working in network environments recovering from equipment failure is more complicated, since the copy of HTML/OS may still be active while a remote networked node is down.

Generally the topic of network recovery requires a lot of thought and planning. Especially when product orders, membership sign-ups, customer requests, and other kinds of critical data are at stake. It is best to develop a preventative scheme that performs two specific duties. First, when a network goes down, the site should write out critical data to a pending area so you can recover it after the network is up again. Second, you need to implement a scheme for bringing the system back to its proper state.

The first step involves isolating the points in your program that write critical data to a networked node. When the remote network is accessed, you need to test whether the network connections succeeded and take action in your code if the network is inaccessible. This is easier than it sounds. To do this you use the return status of the DB tags. The return status, depending on the tag, is either returned or placed in TAGRESULTS variable. In the case of DBADD and DBEDIT, a status result is returned. As an example, suppose you have a DBADD tag that posts critical information to a remote database. The code might be something like this.

```
fieldlist="f1,f2,f3"
temp=DBADD(homeoffice:/mydb",fieldlist)
```

If the homeoffice node goes down, what to do? The best way to handle this is to set up a database identical to the remote database on the local copy of HTML/OS, for example, /pending/mydb. When the network goes down, you posted the record to the local database rather than the networked database. To do this you write the following code:

```
fieldlist="f1,f2,f3"
temp=DBADD(homeoffice:/mydb",fieldlist)
IF temp[1,1] != "TRUE" THEN
    temp=DBADD("/pending/mydb")
/IF
```

If the network goes down, temp[1,1] is not TRUE, so posted information writes to the /pending/mydb database instead of homeoffice:/mydb.

The complicated part is recovering from the network failure. When the node comes up, how do you restore the data? In general there are two ways to do this: You can place a block of code in your program that recovers automatically, or you can set up a recovery page for a system administrator. Both have their advantages and disadvantages. An automated system requires no intervention. However, automated recovery, if not designed and tested properly, can cause more problems than it solves. Also, it is a good idea to check the data before you recover it. You cannot do this with automated systems. For this reason, here we discuss only recovery pages, designed to be used by system administrators. The code for such a page is as follows:

```
<html>
<title>Twelve-line Network Failure Recovery System</title>
<font size=5>Twelve-line Network Failure Recovery
System</font><br><li> Data #1 Status:
<< records=DBFIND("/backup/mydb","",1,5,"record")
```

```
    IF records[1,1] != "" THEN
      N=ROWS(records)
      DISPLAY
        "<font color=red>"+N+" records pending.</font><br>"+
        "<a HREF=recover1>Recover</a>"
      /DISPLAY
    ELSE
     DISPLAY "OK" /DISPLAY
    /IF
>>
</html>
<<overlay recover1
   records=DBFIND("/backup/mydb","",1,5,"record")
   FOR NAME=records ROWNAME=r DO
      temp=DBGETREC("/pending/mydb", r[1])
      IF temp THEN
          t2=DBADD("homeoffice:/mydb",fieldlist)
          IF t2[1,1]="TRUE" THEN
              t3=DBDELETE("/pending/mydb",r)
          /IF
        /IF
    /FOR
/IF
GOTO PAGE
>>
```

The twelve-line recovery system displays a line that says Data #1 Status: OK, or if it finds pending records, it displays the message Data #1 Status: NOK plus a recover link. When the user clicks the link, the on-click Overlay recover1 runs. The DBFIND tag then searches the /pending/mydb database and extracts a list of records. The FOR loop transfers each record in /pending/mydb to the database at the homeoffice node. As the records transfer successfully, they are deleted from the local database, /pending/mydb.

The twelve-line recovery system explained here recovers failed DBADD attempts. To recover failed DBEDIT attempts, you use a similar technique. Suppose you have the following code:

```
fieldlist="f1,f2,f3"
temp=DBEDIT(homeoffice:/mydb,fieldlist)
```

To protect these edits, you need to save the edit to a local database. Here too you create a local database. But unlike the previous example, you also need to store the record number of the record being edited. When setting up the local database, add an extra field to store this record number. Call it newrecord, for example. Once you do that rewrite the code as follows:

```
fieldlist="f1,f2,f3"
temp=DBEDIT("homeoffice:/mydb",record, fieldlist)
IF temp[1,1] != "TRUE" THEN
    fieldlist=f1,f2,f3,newrecord"
    myrec=DBFIND("/pending/mydb2","r2="record,1,1,"newrecord")
    IF myrec=record THEN
      temp=DBEDIT("/pending/mydb2",record,fieldlist)
    ELSE
      temp=DBADD("/pending/mydb2",fieldlist)
    /IF
```

If DBEDIT fails, the record changes are saved to /pending/mydb2. This code creates a new record if it finds a record_pending field already containing record. Otherwise it overwrites the record. The recovery page for this is the same as the recovery page for records for DBADD failures except that the database name here is /pending/mydb2 instead of /pending/mydb.

Summary

In this chapter you learned about database networking. You learned that once a network is set up all you need to do to supply access to a database is to precede the database with the name of the node on which it resides.

You also learned that operating across a network provides both opportunities and potential pitfalls. Pitfalls include the need to manage potential network failures. Advantages include the ability of an organization to provide network database sharing and cooperation between departments—giving departments within an organization greater control and autonomy over their Web operations. Web networking also gives organizations the ability to build systems that sit on both sides of their firewall, allowing Web-sites and intranets to operate even if the other is experiencing network or hardware failures.

Next, in Part IV, *E-Commerce Programming*, you look at how to build world-class shopping carts and shopping system. You'll find that, once again, HTML/OS simplifies and extends your abilities as a Web developer, giving you the power to build the most sophisticated e-commerce sites.

Exercises

In the exercises that follow, you practice setting up Web networks and network-based database systems. These exercises are best performed in a computer lab with multiple, preinstalled copies of HTML/OS. Answers to these exercises are provided on this book's companion Web site as described in the book's Preface.

Exercise 1

Set up a two-node system with full-access between the nodes using what you learned in the "Network Setup" section of this chapter. What happens when you enter a bad IP address, a bad URL, or a bad node name?

Exercise 2

Using the two-node system you built in exercise 1, build a system that takes advantage of server jumping—the ability to create a series of Web pages that span more than one node. Build a page that bounces back and forth between two servers. Use the knowledge base on the **Aestiva** site at http://www.aestiva.com/support/ for a description of server jumping.

Exercise 3

Using the networking techniques you learned, add a Publish button to the six-line editor discussed at the top of Chapter 8, *Building Text Editors*. When the user clicks the Publish button, copy the page to a file of the same name on the remote server. Use the two-node system set up in exercise 1 to accomplish this.

PART IV

E-Commerce Programming

## CHAPTER 16

Designing E-Commerce Systems

E-commerce Web sites vary extremely in size and the features and kinds of product they offer. Some sell memberships, others sell software downloads. Most sell products and services. Some sell only a single product; others sell millions of products. Sites can be B2B, B2C, B2G, G2G, and C2C or a bit of each. (In Web-speak B means Business, C means Consumer, and G means Government.) In Part IV, *E-Commerce Programming*, you learn how to build these kinds of Web sites.

In this chapter you start by learning about the kinds of Web pages used when building e-commerce sites. You begin with a one-page, one product e-commerce site. Then you build a simple database-driven e-commerce site. Then, we provide a list of advanced e-commerce features in preparation for the other chapters of Part IV of this book, where the Web pages used in highly advanced e-commerce sites are explained and brought to life.

A Ten-line E-Commerce Web Site

Consider for starters a one-page Web site where product information and a form to purchase the product are provided on a single Web page. The Web page requires only ten HTML/OS instructions—two in an Overlay that displays a message to the user and eight in an on-click Overlay that does the order processing. The Web page displays product information explicitly typed into the page and an HTML form that captures the purchaser's name and e-mail address, shipping address, and credit card information. The ten-line e-commerce Web site is shown in Figure 16.1 and the code for that page follows.

```
<html>
<title>Ten-line E-commerce Web Site</title>
<font size=5>Buy the official <i>Best Web Sites Made Easy</i>
book.</font><br>
Published by Top Floor Publishing
```

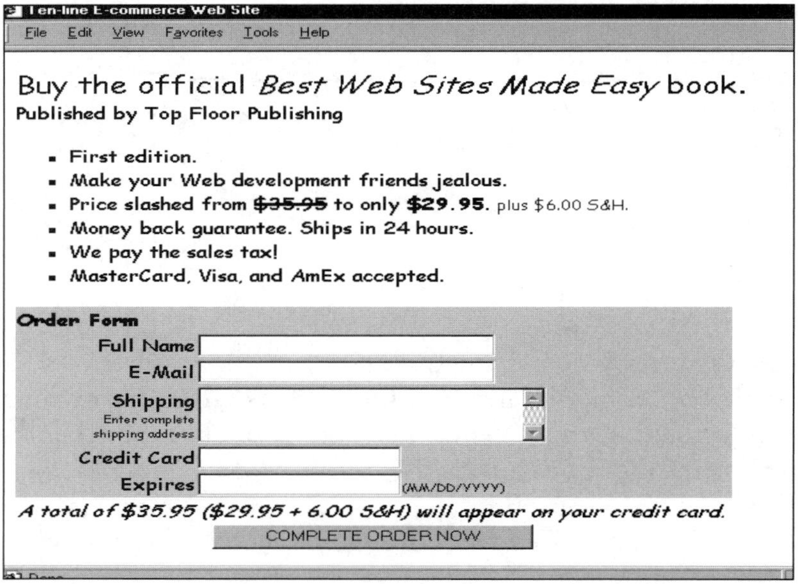

Figure 16.1: The ten-line e-commerce Web site has all the basic capabilities of an e-commerce site.

```
<ul type=square><li>First edition.
<li>Make your Web development friends jealous.
<li>Price slashed from <strike>$35.95</strike>
to only <b>$29.95</b>. <font size=2>plus $6.00 S&amp;H.</font>
<li>Money back guarantee. Ships in 24 hours.
<li>We pay the sales tax!
<li>MasterCard, Visa, and AmEx accepted.
</ul>
<< IF msg != "ERROR" THEN DISPLAY msg+"<br>" /DISPLAY  /IF
    msg="ERROR"
>>
<form method=post ACTION=postorder>
<table bgcolor=#CECECE border=0 cellspacing=0>
<tr><td colspan=2><b>Order Form</b></td></tr>
<tr><td align=right valign=top>Full Name</td>
<td><input type=text name=shop_name size=30></td></tr>
<tr><td align=right valign=top>E-Mail</td>
<td><input type=text name=shop_email size=30></td></tr>
```

```
<tr><td  align=right valign=top>Shipping<br>
<font size=1>Enter complete<br>shipping address</font></td>
<td><textarea name=shop_ship cols=30
rows=3></textarea></td></tr>
<tr><td  align=right valign=top >Credit Card</td>
<td valign=top><input type=text name=shop_card></td></tr>
<tr><td  align=right valign=top >Expires</td>
<td><input type=text name=shop_expires><font
size=1>(MM/DD/YYYY)</font>
</td></tr>
<tr bgcolor=#FFFFFF><td colspan=2 align=center>
<i>A total of $35.95 ($29.95 + 6.00 S&H) will
appear on your credit card.</i></td></tr>
<tr bgcolor=#FFFFFF><td colspan=2 align=center>
<input type=submit value="COMPLETE ORDER NOW">
</td></tr></table></form>
</html>
<<overlay postorder
IF shop_name="" OR shop_email="" OR
   shop_ship="" OR shop_card="" OR
   shop_expires="" THEN
   msg="<font color=red>Missing Info. Try Again.</font>"
ELSE
  myorder=
    "============================="+LF+
    "Order Date: "+TODAY+LF+
    "Full Name: "+shop_name+LF+
    "E-mail: "+shop_email+LF+
    "Card: "+shop_card+" ("+shop_expires+")"+LF+
    "Shipping: "+LF+shop_name+LF+
    "============================="+LF+LF
  MAIL myorder TO ADDRESS="bestwebsales@eastiva.com"
    SUBJECT="Order ("+now+")"
  /MAIL
  APPEND myorder To FILE="order_log.txt" /APPEND
  msg="Order Placed. Thank you. E-mail questions to
       bestwebinfo@aestiva.com."
```

```
shop_card=""
shop_expires=""
shop_ship=""
/IF
GOTO PAGE
>>
```

This page provides the basic functionality required in an e-commerce site. When a user accesses the page, it displays information about a product. The user is presented with an order form to fill out. When the user clicks a Purchase button, the on-click Overlay `postorder` runs, and the order is processed. If one of the entries in the HTML form is missing, an error message is set and the page is redisplayed, informing the user of the error and allowing the user to make the necessary corrections and resubmit the page. If the HTML form is filled out in its entirety, an e-mail message is composed and e-mailed to the sales office using the `MAIL` tag. The `APPEND` tag backs up the order to a file. A *Thank you* message is composed in the code too, so when the page is redisplayed, the user sees the message. You write the entire page with a few `IF-THEN` statements and the four Overlay tags: `DISPLAY MAIL`, `APPEND`, and `GOTO`.

Of course, most e-commerce sites are larger. They sell more products and provide the user a more sophisticated ordering procedure. In the next section you look at splitting this single page e-commerce site into a more typical multipage site.

A Database-Driven E-Commerce Site

When selling multiple products a larger e-commerce site is necessary. To build such a site you split the functionality of the one-page site discussed in the previous section across multiple Web pages. In addition, you add product navigation along with a shopping cart where a temporary order list for the user is saved.

Database-driven e-commerce sites have the defining feature that product information is stored in a database rather than being hard-coded into different HTML documents. This way of constructing an e-commerce site is helpful since it allows you to limit the number of Web pages the site requires. For example, a database-driven Web site with one thousand products may have less than ten Web pages. The same site without the database would have over one thousand pages. As a result, database-driven Web sites are easier to manage than those that are not.

In this section you take a look at a basic database-driven e-commerce site built with the following Web pages:

Page	Primary Purpose
menu.html	Product navigation
detail.html	Product detail
cart.html	Shopping cart
checkout.html	Checkout
thanks.html	Confirmation

Most advanced e-commerce Web sites use these five kinds of Web pages so this section gives you an introduction to the general layout of these kinds of Web pages. The features and makeup of these pages will be different depending on the site being designed but their primary purpose will be the same. In this section you build minimal versions of each of these five Web pages. Later, in the "Advanced Customization" section of this chapter you go into more detail regarding the possible features that you can add to each of these pages.

The minimal versions of these pages, described next, assumes a product database called products with the fields prod_title, prod_price, prod_desc, and prod_image.

A Three-Line Product Navigation Page

A simple product navigation can be one that lists products on the screen. When users click a product, a page provides them detail on the product. You can build a page to do this by starting with the two-line database report discussed in Chapter 12, *Building Query Pages*. Here's the page:

```
<html>
<title>Three-Line Product Navigation Page</title>
<b>My Database-Driven Store</b><br>
Product Menu:<ul>
<table border=0>
<<
myresults=DBFIND("products","",1,50,"record,prod_title,prod_pric
e")
    DISPLAY
        LAYOUT(myresults,"<tr>",
            "<td><a href=detail.html name=rec
value=",[1],">",
```

```
            [2],"</a></td>",
            "<td>",[3],"</td>",
            "</tr>")
    /DISPLAY
>>
</table>
</ul>
</html>
```

Changes are shown in bold. You add a DBFIND search to the page to extract the products. You convert the entries in the first column of the table to hypertext links. When a user clicks a link, the rec variable is set to the record ID of the product and the user is directed to detail.html. This is the same technique used in the "Linking Reports to Detail Page" section at the end of Chapter 13, *Building Database Reports*.

A Six-Line Product Detail Page

A simple product detail page is one that displays information on a selected product along with an Add To Cart button to add the item to a shopping cart. Here is a page that displays the details available on the selected product with a hypertext link to add the item to the cart:

```
<<temp=DBGETREC("products",rec)>>
<html>
<title>Six-Line Product Detail Page </title>
<b>My Database-Driven Store</b><br>
Product Detail:<br>
<a href=menu.html>Return to Menu</a><ul>
<b><<prod_title>></b><br>
<table border=0>
<tr>
<td valign=top>
Price: <<prod_price>></td>
<td valign=top><img src=/images/<<prod_image>>></td>
</tr>
<tr><td colspan=2>
<a href=addtocart name=rec value=<<rec>>>ADD TO
CART</a></td></tr>
</table>
```

```
</ul>
</html>
<<overlay addtocart
   temp=DBGETREC("products",rec)
   APPEND ROW(rec,prod_title,1,prod_price) TO mycart /APPEND
   GOTO "cart.html"
>>
```

The first Overlay on the page uses DBGETREC to load variables from a record in the products database using the record rec, which is set when the user clicks a product link on the menu.html page. The variables loaded from the products record are displayed throughout the page. Then, at the bottom of the page, a hypertext link enables users to add the item to a shopping cart. The shopping cart is really just a variable, called mycart, with four columns and multiple rows—one row per item in the cart. The first column contains the record ID of a product. The second has the product name; the third contains the quantity ordered, and the last column contains the unit price of the item ordered. In more sophisticated carts, this variable has more columns, but the idea is the same.

When a user clicks the Add To Cart link, the database record loads again using the DBGETREC tag to ensure the variables associated with the record match those containing field values. Then the APPEND tag adds a row to mycart. Note how the ROW tag is used as the first parameter of the APPEND tag. This is a good technique for appending multicolumn rows to multicolumn, multirow variables like mycart. Also note that mycart, like all HTML/OS variables, starts with the value ERROR. After a row is appended you still have a row in mycart containing the value ERROR. Here that bad row is left in mycart. It is stripped out of mycart on the shopping cart page. After the APPEND instruction, the user is directed to cart.html to view the contents of the shopping cart.

Note that this detail page is similar to the detail page described in the "Linking Reports to Detail Pages" section at the end of Chapter 13, *Building Database Reports*. The main difference is that here you use a DBGETREC tag instead of a DBGET tag, because here a record ID determines the record instead of a company_name field.

A Twenty-Line Shopping Cart

The previous product detail page used an Add To Cart link. It assumed a shopping cart variable called mycart with four columns. Here is a simple shopping cart page that lists the contents of that mycart variable. This page also includes Delete links to remove items from the cart, a State Tax option to include or not include sales tax, and a Shipping Formula to calculate shipping costs. The code for the page is as follows:

```
<< # Structure of mycart:
   #   column 1 - record ID
   #   column 2 - product name
   #   column 3 - quantity
   #   column 4 - unit price
   /#
   mycart=GETCOLNOTEQ(mycart,1,"ERROR")
   mycart=GETCOLNOTEQ(mycart,1,"")
   IF mycart[1,1]="" THEN GOTO "nocart.html" /IF
   IF ISNUMBER(tax)="FALSE" THEN tax=0 /IF
   shipping=MAX(15,(3+3*rows(mycart)))
>>
<html>
<title>Twenty-Line Shopping Cart Page </title>
<b>My Database-Driven Store</b><br>
Shopping Cart:<br>
<a href=menu.html>Return to Menu</a><ul>
<form method=post ACTION=changecart>
<table border=1><tr>
<td>Product</td><td>Unit
Cost</td><td>Quantity</td><td>Subtotal</td>
</tr>
<< i=1 subtotal=0
   FOR NAME=mycart ROWNAME=x DO
     DISPLAY
       "<tr><td><a href=detail.html name=rec VALUE="+x[1]+">"+
       x[2]+"</a> (<a href=dcart NAME=drec
VALUE="+x[1]+">Delete</a>)"+
       "</td><td>"+x[4]+"</td>"+
       "<td><input type=text name=mycart[3,"+i+"]
size=4></td>"+
       "<td
align=right>"+FORMAT((x[3]*x[4]),"comma")+"</td></tr>"+LF
     /DISPLAY
```

```
      subtotal=subtotal+(x[3]*x[4])
      i=i+1
   /FOR
>>
<tr><td colspan=3>Subtotal</td>
<td align=right><<FORMAT(subtotal,"comma")>></td></tr>
<tr><td colspan=3>State Sales Tax:
<a href=<<page>> NAME=tax value="0.0625">Yes</a>
<a href=<<page>> NAME=tax value="0.0000">No</a>
</td><td align=right><<FORMAT(tax*subtotal,"comma")>></td></tr>
<tr><td colspan=3>Delivery:
</td><td align=right><<FORMAT(shipping,"comma")>></td></tr>
<tr><td colspan=3>TOTAL</td>
<td
align=right><<FORMAT(subtotal+tax*subtotal+shipping,"comma")>></
td></tr>
<tr><td colspan=4 align=right>
<input type=submit name=mybutton value="Recalculate">
<input type=submit name=mybutton value="Checkout">
</td></tr>
</table>
</form>
</html>
<<overlay changecart
   i=1 subtotal=0
   WHILE mycart[1,i] != "" DO
     IF ISINTEGER(mycart[3,i])!= "TRUE" OR
        mycart[3,i] =0 OR mycart[3,i] < 0 THEN
        mycart[1,i]=""
     ELSE
        subtotal=subtotal+mycart[3,i]*mycart[4,i]
     /IF
     i=i+1
   /WHILE
   mycart=GETCOLNOTEQ(mycart,1,"")
   shipping=MAX(15,(3+3*rows(mycart)))
   IF mybutton="Checkout" THEN
```

```
      GOTO "checkout.html"
   ELSE
      GOTO PAGE
   /IF
>>
<<overlay dcart
   mycart=GETCOLNOTEQ(mycart,1,drec)
   GOTO PAGE
>>
```

The top of this page contains an Underlay that serves three functions. First it clears empty rows and the ERROR in the first cell of mycart (as mentioned in the previous section). Then it tests to see whether mycart is empty. If mycart is empty, it directs the user to nocart.html. After that the Underlay initializes the tax variable. Last it runs the following line:

```
shipping=MIN(15,(3+3*rows(mycart)))
```

You can change this shipping formula to fit your needs. This particular formula sets the shipping cost to $3.00 plus $3.00 for each item in the cart, with a maximum shipping cost of $15.00. This sets the shipping cost between $6.00 and $15.00. In more advanced e-commerce systems, multiple shipping options are often provided along with more complex calculations. In the most advanced systems, costs are calculated based on the Zip codes of the organization and destination and data such as total shipping weight is taken into account.

After the Underlay at the top of the page, an HTML table is displayed. First an HTML table header is displayed. After that an HTML table row is displayed for each product in the cart. One row for state tax and a row for shipping follow. The last row displays a total. The part of the Overlay that displays the items in the cart uses the following code:

```
DISPLAY
   "<tr><td><a href=detail.html name=rec VALUE="+x[1]+">"+
   x[2]+"</a> (<a href=dcart NAME=drec
VALUE="+x[1]+">Delete</a>)"+
   "</td><td>"+x[4]+"</td>"+
   "<td><input type=text name=mycart[3,"+i+"] size=4></td>"+
   "<td
align=right>"+FORMAT((x[3]*x[4]),"comma")+"</td></tr>"+LF
/DISPLAY
```

This code is inside a FOR loop. The first part of the DISPLAY statement displays a hypertext link to detail.html. Note the *name-value* pair that sets rec to the record ID. The text in the link is the product name.

This is followed with a similar link that goes to dcart, an on-click Overlay for deleting a product from mycart, which is followed by a unit cost, x[4].

After this you fill an HTML table cell with an HTML form input text box by using the following code:

```
"<td><input type=text name=mycart[3,"+i+"] size=4></td>"
```

Note how the *name* of the input box is dynamically generated. When you are writing input text boxes directly in a page, you can write for example <input type=text name=mycart[3,4]>, which places an input text box on the screen for the name mycart[3,4]. When the user submits the HTML form, the value in this box is saved into mycart[3,4]. Here however, this HTML statement is generated within a DISPLAY statement, so you paste together the line as shown.

To the right of this quantity input, a subtotal is displayed. To ensure numbers are displayed properly you right-align them in the cells of the HTML table, and you use the FORMAT tag to display numbers with two decimal places.

Below the product rows of the HTML table are rows for setting and displaying the state tax, the delivery charge, a subtotal, and a total.

Below this, you provide Recalculate and Checkout buttons. When a user clicks Recalculate, the changecart on-click Overlay runs. This Overlay checks the quantities placed in the cart and recalculates totals. The code uses a WHILE loop that checks each cell possibly modified by the user. If a quantity value is not a positive integer then the first cell in that product row changes to an empty string. Then below the WHILE loop, using a GETCOLNOTEQ tag, deletes all rows with an empty string in the first column. New totals and shipping costs are calculated and depending on whether the on-click Overlay was run by the user clicking Recalculate or Checkout, the page is redisplayed or the user is directed to checkout.html.

Below the changecart on-click Overlay is the dcart on-click Overlay, which runs when the user clicks the Delete link next to a product. This on-click Overlay uses the GETCOLNOTEQ tag to delete the row in mycart with drec in the first column and redisplays the page.

A Nine-Line Checkout Page

When the Checkout button on the previous Shopping Cart page is clicked the user is sent to a page where the user can complete the order. The checkout process typically does the following:

- Collects delivery information
- Collects payment information
- Sends order to company for fulfillment
- Backs up order

You can build a simple page that performs these tasks by starting with the page discussed in the "Ten-Line E-Commerce Web Site" section at the beginning of this chapter. Deleting the unnecessary parts of the page (with new or modified elements in bold), you get the following code:

```
<html>
<title>Checkout Page</title>
<b>My Database-Driven Store</b><br>
Checkout Form:<br>
<a href=menu.html>Return to Menu</a><ul>
<< IF msg != "ERROR" THEN DISPLAY msg+"<br>" /DISPLAY  /IF
    msg="ERROR"
    total=subtotal + tax x subtotal + shipping
>>
<form method=post ACTION=postorder>
<table bgcolor=#CECECE border=0 cellspacing=0>
<tr><td colspan=2><b>Checkout Form</b></td></tr>
<tr><td align=right valign=top>Full Name</td>
<td><input type=text name=shop_name size=30></td></tr>
<tr><td align=right valign=top>E-Mail</td>
<td><input type=text name=shop_email size=30></td></tr>
<tr><td  align=right valin=top>Shipping<br>
<font size=1>Enter complete<br>shipping address</font></td>
<td><textarea name=shop_ship cols=30
rows=3></textarea></td></tr>
<tr><td  align=right valign=top >Credit Card</td>
<td valign=top><input type=text name=shop_card></td></tr>
<tr><td  align=right valign=top >Expires</td>
<td><input type=text name=shop_expires><font
size=1>(MM/DD/YYYY)</font>
</td></tr>
<tr bgcolor=#FFFFFF><td colspan=2 align=center>
<i>A total of <<FORMAT(total,"comma")>>(
```

```
<<FORMAT(subtotal,"comma")>> + <<FORMAT(shipping,"comma")>>
S&H)
will appear on your credit card.</i></td></tr>
<tr bgcolor=#FFFFFF><td colspan=2 align=center>
<input type=submit value="COMPLETE ORDER NOW">
</td></tr></table></form>
</html>
<<overlay postorder
IF shop_name="" OR shop_email="" OR
   shop_ship="" OR shop_card="" OR
   shop_expires="" THEN
   msg="<font color=red>Missing Info. Try Again.</font>"
ELSE
  myorder=
    "==========================="+LF+
    "Order Date: "+TODAY+LF+
    "Full Name: "+ship_name+LF+
    "E-mail: "+ship_name+LF+
    "Card: "+ship_card+" ("+ship_expires+")"+LF+
    "Shipping: "+LF+ship_name+LF+
    "ITEMS ORDERED:"+LF
  FOR NAME=mycart ROWNAME=x DO
    myorder=myorder+
    " Qty "+x[3]+" of "+x[1]+": "+FORMAT(x[3]*x[4],"comma")+LF
  /FOR
  myorder=myorder+
    "SUBTOTAL: "+ FORMAT(subtotal,"comma")+LF+
    "Shipping: "+ FORMAT(shipping,"comma")+LF+
    "TOTAL: "+ FORMAT(total,"comma")+LF+
    "==========================="+LF+LF
  MAIL myorder TO ADDRESS="salesorders@mycompany.com"
    SUBJECT="Order ("+now+")"
  /MAIL
  APPEND myorder To FILE="order_log.txt" /APPEND
  msg="Order Placed. Thank you. E-mail questions to
       salesquestions@mycompany.com."
```

```
    shop_card=""
    shop_expires=""
    shop_ship=""
/IF
GOTO "thanks.html"
>>
```

This code collects contact and shipping information, and credit card information. When the user clicks the Complete Order button, the `postorder` on-click Overlay runs. It uses an `IF-THEN` statement to check the submitted information. If the data is validated, the code composes the text for the order, placing it in the `myorder` variable. It then e-mails `myorder` to the owner of the site, backs up the `myorder` to a file using the `APPEND` tag, and then directs the user to the thank you page, `thanks.html`. Note that more sophisticated pages would also send a confirmation e-mail to the user of the site. This is left as an exercise at the end of this chapter.

A One-Line Confirmation Page

The thank you or confirmation page is needed so the user knows that the order has been processed. It is best to separate the page from the checkout page to ensure the user gets the feedback that the order was successfully placed. A simple confirmation page is as follows:

```
<< mycart="" >>
<html>
<title>Thank You Page</title>
<b>My Database-Driven Store</b><br>
<a href=menu.html>Return to Menu</a>
<ul><br><br>
<font size=2>Your order has been processed.</font><br>
<font size=5>Thank you.</font><br><br>
If you have questions please call 1-212-555-6789<br><br>
- Staff</ul>
</html>
```

The only HTML/OS instruction used on this page is the one at the top that sets `mycart` to the empty string. The rest of the page is a simple document that displays a *Thank you* message for the user. Additional helpful features can be added to pages like this. These are just some of the advanced features covered in the next section.

Advanced E-Commerce Sites

In the previous section you looked at the construction of a database-driven e-commerce site. The site was composed of five pages, each with a different purpose. The navigation page was used to select a product. The product detail page provided detail on selected products. The shopping cart page informed the users of their selections, and a checkout page processed the order. The confirmation page provided information to the users after order placement.

Highly sophisticated e-commerce sites provide additional pages of use by those running the site. They also improve on the pages discussed in this chapter, often placing multiple features on the same page. Web sites, such as **Puritan's Pride** (http://www.puritanspride.com/) in Figure 16.2, place multiple navigation tools and product detail on the same page.

Figure 16.2: Sophisticated e-commerce sites merge navigation and product information together on the same page.

In this section you look at the main components of more sophisticated e-commerce sites and the kinds of features you may want to add to your site. This section can serve as a source of ideas. In the remaining chapters of Part IV, *E-Commerce Programming*, you learn how to build many of the features discussed in this section.

The Main System Components

When building an advanced e-commerce site you work with three main system components: Web pages, databases, and settings data. Web pages provide presentation and functionality but depend on underlying data. You store the underlying data in databases and settings files. Until now, the only database discussed in this chapter was a product database and no settings files were used. A sophisticated site uses multiple databases and settings files to store configuration information.

Site Databases and Settings Files

Sophisticated e-commerce sites often include the following databases:

- Product database
- Order database
- Order Items database
- User database

The Product database stores information on each product. You expand the fields in each record to include any and all information directly associated with each product. In addition to the basic fields, such as product name and price, fields for product options, related products, special pricing options, and special shipping surcharges are stored here.

The Order database is where you store orders the user has placed. It gives you an archive of orders. You save customer information, shipping information, the date the order was placed, and other information pertaining to the order here. The Order database goes along with an Order Items database, which stores the specifics of each line item ordered. If a user places an order containing four products, for example, a record is added to the order database and four other records, one for each item ordered, are added to the Order Items database. The Order Items database record would include a field that stores a unique order number, relating the records back to its associated record in the order database.

The User database is where you store information on specific users. You usually store fields for a login ID, password, and an e-mail address in this database. Other fields may store a pricing level (retail or wholesale, for example), the date of the user's last order, the total number of orders placed, and so on.

Settings files are standard text files used by the HTML documents on the Web site. These text files make it easier to manage a Web site. For example, you can use settings files to store a table of shipping options in a pull-down menu for providing users with shipping options. They can contain a cross-reference between two-letter U.S. state codes, and the full names of states, again in a pull-down menu format. Setting files can be e-mail templates—files that store the content of messages that are automatically e-mailed to users when they order a product or when staff members process their order.

The Web Pages

Web pages are the presentation and dynamic elements of a site. In the previous section you familiarized yourself with five kinds of Web pages. In addition to them, sophisticated sites may have Web pages for customer-order tracking, providing receipts, printing purchase orders, and providing staff functions such as product record editing, determining which products are on sale or should be highlighted, issuing sales reports, and more. In the following section you look at the many of the features possible when building a sophisticated Web site.

Advanced Customization

Sophisticated e-commerce sites serve as interfaces between organizations and their customers, staff, and visitors. They reflect the individuality of an organization. No two e-commerce sites are they same. The features and Web pages need to be changed and updated as operations and organizational policies change. An advanced e-commerce site requires constant attention, improvement, and customization.

When building a new e-commerce site, it is important to realize you cannot build it over night. A lot of thought is needed—the same kind of thought needed when making everyday organizational decisions. You must carefully select the ideas and features that go into a site from hundreds of possibilities.

With so many possible designs and features, a good starting point when designing an e-commerce site, is to select those features or design elements you want on each page of the e-commerce part of the site. Narrowing down the features and designs you want can prevent you from skipping those that are truly important to the site. The following is a general wish list you can use for this purpose. Features are organized by the kind of Web pages typically found in the e-commerce section of a Web site. We do not list those Web site features that are purely informational or those disconnected from transactions associated with the buying of products or services.

Product Navigation Pages

Dynamic categories. Category lists that display only those categories containing products.

Image grid. Products that display a multicolumn table of images.

Search box. A text box component that yields a search result page.

Multiple categories. A category search that attaches to a subcategory search.

Multiselection feature. Product lists that allow the user to select multiple products at a time.

Prioritization. Product lists sorted by a priority key so that certain products always appear at the top.

Add to cart. Add To Cart buttons that appear on navigation pages.

Product Detail Pages

Variable pricing. Automatic pricing based on user type.

Options. Product options, such as color of a sweatshirt, applied by users when they add the item to the shopping cart. Options are factors that don't change the price of a product.

Add-ons. Add-ons to a product, such as 50X zoom lens, applied by users when they add the item to the shopping cart. Add-ons change the price of the purchase.

Product collections. Detail pages that display series of products, all with a common description. Each product has its own description and an Add To Cart button.

Real-time inventory. Detail pages that test the availability of an item, notifying the user if the item is unavailable.

Related items. Lists of products related to the one displayed, typically displayed at the bottom of a detail page.

Extra detail. Extra detail related to the current detail displayed on the page, typically displayed at the bottom of the page or as a link to a pop-up page.

Zoom and related photos. Links that allow the user to zoom into graphics elements already on the page.

Sales announcements. Special messaging on a page containing promotional content relating to the product being viewed. A message may include information on possible savings if minimum quantities are ordered, or if orders are placed by a specific date, for example.

Shopping Cart Pages

Related products. Related products that display along side the cart when certain items appear in the shopping cart. For example, if a toy is found in the cart, a link for purchasing batteries is provided.

Specials and promotions. Specials and promotions that display on the page. For example, if free shipping is provided on orders over $50 then a cart with $35 worth of merchandise in the cart might display: "Free shipping on orders over $50. Add a few more items to your order and save."

Printable purchase order. A printable purchase order for use by business customers.

Cookied carts. Shopping cart entries that are saved so that, even if they are abandoned, upon returning to the site days or weeks later, the items remain in the user's cart.

Reminder service. An option to permit users to compose a reminder e-mail with links to re-order specific items in their cart or remind them of specific holidays.

Checkout Pages

Login. A page with a *Forgot your password?* feature so users can re-use information previously entered, such as shipping and billing information, in the checkout process.

Real-time authorization. A feature that allows credit card or checks to be issued over the Web. When a user places an order, a connection is made to a bank, completing a bank transaction on the fly, without the need to process the order at a later date.

Automated download feature. A product download button for sites that sell software or information.

Shipping calculators. Useful when building sites that give users multiple shipping options. For example, sites that give the user the ability to choose among Ground, Next Day, and Two-Day delivery options.

Address book. An address book entry that avoids requiring the user to type in shipping addresses on repeat orders.

Confirmation Pages

Receipt page. A page that provides the user a printable receipt of the order.

Reminder notification. A page that gives users the ability to send themselves a reminder to buy another product. The user specifies a date, and the site sends them a reminder on that date with the message they specified.

Other Pages

Order tracking. Pages that allow customers to see whether the products they ordered shipped out. May include a FedEx, UPS, or U.S Postal Service tracking numbers and links.

Customer order history. A page where customers can view past orders. Orders can be summarized and include an Add To Cart button for easy re-ordering.

Order pickup. A page for staff to pickup and process orders.

Database editors. Record editors for modifying product and user information.

Settings pages. Pages for setting categories, products on sales, editing e-mail templates, and setting configuration parameters.

Reporting. Reports on page access, failed user searches, the use of sales promotions, and so on.

Coupons. A feature that provides users the ability to manage a coupon database. Goes along with a Coupon entry box placed on a checkout page.

This list includes many of the features you have grown to expect from the world's largest and most sophisticated e-commerce sites. You will want to add many of them to your e-commerce site. In addition you will want to add features specific to your industry and drop those features not applicable to your situation. Finally, since this list is long, you will want to prioritize the list to meet objective time and delivery goals.

Summary

This chapter introduced the world of e-commerce sites. You learned that building advanced database-driven Web sites is not rocket science—that such sites can be built using five types of Web pages, each requiring on average, about a dozen lines of HTML/OS instructions. You also learned that those pages can vary greatly because of the variety of features you can add to them.

In practice, the individuality you give your site will reflect the individuality of your organization. Construction will take a lot longer than the time it takes to cut and paste the pages here into a site and get them to work together. You will want to pay careful attention to how each is constructed and vary them to fit your individual needs. Furthermore, you will want to experiment with different features and designs.

In the next five chapters of Part IV, *E-Commerce Programming*, you'll learn how to build many of the features listed in the "Advanced Customization" section of this chapter. Next, in Chapter 17, *Building Product Navigation Pages*, you learn how different navigation pages are built.

Exercises

In the following exercises you extend the capabilities of the ten-line e-commerce Web site provided near the beginning of this chapter. Answers to these exercises are provided on this book's companion Web site as described in the book's Preface.

Exercise 1

The "Ten-Line E-commerce Web Site" section of this chapter provides the code for a single page e-commerce site. The page avoids tax calculation by saying tax is included. Expand this page so it supports tax calculation.

Exercise 2

The ten-line e-commerce site does not do sophisticated data validation. Use the data validation techniques described in the "Commonly Used Validation Schemes" section of Chapter 10, *HTML Forms Processing* to accomplish this goal.

Exercise 3

The ten-line e-commerce site does not e-mail a confirmation to the user when a purchase is made. Add this feature to the page.

## CHAPTER 17

Building Product Navigation Pages

Chapter 16, *Designing E-Commerce Systems* introduced a three-line navigation page in the "Your First Database-Driven E-Commerce Site" section. In this chapter you explore the different ways to construct navigation pages. An emphasis is placed on e-commerce sites but you can also apply what you learn here to the needs of information databases, portal Web sites, and article archives. The concepts are universal.

You start by exploring the kinds of features typically included on a navigation page and how to build them. Then you build an image-based navigation page. After that you learn about navigation pages that allow users to select multiple products at a time. This is followed with discussions on category lists, hierarchical trees, and search boxes.

Use Navigation Pages Only When Necessary—Product navigation pages are not required on sites with few products. Do not introduce navigation components unless they are useful to the user visiting the site. If you have only a few products it is doubtful the user needs navigation aids. If you plan on having many products don't introduce the navigation elements until they are needed.

Selecting Navigation Features

One of the most important considerations when building an e-commerce site is how to make products on the Web site easy to locate. The process must be intuitive and natural. The amount of energy and thought required on the part of a user to find a product should be minimized. The best navigation pages are single uncluttered Web pages that allow the users to find what they are looking for. Well-designed navigation pages include any combination of the following four navigation components:

- Products capsules
- Product lists
- Category lists
- Search boxes

The way you arrange these different components depends on the number of products you have and the ability you have to support navigation components. Sites may need only one of these components. Other sites will give the user many options, such as the **King Arthur Flour** Web site (http://www.kingarthurflour.com/) shown in Figure 17.1. The Web page shown includes two category lists and a sophisticated search box. Let's look at each component and see how and when it should be used.

Figure 17.1: The recipe book on this Web site uses multiple navigation tools to ensure recipes are easy to find.

Product capsules are mini product detail pages that point to pages with greater detail. A product capsule can include a small graphic, a one-line product title, and perhaps a one-line description. If the product is a commodity that is well recognized by the user, the capsule can include an Add To Cart link. If not, you should include a link to a detail page in the capsule.

Product capsules are a great way to give selected products in your inventory preferred visibility, however they interfere with the navigation aspect of the page. Only a limited number of product capsules can be placed on a navigation page before the page becomes too busy. Also, product capsules need to be managed. They should change at least daily. You can do this automatically by randomly selecting products, when the page is launched, from a list of products reserved for placing on the product navigation page, or you can do this manually by providing a back-end tool for selecting the product capsules you want on the page.

Product lists are typically lists of single-line product names that link to product detail pages. On a Web site with less than 20 products the navigation page is often a product list. Other components are not necessary. When you have so many products that you can split them into distinct categories, product lists are no longer effective navigation aids; replace them with a list of categories. When the number of products grows further, perhaps to thousands, product lists become necessary once again—but not as a primary navigation tool. You use such lists as alternatives to product capsules. Use them like product capsules—as a way to focus special attention on specific products.

Category lists are typically lists of category names presented on a navigation page that link to a list of products. Product categorization is useful when you have more than 20 products. If you have thousands of products, a category list may have different levels. First the user selects a main category. Then the user selects a subcategory, and so on. The depth of the categories depends on the number of products you have.

Search boxes are most often input boxes with a Find button for searching the inventory of a Web site. The best search boxes are simple, requiring the user simply to place one or more words in the box to perform a search and yield a product list of results. Search boxes are useful on sites with hundreds or thousands of products. In most cases they are not useful when you have fewer products because, in those cases, product categorization works better—always yielding a search result for the user. The exception to this rule is the site that features complex products that cannot be described by their product name. For example, a site that sells about one hundred works of art may provide a search that allows the user to specify a topic, or an artist name.

Perhaps the most important aspect of search boxes is not what the user sees, but how you actually process the search request. The best searches are intelligent—meaning you create an algorithm that searches your products and yields results in most circumstances, placing the most appropriate search result at the top of the page. This is easier said than done and highly dependent on the nature of the data being searched. However, you do get some tips on how to build intelligent searches in the "Building Search Boxes" section later in this chapter.

Building Product Lists

The "A Database-Driven E-Commerce Site" section of Chapter 16, *Designing E-Commerce Systems*, introduced a three-line navigation page. The page displays a simple list of products. Here you display a product list consisting of images, lists that are prioritized, lists that display specials, lists with Add To Cart links next to each item in the list, and lists where the users can select more than a single item. You can also extend the examples provided here with Page Up and Page Down features. To do that, use the technique described in the "Seven-Line Database Report" section of Chapter 13, *Building Database Reports*.

A Twelve-Line Image Selection Page

To display a list of images, you could take the three-line navigation page and substitute product names with images. In doing so however, the images would appear in a single column. More often you want to display the images in multiple columns across the page. To do this, you convert the LAYOUT tag used in the navigation page with a WHILE loop. The code follows:

```
<title>Twelve-line Image Navigation Page </title>
<b>My Database-Driven Store</b><br>
Image Menu:<ul>
<table border=0>
<<
x=DBFIND("products",1,50,"record,prod_title,prod_price,prod_imag
e")
    i=1 j=1 no_cols=3
     WHILE myresults[1,I] != "" DO
       IF j=1 THEN DISPLAY "<tr>" /DISPLAY /IF
       DISPLAY
         '<td><a href=detail.html name=rec
value="'+myresults[1, i]+'">'+
         '<img border=0 src="/images/'+myresults[4]+'
'</a><br>'+
          x[2]+ '</td>'
       /DISPLAY
       IF j=no_cols THEN DISPLAY "</tr>" /DISPLAY /IF
       i=i+1 j=j+1
       IF j > no_cols THEN j=1 /IF
     /WHILE
     IF j != 1 THEN DISPLAY "</tr>" /DISPLAY /IF
>>
</table>
</ul>
</html>
```

This page displays images, each with a product title underneath it, three columns wide. The number of columns is adjustable. The trick here is to use three different DISPLAY statements in a WHILE loop: one to display the HTML <tr> tag when needed, one to display the content of each cell, and one to display the HTML </tr> tag, when needed.

Sites such the **Schweitzer Linen** (http:// www.schweitzer-lenen.com) shown in Figure 17.2, use image selection. Here images are more helpful navigation tools than words.

Figure 17.2: This Web site uses images as a navigation tool.

A Six-Line Product List with Product Specials

When displaying products, it is often useful to give increased visibility to certain products. Two ways to do this are by placing select products in bold and placing certain products at the top of the list. To place certain products at the top of the list, you sort the products returned from DBFIND using a sort key. Alternatively, you can use the DBFINDSORT tag. To emphasize items on sale, you display them in bold. Both cases are accomplished using special fields in the database. The prod_key field creates sort prioritization. The prod_onsale field determines the products to display in bold. Here's the code to do that:

```
<html>
<title>Six-Line Product List With Specials</title>
<b>My Database-Driven Store</b><br>
Product Menu:<ul>
<table border=0>
<< myresults=DBFIND("products",1,50,
        "record,prod_title,sort_key,prod_onsale")
   myresults=SORTCOL(myresults,3)
   FOR NAME=myresults ROWNAME=x DO
      IF x[4]="TRUE" THEN b[1]="<b>" b[2]="</b>" ELSE b="" /IF
      DISPLAY "<tr><td>"+b[1]+
              "<a href=detail.html name=rec value="+x[1]+">"+
              x[2]+"</a>"+b[2]+"</td><td>"+x[3]+"</td></tr>"
      /DISPLAY
   /FOR
>>
</table>
</ul>
</html>
```

The first line in bold sorts the results of the DBFIND tag. The second bolded line sets up b, a two-column by one-row variable. If the line belongs to an item on sale, the two cells in the b variable are filled with the `<b>` and `</b>` HTML bold tags. If not, b is set to the empty string. As a result, products on sale appear bold while others remain unchanged. The technique used here is an example of how you add fields to a database to give you greater control over the display of the products. In general, product emphasis requires the addition of special fields in the product database. How you use those fields when you display the products is up to you. The same fields, for example, can be used to display on-sale images next to items on sale.

A Seven-Line Multiselect Product List

Product navigation is about finding and locating a product or service. In some cases however, the concept is also about giving the user the ability to select multiple products and view them side by side on a detail page. This requires you give the user the ability to select multiple products at once from a menu. At other times you may want to allow the user to select multiple products at once and add them to a shopping cart.

In both of these cases you need to give users the ability to select multiple products from a list. To do this, you use check boxes. Instead of providing a list of hypertext links, you provide the user Compare and Add To Cart buttons, and check boxes next to each item. Because a multiselect feature is more often an add-on to a standard product list, the links used to select an individual product are best retained. The code for this is as follows:

```
<html>
<title>Seven-Line Multi-Select Product List </title>
<b>My Database-Driven Store</b><br>
Product Menu:<ul>
<form method=post ACTION=redirect>
<input type=submit name=mybutton value="Compare">
<input type=submit name=mybutton value="Add To Cart"><br>
<table border=0>
<< myresults=DBFIND("products",1,50, "record,prod_title")
    FOR NAME=myresults ROWNAME=x DO
        DISPLAY '<tr>'+
          '<td><input type=checkbox name=myrecords
value="'+x[1]+'"></td>'+
            "<td><a href=detail.html name=rec value="+x[1]+">"+
            x[2]+"</a></td></tr>"
        /DISPLAY
    /FOR
>>
</table>
</form>
</ul>
</html>
<<overlay redirect
    IF mybutton="Compare" THEN
      GOTO "mdisplay.html"
    ELSE
      GOTO "cart.html"
    /IF
>>
```

This Web page starts with an HTML form linked to the `redirect` on-click Overlay, which, depending on the button the user clicks, redirects the user to `mdisplay.html` or `cart.html`. This Web page is similar to the page discussed in the previous "A Six-line Product List with Product Specials" section except it includes an HTML form with check boxes and two submit buttons.

This page uses multiple check boxes with the `myrecords` name. It is important to remember that, when the HTML form is submitted, this `myrecords` name will be a single column, multirow variable filled with record numbers—one for each selection. See the section "Using Checkbox" in Chapter 10, *HTML Forms Processing* for more information on how this HTML form component works.

After the HTML form is submitted, the user is directed to either `mdisplay.html` or `cart.html`. The purpose of this page is to create and fill the `myrecords` variable. How the `myrecords` variable is handled is up to the code placed in `mdisplay.html` and `cart.html`. The code to do that is left as an exercise at the end of this chapter.

Building Category Lists

Category lists can be written manually, read from a text file, or composed on the fly from the products database. In this section you learn all three methods. At the end of this section you also look at category lists that have depth—meaning, categories with subcategories with subcategories, etc.

A Zero-Line Category List

First, consider building a category list manually. Here you add a field to the products database called `prod_cat` that stores the name of a category. Then you manually type into the HTML document a list of hypertext links, one for each category. You use no Overlays, producing a zero-line category list as shown in the following example:

```
<html>
<title>Zero-Line Category List </title>
<b>My Database-Driven Store</b><br>
Categories:<ul>
<a href=list.html name=mycat value="tshirts">T-Shirts</a><br>
<a href=list.html name=mycat  value="pants">Pants</a><br>
<a href=list.html name=mycat  value="shorts">Shorts</a><br>
</ul>
</html>
```

Here each link, when clicked, sets the `mycat` variable and directs the user to `list.html`, a product listing page. That page lists the products in the selected category. To do that, you replace the `DBFIND` tag on any product listing page with one that extracts only those products in the selected category. For example, starting with the three-line navigation page introduced in the "Your First Database-Driven E-Commerce Site" section of Chapter 16, *Designing E-Commerce Systems*, you get the following:

```
<html>
<title>Three-Line Product List From Category</title>
<b>My Database-Driven Store</b><br>
Category: <b><<mycat>></b><ul>
<table border=0>
<< s='prod_cat="'+mycat+'"'

myresults=DBFIND("products",s,1,50,"record,prod_title,prod_price
")
    DISPLAY
        LAYOUT(myresults,"<tr>",
            "<td><a href=detail.html name=rec value=",[1],">",
            [2],"</a></td>",
            "<td>",[3],"</td>",
            "</tr>")
    /DISPLAY
>>
</table>
</ul>
</html>
```

Changes are shown in bold. A category name is displayed at the top of the page and a search string appears in the second parameter of the `DBFIND` tag to limit searches to items in the selected category.

Editable Categories

The zero-line category list is fine if categories do not change. But on large sites they may change often. In that case you may want to store the possible categories in a text file and allow staff members to edit the text file, which they can do using an HTML editor, like those discussed in Chapter 8, *Building Text Editors*, or using a comma-delimited text file editor like that discussed in the "Fifteen-Line Spreadsheet Editor" section of Chapter 10, *HTML Forms Processing*.

The category page reads the category text file and displays the category lines using a `layout` tag. Replace the three hypertext links in the zero-line category page with the following Overlay:

```
<<
COPY FILE="mycats.txt" TS="|" TO mycats /COPY
DISPLAY
   LAYOUT(mycats,'<a href=list.html name=mycat value="',[1],
      '">',[1],'</a><br>')
/DISPLAY
>>
```

The Overlay reads the text file into the `mycats` variable. That variable is used in a `LAYOUT` tag to display the category listing lines dynamically. Now staff members have a text file to edit that is divorced from the Web page. Changing the text file changes the list of categories listed on the Web page without you having to edit the Web page itself.

Dynamic Categories

Another way to build a category list is by extracting the possible categories from the `products` database. This method has the advantage that empty categories are not listed. It is most definitely a Web *faux pas* to display empty categories on Web pages. To extract the categories used in a product database, you use the `DBUNIQUE` tag. Replace the three hypertext links in the zero-line category page with the following Overlay:

```
<<
mycats=DBUNIQUE(products,"","prod_cat")
DISPLAY
   LAYOUT(mycats,'<a href=list.html name=mycat value="',[1],
      '">',[1],'</a><br>')
/DISPLAY
>>
```

This piece of code is identical to the previous code used when extracting categories from a text file, except here, the categories are extracted from the database.

Hierarchical Categories

On large Web sites category lists may lead to other category lists. Products may appear at every level. Portals and search engines often organize information this way. The **Famous UncleWebster** Web site at http://www.unclewebster.com/ does this, for example. See Figure 17.3.

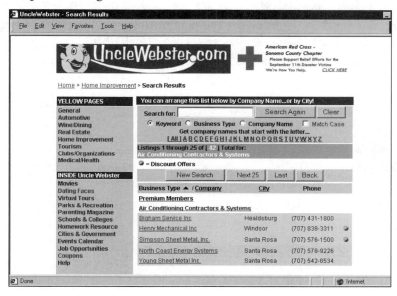

Figure 17.3: The UncleWebster Web site uses a hierarchical tree as a navigational aid.

Each category leads to more categories that lead to more categories. This is also known as a hierarchical tree. When coding this kind of drill-down navigation, it is useful to define the location of the product in the hierarchical tree using a `prod_cat` field. You use a single field. Define the entry as a category path, preceded with the depth of the path. For example:

4|Macintosh|Monitors|Color|15 Inch

This indicates a category with four levels. The main category is *Macintosh*. Within this is the category *Monitors*, and within that is the category *Color*, and within that is the category *15 Inch*. The category depth (4) is placed at the beginning of this field as a convenience. It becomes useful when you are extracting categories of a particular depth—a task you need to perform later on in the programming.

Navigation involves three distinct user aids. First, you provide users a clickable category tree that tells them their current category. Clicking a category name in the tree allows users to navigate up the tree. Second, you provide users a list of categories to access. Last, you provide the users a list of products.

Building the Clickable Tree

The clickable tree that displays on the screen depends on the current category and category depth of the user. The user starts in the home category at depth 0. You begin the link with a link to this home directory and follow that with links to each of the subcategories defined in the prod_cat field. The code is as follows:

```
<< mycatcol=LISTTOCOL(mycat,"|")
   mylevel=mycatcol[1,1]
   IF ISINTEGER(mylevel)!="TRUE" THEN mylevel=0 mycatcol=0 /IF
   DISPLAY
      '<A HREF="'+page+'" NAME=mycat value="0">Home</a>&gt;'
   /DISPLAY
   i=1
   WHILE i <= mylevel DO
      x=GETTABLE(mycatcol,1,1,2,i+1)
      x=i+"|"+COLTOLIST(x,1,"|")
      y=mycatcol[1,i+1]
      DISPLAY
         '<A HREF="'+page+'" NAME=mycat
value="'+x+'">'+y+'</a>&gt;'
      /DISPLAY
      i=i+1
   /WHILE
>>
```

The LISTOCOL tag converts the vertical bar-separated list into a one-column table. This makes the data easier to manage. The first cell of this variable is the depth level. If the mycat variable has not yet been set (the first time on the page) then the level is set to 0. This is followed by the display of a link to the home category, which is followed by a WHILE loop that displays the links stored in the mycatcol variable. Each time through the loop a link is displayed. The tricky part of the loop is correctly setting the value for the mycat variable (x) and the value displayed (y). If, for example, the current value of mycat is 3|Macintosh|Monitors|Color, you want to set x to 1|Macintosh in the first link. The second time through the loop, you want to set x to 2|Macintosh|Monitors, and so on. To do this, you use the GETTABLE tag to extract the first up to the i'th column of mycatcol. Then you create x by pasting together the category depth, a vertical bar, and a vertical bar-separated list. You create the list with the COLTOLIST tag. See Appendix D, *HTML/OS Tag Reference Guide*, for details on this Overlay tag. Finally, i is incremented and the loop is repeated. The final result is a link that looks as follows:

Home>*Macintosh*>*Monitors*>*Color*>

A user clicking a link in this navigation component sets mycat to a value like those stored in prod_cat fields.

Building the Category List

The list of categories in the current category is extracted from the database using the DBUNIQUE tag, the same tag used earlier in the "Dynamic Categories" section of this chapter. Here however you are looking for subcategories, not a specific category specified on a previous page. The technique is the same except that here, if the current category is 2|Macintosh|Monitors, for example, then you seek all categories beginning with 3|Macintosh|Monitors. The code for this is as follows:

```
s=REPLACE(mycat,mylevel+"|",(mylevel+1)+"|")
s='prod_cat ~ "'+s+'"'
mycats=DBUNIQUE(products,s,"prod_cat")
IF mycats[1,1] != "" THEN
   DISPLAY "Categories:<br>" /DISPLAY
   FOR NAME=mycats ROWNAME=x DO
      y=CUT(x[1],(mylevel+1)+"|")
      y=REPLACEALL(y,"|","&gt;")
      DISPLAY
         '<A HREF="'+page+'" NAME=mycat
value="'+x[1]+'">'+y+'</a><br>;'
      /DISPLAY
   /FOR
/IF
>>
```

The first REPLACE tag increments the leading category depth in the mycat variable so a search string can be composed and used in the following DBUNIQUE tag. The DBUNIQUE tag extracts unique subcategories, which a FOR loop then displays. Note that for this technique to work at least one product must be in the database at this level. If you are not placing products at every level, be sure to place a blank record at each level. Note also how the CUT and REPLACEALL tags convert the category lists extracted from the database into categories you can display on the screen.

Building the Product List

You use the DBFIND tag to extract the products at the current category level. The code is similar to that used in the three-line product list from category page, described earlier in this section. The code is as follows:

```
y=CUT(x[1],(mylevel+1)+"|")
y=REPLACEALL(y,"|","&gt;")
DISPLAY "Category: <b>"+y+"</b><br>" /DISPLAY
s='prod_cat="'+mycat+'"'
myresults=DBFIND("products",s,1,50,"record,prod_title,prod_price
")
DISPLAY
  LAYOUT(myresults,"<tr>",
      "<td><a href=detail.html name=rec value=",[1],">",
      [2],"</a></td>",
      "<td>",[3],"</td>",
      "</tr>")
/DISPLAY
```

Changes are shown in bold. The main change converts the mycat variable into text that can be displayed. This code, along with the code provided in this section for displaying a navigation tree and a list of categories are needed when you are building sophisticated hierarchical navigation pages for use in large e-commerce sites and directory portals.

Building Search Boxes

Search boxes are useful on sites with many products. Often they are placed on pages that also include product lists and category lists. The Overlays used when building search boxes are the same as those used when building query pages—like those discussed in Chapter 12, *Building Query Pages*.

When building search boxes, it is best to keep the search simple—at least for the user. A single input text box is preferred. The fields actually searched, and the algorithm behind the search, do not need to be simple however.

At the least, you want the words placed in the search box to be matched against words in one or more fields of the products database. To do that, set up your search as a group search. Setting up group searches is discussed in the "Using Group Fields" section of Chapter 12. This is known as an *intelligent* search since the multiple words are matched against words in multiple fields. Users are not required to think about the nature of the words they type into the search box.

A more intelligent search is obtained by automatically changing the search result if no search results are found, or if too many results are found. We leave this as an exercise at the end of this chapter.

Summary

In this chapter you learned how to build navigation pages. You learned that product navigation is generally customized to fit the needs of each site. While this chapter provides you with many sophisticated ways to build navigation pages, this chapter is not, and cannot be, exhaustive. In general, navigation pages are limited only by your imagination.

You've also seen that navigation elements are often not stand-alone pages. In this book we have separated the different e-commerce components into different pages for convenience, but in highly sophisticated sites these components are intermingled.

The main thing to remember when building your site is to provide the user options that fit the needs of your site. The elements should be intuitive, and lead your users to the products or services they seek with a minimum of thought, a minimum of hunting around, and as few clicks as possible.

Next, in Chapter 18, *Building Product Detail Pages*, you learn the different ways to display content on the page once a user has been able to locate a product. That next chapter, along with this one, gives you the ability to build a wide variety of navigation and product detail pages—an important part of e-commerce applications.

Exercises

In the following exercises you extend and build additional navigation pages using what you learned in this chapter. Answers to these exercises are provided on this book's companion Web site as described in the book's Preface.

Exercise 1

The multiselect product list, which was discussed in the "A Seven-Line Multiselect Product List" section of this chapter, links to `mdisplay.html` and `cart.html`. Set up a `products` database and the pages `mdisplay.html` and `cart.html`, so that together, the three pages constitute a functional Web site. To test your creation, fill the database with at least three or four records.

Exercise 2

The discussion in the "Building Search Boxes" section near the end of this chapter recommends building a search box using the techniques learned in the "Using Group Fields" section of Chapter 12, *Building Query Pages*. Add a search box that takes advantage of group fields to the Web page you built in Exercise 1. In your query, use the `=&` comparison operator.

Exercise 3

Make the search in Exercise 2 more intelligent by doing the following: If the number of search results found is less than five, repeat the search using a `~&` operator. If after searching within this operator, you still get too few results, use a `~|` operator. Take the results you find with these searches and combine them together. Display the results found using the first search operator above those found using the second type of search operator. Now you have a highly intelligent search with results sorted by relevance.

CHAPTER 18

Building Product Detail Pages

Product detail pages can vary a lot in sophistication. Most e-commerce sites simply display the information about a product along with an Add To Cart link. The page described in the "A Six-Line Product Detail Page" section of Chapter 16, *Designing E-Commerce Systems*, is such an example.

As you get more sophisticated however, you learn that these pages can offer a lot more to users. Extra information can include manufacturer articles, specification sheets, reviews, photos, and links to related Web pages or Web sites.

You also learn that products are often related to other products. Users interested in one product may be interested in other products by the same manufacturer, other products (perhaps hot sellers) in the same category, other products priced similarly to the one they selected, and so on.

In this chapter you look at some of the ways you can expand and improve detail pages. You also look at how to display products with options or add-ons and how those products work with shopping carts.

Adding Extra Detail

Extra detail is most often added to Web pages in three ways. You can add links to other Web pages containing the extra information, add the information in sections at the bottom of the page, or add the extra detail to the main part of the page. In this section you explore all three of these situations.

The Image Zoom

The saying "a picture is worth a thousand words" holds true on the Web as well as off the Web. However, large pictures slow down the rendering of Web pages. As a result, it is often a good idea to limit image photos on detail pages to 15 kilobytes or smaller, and link them to larger photos. This is known as image zoom. Many e-commerce sites use a standard hypertext link to provide the image zoom. The HTML instruction looks something like the following line:

```
<a href=p_01_big.jpg><img border=0 src=p_01.gif></a>
```

When the user clicks the image on the product detail page, a larger image is displayed. The image appears in the upper-left corner of the browser. It is displayed without a title. To return to the page, the user must click the browser's Back button. This is a somewhat crude way to do image zooms.

A better way to do this is to display the larger photo on a Web page, centered, along with a product title and a link back to the previous page. To do this you link the image in the detail page to a zoom page. You write the following:

```
<a href=zoom.html name=rec value=<<rec>>><img border=0
src=p_01.gif></a>
```

When the user clicks the image, the zoom.html page is displayed. You write that page as follows:

```
<html>
<title>One-Line Zoom Image Page</title>
<<temp=DBGETREC("products",rec)>>
<html>
<title>Six-Line Product Detail Page </title>
<table border=0 width=100% height=100%>
<tr valign=center><td align=center>
<table border=1 cellpadding=10 cellspacing=0>
<tr><td><img src=/images/<<prod_image_big>>><br>
<<prod_title>><br>
<a href=detail.html>Continue Shopping</a><br>
</td></tr></table>
</td></tr></table>
</html>
```

The first and only HTML/OS instruction on this page loads the specified record. You include the image and title by displaying field values and provide a link so the user can return to the detail.html page. Using HTML tables lets you center the image on the page.

Related Items

Related items are products of interest to those viewing the currently selected product. Related items are an example of cross-referencing as explained in the accompanying note, "Cross-Referencing." They are most often displayed below the product detail. You can store them in the `products` database as a list of SKUs (product IDs). Assume a database with a `prod_related` field for this. Assume also that each record has a `prod_sku` field for the product SKU.

When the product loads on the product detail page, you wish to convert the `prod_related` field into a list of related products. To do that you must find all the records in the `products` database with matching SKUs. One way to do this is to create a group field called `prod_skugroup` with the member `prod_sku`. By doing this, you make it easy to extract a list of SKUs. For example, the search string for a group field search might be

```
prod_skugroup = "111,222,333"
```

That would extract records with SKUs equal to `111`, `222`, and `333` respectively. See the "Using Group Fields" section in Chapter 12, *Building Query Pages*, for an explanation. Using this technique, the code for displaying a list of related products on a detail page is as follows:

```
IF prod_related="" THEN
   myresults=""
ELSE
   s='prod_skugroup =| "' + prod_related + '"'
   myresults=DBFIND(products,s,1,10,"record,prod_title")
   DISPLAY "Related Products:<br>" /DISPLAY
   DISPLAY LAYOUT(myresults,
      "<A HREF=detail.html NAME=rec VALUE=",[1],">",
      [1],"</a><br>"
   /DISPLAY
/IF
```

Here, if the `prod_related` variable is empty, related products are not listed. If one or more SKUs are in the `prod_related` variable, a `DBFIND` search is done and the products are listed, each with a link to the `detail.html` product page.

Cross-referencing—*Displaying related items is an example of cross-referencing. You can use the same technique used here to link a detail page to other kinds of cross references. For example, a video database can contain fields with names of actors in the video. Instead of displaying related products, one displays the names of the actors in the video. Clicking an actor's name can bring up information on the actor along with other videos featuring the same actor.*

Real-Time Inventory

Real-time inventory is an example of extra product detail that's merged into the primary display on the page. Typically you accomplish this by looking at an inventory field in the `products` database. You can display the inventory, but more importantly, in the event the inventory for an item is unavailable, you notify the user and deactivate the Add To Cart button. This is all you need to do on the detail page to handle real-time inventory. The two Overlays to do this can be as simple as those shown here:

```
<< # Overlay to inform user whether item is in stock /#
DISPLAY "Inventory: " /DISPLAY
  IF prod_inventory=0 THEN
    DISPLAY "<font color=red>Not In Stock</font>" /DISPLAY
ELSE
  DISPLAY "<font color=red>In Stock</font>" /DISPLAY
/IF
>>
<< # Overlay to display Add To Cart button /#
IF prod_inventory != 0 THEN
  DISPLAY
    '<input type=submit name=mybutton value="Add To Cart">'
  /DISPLAY
ELSE
  DISPLAY
    '<input type=submit name=mybutton value="Not In Stock">'
  /DISPLAY
/IF
>>
```

This first Overlay uses an IF-THEN statement to inform the user whether the item is in stock. The second Overlay also uses an IF-THEN statement, this time changing the Add To Cart button to a Not In Stock button if `prod_inventory` is 0. Most of the programming associated with real-time inventory is not here but in the final checkout process. There you need to ensure inventory is available at order time. There is no need to do checking of this kind in this page or any page preceding final checkout. The checkout process is described in Chapter 20, *Building Checkout Pages*.

Product Collections

In many Web sites it makes more sense to display many products on a single detail page than place the products on different Web pages. This is particularly important when the products are similar or need to be compared against each other. These pages are called product collections. The **Baby Heirlooms** site (http://www.babyheirlooms.com/) shown in Figure 18.1 demonstrates the use of product collections.

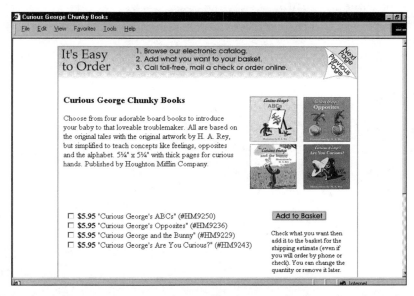

Figure 18.1: This baby store uses product collections to display related products on the same Web page.

When working with product collections, it is important to organize the fields in the products database correctly. The recommended way to do this is as follows:

- Place each product in a collection in a different record.
- Define a collection ID that's the same for each record in a collection.
- Define a collection title field that's the same for each.
- Define a product suffix field that's unique to each.
- Define a collection description field that's the same for each.
- Define a product description field that's unique to each.

Displaying multiple products on a page is a matter of displaying the duplicated fields of one of the records at the top of the page and following that with smaller detail pages, one for each record in the collection, each with its own Add To Cart button. The code for this is left as an exercise at the end of this chapter.

Displaying product collections may require added programming in the product navigation page. If you wish to display each product in a collection, modification is unnecessary although you will want to display product titles as the concatenation of the collection title and individual product title. To display one listing per collection you will need to delete duplicate entries. To do this you use the following algorithm:

```
# myresult format:
# column 1 - collection ID
# column 2 - product ID
# column 10 - unused
/#
myresult=SORTCOL(myresult,1)
i=1 last_cid="*"
WHILE myresult[1,i] != "" DO
  IF myresult[1,i] != last_cid THEN
      last_cid=myresult[1,i]
  ELSE
      IF last_cid != "" THEN myresult[10,i]="DELETEME" /IF
  /IF
  i=i+1
/WHILE
myresult=GETCOLNOTEQ(myresult,10,"DELETEME")
```

This code takes myresult, a generic search result, and sorts it by the collection ID. Then, using a WHILE loop, it scans the search result, marking column 10 with the value DELETEME when a collection ID has changed, provided the collection ID is not empty. After the loop, the GETCOLNOTEQ tag deletes the marked entries. This code is general in nature. You can use it any time you need to delete duplicated entries from a list.

Displaying product collections may also require added programming when building record editors for the database. In your record editor, when you edit a duplicated field in a record, you will want to make sure you apply the same modification to the duplicated fields of all records in the same collection. Back-end systems, the pages used by office staff members to manage their site, are described further in Chapter 21, *Building Back-End Management Systems*. Record editors are described in Chapter 14, *Building Database Editors*.

Options and Add-Ons

Many e-commerce sites sell products and services with options and add-ons that need to be determined at the time the item is added to a shopping cart. When the user selects options or add-ons, the same item is added to the cart except that the item description is changed perhaps along with its price. The distinction between an option and an add-on for purposes of this book's discussion is covered in the accompanying "Options versus Add-On" note.

Options versus Add-On—In this book the word option *specifically refers to a product attribute that needs to be selected at purchase time but does not change the price of the selection, for example, the color of an iMac computer. An* add-on *is an item that the user may add to the same product, at purchase time. Each add-on adds a surcharge to the base price of the product, for example, an extended warranty for the iMac.*

You store the specification of available options and add-ons in fields in the record for the product. There are a number of ways to do this. In each case, you need to consider the following three development issues:

- How to format the data in the options or add-on field
- How to convert this field into HTML form components on the Web page
- How to add the user selection to the shopping cart

Formatting Your Data

The first issue relates to how the options or add-ons are stored in the `products` database. If your `products` database only needs to support a single kind of option, a field called `prod_options` that contains a comma-delimited list of option values is sufficient. In this case you format the content of the field as follows:

`option1,option2,option3`

If there's a chance an option might contain a comma (,) character, use a vertical bar as your delimiter. If your `products` database needs to support two kinds of options, add another options field. For example, a clothing database might have options for sizes and colors. Defining the fields `prod_sizeoptions` and `prod_coloroptions` could handle that situation.

In larger databases you might have an arbitrary number of options. For example, some products might be clothing. Other products might be electrical appliances that require that the user to select between American and European voltages (110 vs. 220 volts). Still other products may have other kinds of options. In this case you want more flexibility. You can do this by defining one field that lists your option types and another that lists the option values for each. The field name and format of the two fields would be as follows:

```
prod_opt_titles     title1,title2
prod_opt_values     opt1,opt2,opt3|opt1,opt2,opt3
```

For example, the fields of one record may have the values:

```
prod_opt_titles     Colors, Sizes
prod_opt_values     Red,White,Black|Small,Medium,Large,Xlarge
```

Another record in the same database may have fields with the following values:

```
prod_opt_titles     Voltage
prod_opt_values     110 (USA),220 (European)
```

The `prod_opt_values` field contains two option lists. It uses two separators. Here a comma separates one option from the next, and a vertical bar separates one set of options from the next.

When working with add-ons, you can define the two fields, `prod_addon_values` and `prod_addon_surcharge`. The format would be as follows:

```
prod_addon_values     1 Year Warranty, 4 Year Extended Warranty
prod_addon_surcharge  0,85.00
```

Both are comma-delimited lists. The first contains the titles of each add-on. The second contains the surcharges associated with each.

Converting to HTML Form Components

Once you know how your data is stored in your options or add-on fields, you are ready to take that data and convert it to HTML components on your product detail page. You can convert these fields to pull-down menus or radio button. Here you convert the data to pull-down menus.

Consider the case of a single options list formatted as a comma-delimited list. Such a page is shown in Figure 18.2.

You provide the options using a pull-down menu placed beside the Add To Cart button. The options are specified when a user adds the item to the shopping cart. To build this page, you can start with the page described in the "A Six-Line Product Detail Page" section of Chapter 16, *Designing E-Commerce Systems*." The code for that page, modified to display product options, is as follows:

```
<<temp=DBGETREC("products",rec)>>
```

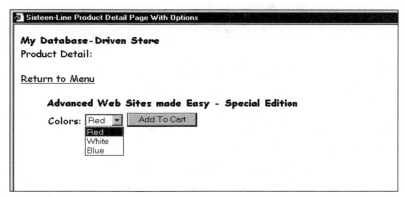

Figure 18.2: Product detail pages can be outfitted with product option menus, as shown here.

```
<html>
<title>Sixteen-Line Product Detail Page With Options</title>
<b>My Database-Driven Store</b><br>
Product Detail:<form method=post ACTION=addtocart>
<a href=menu.html>Return to Menu</a><ul>
<b><<prod_title>></b><br>
<table border=0>
<tr>
<td valign=top><<prod_desc>></td>
<td valign=top>
<<IF ISFILE("/images/"+prod_image) THEN
     DISPLAY "<img border=0 src=/images/"+prod_image+">"
/DISPLAY
  /IF
>>
</td>
</tr>
<tr><td colspan=2>
<<IF prod_coloroptions != '' THEN
    DISPLAY "Colors: <select name=addopt>" /DISPLAY
    myopts=LISTTOCOL(prod_coloroptions,",")
    DISPLAY
      LAYOUT(myopts, '<option value="',[1], '">',[1])
```

```
    /DISPLAY
    DISPLAY "</select>" /DISPLAY
 /IF>>
<input type=submit value="Add To Cart"></td></tr>
</form></ul>
</html>
<<overlay addtocart
   temp=DBGETREC("products",rec)
   IF addopt != "ERROR" AND addopt != "" THEN
      prod_title=prod_title+' ('+addopt+')'
   /IF
   APPEND ROW(rec,prod_title,1,prod_price) TO mycart /APPEND
   addopt=''
   GOTO "cart.html"
>>
```

Changes are shown in bold. First the code replaces the Add To Cart link with an Add To Cart button in an HTML form. An image is displayed only if it is found using an IF-THEN statement. Then the Overlay displays an Options pull-down menu (in the event options are found). The LISTTOCOL tag in the Overlay converts the list of options into myopts, a one-column variable. Then the top of an HTML select component, which sets the addopt variable, is displayed in the page. Using the LAYOUT tag, the option lines in the select statement (formatted as <option value=*option*>*option*) are displayed. This is followed by the close of the select statement. For information on this HTML form component, see the "Form Components" section of Chapter 10, *HTML Forms Processing*.

After the user submits the HTML form, addopt changes the product title of the item added to the cart. If the user specifies an option or add-on, the title of the item is modified to reflect the option selected.

If the data in the options fields is more complex, you need more coding to convert the data to pull-down elements. Consider the case of add-ons. The code to do that conversion is as follows:

```
IF prod_addon_values != '' THEN
   addon_titles=LISTTOCOL(prod_addon_values,",")
   addon_surcharges=LISTTOCOL(prod_addon_surcharges,",")
   DISPLAY "<select name=add_addon>" /DISPLAY
   DISPLAY '<option value="">select addon' /DISPLAY
   i=1
```

```
WHILE addon_titles[1,i] != "" DO
  DISPLAY
    '<option
value="'+addon_titles[1,i]+'">'+addon_titles[1,i]+
       ' (Add $'+FORMAT(addon_surcharges[1,I],"money",2) +
')'
  /DISPLAY
  i=i+1
/WHILE
DISPLAY "</select>" /DISPLAY
/IF
```

Here both fields are converted to one-column variables using LISTTOCOL tags. Here too a pull-down menu is displayed. This code uses a WHILE loop. Note that each pull-down element is displayed with its corresponding surcharge. Using this code, a product detail page with support for product add-ons follows this paragraph. The addtocart on-click Overlay needed to process this is similar to the one used in the sixteen-line, product detail page with options page described earlier in this section. Here however, you must extract surcharges and apply them to the cart. The code for the on-click Overlays is as follows:

```
<<overlay addtocart
   temp=DBGETREC("products",rec)
   IF add_addon != "ERROR" AND add_addon != "" THEN
      col1=LISTTOCOL(prod_addon_values,","),
      col2=LISTTOCOL(prod_addon_surcharges,","),
      temp=MERGE(col1,col2)
      temp=GETCOLEQ(temp,1,add_addon)
      IF ISNUMBER(temp[2]) THEN
         prod_title=prod_title+' ('+temp[1]+')'
         prod_price=prod_price+temp[2]
      /IF
   /IF
   APPEND ROW(rec,prod_title,1,prod_price) TO mycart /APPEND
   add_addon=''
   GOTO "cart.html"
>>
```

In this on-click Overlay the add_addon variable contains the title of the add-on selected. Here LISTTOCOL tags convert the values in the add-on fields into two one-column variables that are then pasted together using the MERGE tag. The MERGE tag is similar to the APPEND tag, except it appends horizontally rather than vertically. After the two columns are merged, the add_addon variable in the GETCOLEQ tag extracts the row from the merged table with the selected add-on. The title and surcharge are extracted and used to adjust the values of prod_title and prod_price, which are added to the mycart variable in the subsequent APPEND tag.

Summary

In this chapter you learned how to build advanced product detail pages. Like the navigation pages described in the previous chapter, here too you can customize the pages to fit the individual needs of the site. Perhaps the most important technique you learned is how to work with options and add-ons. Although a tricky area, the ability to handle options and add-ons is a must-learn for the advanced Web developer

It should be noted that this chapter introduced a few ways to process options and add-ons. You may need to change the way you add the options or add-ons to your shopping cart. For example, instead of altering the content of the product title and price, you may want to add the data to new columns in mycart, used specifically for storing options or add-ons. This gives you more flexibility in the way mycart is displayed on the shopping cart page.

The shopping cart is the topic of Chapter 19, *Building Shopping Cart Pages*, coming up next. There you learn how to build different kinds of shopping carts.

Exercises

In the following exercises, you build other kinds of detail pages using what you learned in this chapter. Answers to these exercises are provided on this book's companion Web site as described in the book's Preface.

Exercise 1

Build a product detail page for a hypothetical Web site for selling books. The detail page should list the title of the book and the author along with other titles by the same author. Make each title a link.

Exercise 2

In Exercise 1 you built a small on-line bookstore. Using the outline provided in the "Product Collections" section of this chapter, build a database to support book collections. When a book's detail page is displayed, present information on the book and an Add To Cart link for each book in the collection. Using what you learned in Chapter 17, *Building Product Navigation Pages,* build a product list page that links to this detail page. Modify the page so only one book is displayed per collection.

Exercise 3

The "Options and Add-ons" section of this chapter describes how to set up the fields for product databases with unlimited types of options. Build a product page that takes the values in the two fields used to store these options and convert them to one or more pull-down menus, preceding each with the title for that option. Make sure the `addtocart` on-click Overlay works as well. Hint: Break up the options into multiple options lists and use a FOR loop to loop across all of the option lists, each time generating a pull-down menu.

CHAPTER 19

Building Shopping Cart Pages

Fundamentally, a shopping cart is a temporary holding area for products being purchased. It's also the place where users make adjustments to an order and you calculate the costs and display them on the page for the user. The page described in the "Twenty-Line Shopping Cart" section of Chapter 16, *Designing E-Commerce Systems*, does all those things.

However, as a site gets more advanced, the purpose of the shopping cart expands. It becomes a place to post promotional messages that inform the user of sales, and special opportunities. The cart is not simply a temporary area that disappears when the user leaves the site, but a personal area the user can return to in the future. Figure 19.1 shows a shopping cart page for **Courtesy CareFree Garden** (http://www.carefreegardens.com/) with highlighted product capsules. In this chapter you explore how to extend the capabilities of shopping carts to include these capabilities.

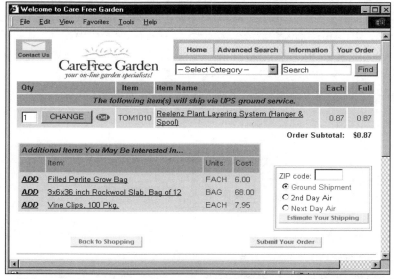

Figure 19.1: This garden supply store displays promotional products on its shopping cart page.

Promotional Messages

Promotional messages are a type of on-page marketing. By reminding the user of certain specials or related products, the Web site may increase sales. As an example, when buying a toy, it is easy to forget the need to buy batteries. Reminding the user to buy batteries is helpful to the buyer and the Web site. Note that you can display these reminders on the product page, as explained in the "Related Items" section of Chapter 18, *Building Product Detail Pages*. But you can also display them on the shopping cart page.

Another type of sales reminder might prompt the user to take advantage of a special offer. For example, when users buy one item, you might want to inform them that if they buy another they get it at fifty percent off. Or, for example, when users place items totaling more than $100 in their cart, they get free shipping. Most on-page promotions fall into the following three categories:

Product specific promotions—A Click Here To Buy Batteries button is an example of a product-specific promotion.

Category-triggered promotions—A banner that advertises printer paper whenever the cart contains a printer, is an example of a category-triggered promotion (the category being *printers*).

Cart-triggered promotions—Get Free Shipping on Orders Over $100 is an example of a cart-triggered promotion.

Twenty-Four Line Cart with Shipping Promotion

To add a free shipping promotion, you need to do two things: First you need to modify your shipping calculation to reflect the promotion. Second you need to alert the user of the promotion. Starting with the code provided in the "Twenty-Line Shopping Cart Page" section of Chapter 16, *Designing E-Commerce Systems*," you get the following:

```
<< # Structure of mycart:
   #   column 1 - record ID
   #   column 2 - product name
   #   column 3 - quantity
   #   column 4 - unit price
   /#
   mycart=GETCOLNOTEQ(mycart,1,"ERROR")
   mycart=GETCOLNOTEQ(mycart,1,"")
   IF mycart[1,1]="" THEN GOTO "nocart.html" /IF
   IF ISNUMBER(tax)="FALSE" THEN tax=0 /IF
   shipping=MAX(15,(3+3*rows(mycart)))
```

```
>>
<html>
<title>Twenty Four-Line Cart With Shipping Promotion</title>
<b>My Database-Driven Store</b><br>
Shopping Cart:<br>
<a href=menu.html>Return to Menu</a><ul>
<form method=post ACTION=changecart>
<table border=1><tr>
<td>Product</td><td>Unit
Cost</td><td>Quantity</td><td>Subtotal</td>
</tr>
<tr><td colspan=4 align=center>
<b>Free Shipping On All Orders Over $100</b></td>
</tr>
<< i=1 subtotal=0
   FOR NAME=mycart ROWNAME=x DO
     DISPLAY
       "<tr><td><a href=detail.html name=rec VALUE="+x[1]+">"+
       x[2]+"</a> (<a href=dcart NAME=drec
VALUE="+x[1]+">Delete</a>)"+
       "</td><td>"+x[4]+"</td>"+
       "<td><input type=text name=mycart[3,"+i+"]
size=4></td>"+
       "<td
align=right>"+FORMAT((x[3]*x[4]),"comma")+"</td></tr>"+LF
     /DISPLAY
     subtotal=subtotal+(x[3]*x[4])
     i=i+1
   /FOR
   IF subtotal > 100 THEN
    shipping=0
   /IF
>>
<tr><td colspan=3>Subtotal</td>
<td align=right><<FORMAT(subtotal,"comma")>></td></tr>
<tr><td colspan=3>State Sales Tax:
<a href=<<page>> NAME=tax value="0.0625">Yes</a>
<a href=<<page>> NAME=tax value="0.0000">No</a>
```

```
</td><td align=right><<FORMAT(tax*subtotal,"comma")>></td></tr>
<tr><td colspan=3 name=shipping>Delivery:
</td><td align=right><<FORMAT(shipping,"comma")>></td></tr>
<tr><td colspan=3>TOTAL</td>
<td
align=right><<FORMAT(subtotal+tax*subtotal+shipping,"comma")>></
td></tr>
<tr><td colspan=4 align=right>
<input type=submit name=mybutton value="Recalculate">
<input type=submit name=mybutton value="Checkout">
</td></tr>
</table>
</form>
</html>
<<overlay changecart
   i=1 subtotal=0
   WHILE mycart[1,i] != "" DO
     IF ISINTEGER(mycart[3,i])!= "TRUE" OR
        mycart[3,i] =0 OR mycart[3,i] < 0 THEN
        mycart[1,i]=""
     ELSE
        subtotal=subtotal+mycart[3,i]*mycart[4,i]
     /IF
     i=i+1
   /WHILE
   mycart=GETCOLNOTEQ(mycart,1,"")
   shipping=MAX(15,(3+3*rows(mycart)))
   IF subtotal > 100 THEN shipping=0 /IF
   IF mybutton="Checkout" THEN
      GOTO "checkout.html"
   ELSE
      GOTO PAGE
   /IF
>>
<<overlay dcart
   mycart=GETCOLNOTEQ(mycart,1,drec)
   GOTO PAGE
>>
```

Changes are shown in bold. The first change modifies the shipping variable after the total in the cart is known. A simple IF-THEN statement accomplishes this. Then an HTML table row alerts the user of the shipping promotion. Then, in the changecart on-click Overlay, an IF-THEN statement, like earlier on the Web page, modifies the shipping calculation. This is an example of a cart-specific promotion.

Thirty-Five Line Cart with Product Promotion

Product-specific promotions require that you first add a field to the product database to indicate the promotion being applied to the item. Typically it's a good idea to give promotions their own codes so you can develop multiple product promotions. For example, suppose the product promotion is called "A." You can add code to the shopping cart page that provides information on the promotion when such a product is detected and you change your calculations accordingly. For example, if your offer is a buy one and get the next 50 percent off promotion, you write the shopping cart instructions as follows:

```
<< # Structure of mycart:
    #   column 1 - record ID
    #   column 2 - product name
    #   column 3 - quantity
    #   column 4 - unit price
    #   column 5 - promotion code
    /#
    mycart=GETCOLNOTEQ(mycart,1,"ERROR")
    mycart=GETCOLNOTEQ(mycart,1,"")
    IF mycart[1,1]="" THEN GOTO "nocart.html" /IF
    IF ISNUMBER(tax)="FALSE" THEN tax=0 /IF
    shipping=MAX(15,(3+3*rows(mycart)))
    promos=GETCOLNOTEQ(mycart,5,"")
    promo_message=""
    IF promos[1,1]!= "" THEN
        FOR NAME=promos ROWNAME=promo DO
            IF promo[5]="A" THEN
                promo_message=promo_message+
                    "Buy One <u>"+promo[2]+"</u> and get the next half
off!<br>"
            /IF
```

```
      /FOR
    /IF
>>
<html>
<title>Thirty Five-Line Cart With Shipping Promotion</title>
<b>My Database-Driven Store</b><br>
Shopping Cart:<br>
<a href=menu.html>Return to Menu</a><ul>
<form method=post ACTION=changecart>
<table border=1><tr>
<td>Product</td><td>Unit
Cost</td><td>Quantity</td><td>Subtotal</td>
</tr>
<< IF promo_message != "ERROR" THEN
     DISPLAY "<tr><td colspan=4 align=center><b>"+
       promo_message+"</b></td></tr>" /DISPLAY
    /IF
>>
<< i=1 subtotal=0
    FOR NAME=mycart ROWNAME=x DO
      DISPLAY
        "<tr><td><a href=detail.html name=rec VALUE="+x[1]+">"+
        x[2]+"</a> (<a href=dcart NAME=drec
VALUE="+x[1]+">Delete</a>)"+
        "</td><td>"+x[4]+"</td>"+
        "<td><input type=text name=mycart[3,"+i+"]
size=4></td>"+
        "<td align=right>"
      /DISPLAY
      IF x[3]<2 THEN
        DISPLAY FORMAT((x[3]*x[4]),"comma")+"</td></tr>"+LF /DISPLAY
        +=0
      ELSE
        t=ROUNDDOWN(x[3]/2)*x[4]*0.50
        DISPLAY
          FORMAT(((x[3]-t)*x[4]),"comma")+"</td></tr>"+LF
        /DISPLAY
      /IF
```

```
        subtotal=subtotal+((x[3]-t)*x[4])
        i=i+1
     /FOR
>>
<tr><td colspan=3>Subtotal</td>
<td align=right><<FORMAT(subtotal,"comma")>></td></tr>
<tr><td colspan=3>State Sales Tax:
<a href=<<page>> NAME=tax value="0.0625">Yes</a>
<a href=<<page>> NAME=tax value="0.0000">No</a>
</td><td align=right><<FORMAT(tax*subtotal,"comma")>></td></tr>
<tr><td colspan=3 name=shipping>Delivery:
</td><td align=right><<FORMAT(shipping,"comma")>></td></tr>
<tr><td colspan=3>TOTAL</td>
<td
align=right><<FORMAT(subtotal+tax*subtotal+shipping,"comma")>><//
td></tr>
<tr><td colspan=4 align=right>
<input type=submit name=mybutton value="Recalculate">
<input type=submit name=mybutton value="Checkout">
</td></tr>
</table>
</form>
</html>
<<overlay changecart
   i=1 subtotal=0
   WHILE mycart[1,i] != "" DO
     IF ISINTEGER(mycart[3,i])!= "TRUE" OR
        mycart[3,i] =0 OR mycart[3,i] < 0 THEN
        mycart[1,i]=""
     ELSE
        IF mycart[4,i] = "" THEN
          subtotal=subtotal+mycart[3,i]*mycart[4,i]
        ELSE
           t=ROUNDDOWN(x[3]/2)*x[4]*0.50
           subtotal=subtotal+((x[3]-t)*x[4])
        /IF
     /IF
```

```
   i=i+1
 /WHILE
 mycart=GETCOLNOTEQ(mycart,1,"")
 shipping=MAX(15,(3+3*rows(mycart)))
 IF mybutton="Checkout" THEN
     GOTO "checkout.html"
 ELSE
     GOTO PAGE
 /IF
>>
<<overlay dcart
 mycart=GETCOLNOTEQ(mycart,1,drec)
 GOTO PAGE
>>
```

Changes are shown in bold. The Underlay uses GETCOLNOTEQ to extract those lines in the cart with a promotion. If a promotional item is found, a promotion message is composed. Note the IF-THEN statement placed inside the FOR loop. It sets a message for promotion type A. If you have other promotion codes, add more IF-THEN statements in the FOR loop to handle them.

Later in the document the promo_message variable is displayed. Then, in the changecart on-click Overlay, the subtotal calculation is modified to take into account the type A promotion. You can add more promotion types along side this IF-THEN statement to perform the necessary calculations.

Saving Shopping Carts Using Cookies

Saving a shopping cart so it is not lost when the user leaves your sites (abandons the cart), can be accomplished by using the Cookie Tracking feature built into HTML/OS. Cookie Tracking is explained in the "Cookie Tracking" note.

Cookie Tracking—*Cookie Tracking is a setting you can turn on in the HTML/OS Control Panel. When you turn it on, if HTML/OS is able to read a cookie successfully, it sets* ISCOOKIE *to* TRUE. *HTML/OS also gives the user a unique ID, which it saves in the* HTMLOS.COOKIEID *variable. Once* HTMLOS.COOKIEID *is saved in a cookie, HTML/OS does not change it, so it can reliably identify a specific computer returning to the site. To use this feature, access the Control Panel from the HTML/OS desktop. Click* **System**. *Click* **Cookies**. *Then select* **On** *and click the* **Save Settings** *button. Now Cookie Tracking is on.*

Cookie tracking requires that a user's cart, previously saved in a file, be loaded when the user first enters the site. Then, as the cart is changed, this file is updated, ensuring that users who abandon their carts can return later. The code for the entrance page of the site is as follows:

```
IF mycart="ERROR" THEN
    IF ISCOOKIE="TRUE" THEN
      IF ISFILE("/cookies/"+HTMLOS.COOKIEID+".txt") THEN
        COPY FILE="/cookies/"+HTMLOS.COOKIEID+".txt" TS="," TO
mycart /COPY
    ELSE
      mycart=""
    /IF
/IF
```

This code initializes the cart using the cookie file containing the cart. Note that we arbitrarily named the cookie file with the name of the `HTMLOS.COOKIEID` variable followed with a `.txt` extension and we placed it in the `/cookies` directory. In the cart itself, or whenever the `mycart` variable is modified, you need the following code to update this file:

```
IF ISCOOKIE="TRUE" THEN
  COPY mycart TO FILE="/cookies/"+HTMLOS.COOKIEID+".txt" TS=","
/COPY
/IF
```

This ensures that users can leave the site at any time and return to find their carts intact. The algorithm outlined here works fine except for two problems. First, what happens when you have so many people visiting your site that the `/cookies` directory fills up with tens of thousands of files? This is dangerous since directories with so many files can slow down a site. Second, what if the returning users have products in their carts that are no longer available, or products with out-of-date prices?

To solve the first potential problem it is important to understand that most hardware operating systems slow down when a directory has too many files in it, because responses to file requests slow down. Most operating systems organize files internally as series of lists. The more files, the longer the lists are that have to be scanned when a file needs to be located on the hardware. One solution is to limit the number of files you have in a directory by spreading them across many directories. If you have too many directories, limit the number of directories by nesting them within one another. Now, when the hardware operating system looks for a file, it needs to scan a few short lists rather than one very long list spread all across the hard disk.

To code a solution, you will need to set up different directories for your cookies so that no single directory has too many files. This is left as an exercise at the end of this chapter.

To ensure that items in the cart are still valid, the previous code placed at the entrance of the site needs to contain additional code that checks each item in the cart. If an item is no longer in the `products` database, it is omitted from the cart. If it is found, settings such as price are updated. The code for this is as follows:

```
IF mycart="ERROR" THEN
   IF ISCOOKIE="TRUE" THEN
     IF ISFILE("/cookies/"+HTMLOS.COOKIEID+".txt") THEN
       COPY FILE="/cookies/"+HTMLOS.COOKIEID+".txt" TS="," TO
mycart /COPY
       i=1
       FOR NAME=mycart ROWNAME=x DO
         sstr='prod_name="' + x[2] + '"'
         r=DBFIND("products",sstr,1,1,"record,prod_price")
         IF r[1,1]!="" THEN
           mycart[1,i]=r[1]
           mycart[4,i]=r[2]
         ELSE
           mycart[1,i]=""
         /IF
         i=i+1
       /FOR
       mycart=GETCOLNOTEQ(mycart,1, "")
   ELSE
     mycart=""
   /IF
/IF
```

Changes are shown in bold. The DBFIND tag searches the `products` database. If an item is found, it updates the first and fourth column entries. If not, it places an empty string in the first column entry of the cart. Those rows marked with an empty string are later deleted using a GETCOLNOTEQ tag immediately following the end of the FOR loop.

Building Advanced Shipping Options

Most shopping systems give the user the ability to select from a list of shipping options. The options are presented to the user on the shopping cart page or on a checkout page. By placing the shipping information on the shopping cart page, you give the user the ability to determine a true cost for the items in the cart. By placing the option on a checkout page, you deny the user a true cost but you simplify the cart for the user and merge the function with related tasks, such as capturing a shipping address. In some cases the shipping cost will depend on the destination requiring you place it on a checkout page. Here you look at placing shipping options on the shopping cart page. Specifically, you look at giving a user the ability to select ground, overnight, or express shipping.

Adding shipping options is similar to adding a tax calculation to a shopping cart page except that you use a pull-down menu to offer the selections (rather than some hypertext links) and that you must change the shipping charge accordingly. Starting with the twenty-line shopping cart of Chapter 16, *Designing E-Commerce Systems*, you get the following page:

```
<< # Structure of mycart:
   #   column 1 - record ID
   #   column 2 - product name
   #   column 3 - quantity
   #   column 4 - unit price
   /#
   mycart=GETCOLNOTEQ(mycart,1,"ERROR")
   mycart=GETCOLNOTEQ(mycart,1,"")
   IF mycart[1,1]="" THEN GOTO "nocart.html" /IF
   IF ISNUMBER(tax)="FALSE" THEN tax=0 /IF
   IF shipcode="ERROR" THEN shipcode="A" /IF
   IF shipcode="A" THEN
      shipping=MAX(15,(3+3*rows(mycart)))
   ELIF shipcode="B" THEN
      shipping=MAX(25,(8+4*rows(mycart)))
   ELSE
      shipping=MAX(49,(15+5*rows(mycart)))
   /IF
>>
<html>
<title>Thirty-Line Cart With Shipping Options</title>
```

```
<b>My Database-Driven Store</b><br>
Shopping Cart:<br>
<a href=menu.html>Return to Menu</a><ul>
<form method=post ACTION=changecart>
<table border=1><tr>
<td>Product</td><td>Unit
Cost</td><td>Quantity</td><td>Subtotal</td>
</tr>
<< i=1 subtotal=0
    FOR NAME=mycart ROWNAME=x DO
      DISPLAY
        "<tr><td><a href=detail.html name=rec VALUE="+x[1]+">"+
        x[2]+"</a> (<a href=dcart NAME=drec
VALUE="+x[1]+">Delete</a>)"+
        "</td><td>"+x[4]+"</td>"+
        "<td><input type=text name=mycart[3,"+i+"]
size=4></td>"+
        "<td
align=right>"+FORMAT((x[3]*x[4]),"comma")+"</td></tr>"+LF
      /DISPLAY
      subtotal=subtotal+(x[3]*x[4])
      i=i+1
    /FOR
>>
<tr><td colspan=3>Subtotal</td>
<td align=right><<FORMAT(subtotal,"comma")>></td></tr>
<tr><td colspan=3>State Sales Tax:
<a href=<<page>> NAME=tax value="0.0625">Yes</a>
<a href=<<page>> NAME=tax value="0.0000">No</a>
</td><td align=right><<FORMAT(tax*subtotal,"comma")>></td></tr>
<tr><td colspan=3>
Shipping: <select name=shipcode>
<option value="A">Ground
<option value="B">Two-Day
<option value="C">Overnight
</select>
</td><td align=right><<FORMAT(shipping,"comma")>></td></tr>
```

```
<tr><td colspan=3>TOTAL</td>
<td
align=right><<FORMAT(subtotal+tax*subtotal+shipping,"comma")>></
td></tr>
<tr><td colspan=4 align=right>
<input type=submit name=mybutton value="Recalculate">
<input type=submit name=mybutton value="Checkout">
</td></tr>
</table>
</form>
</html>
<<overlay changecart
   i=1 subtotal=0
   WHILE mycart[1,i] != "" DO
     IF ISINTEGER(mycart[3,i]) != "TRUE" OR
        mycart[3,i] =0 OR mycart[3,i] < 0 THEN
        mycart[1,i]=""
     ELSE
        subtotal=subtotal+mycart[3,i]*mycart[4,i]
     /IF
     i=i+1
   /WHILE
   mycart=GETCOLNOTEQ(mycart,1,"")
   IF shipcode="A" THEN
       shipping=MAX(15,(3+3*rows(mycart)))
    ELIF shipcode="B" THEN
       shipping=MAX(25,(8+4*rows(mycart)))
    ELSE
       shipping=MAX(49,(15+5*rows(mycart)))
    /IF
   IF mybutton="Checkout" THEN
      GOTO "checkout.html"
   ELSE
      GOTO PAGE
   /IF
 >>
 <<overlay dcart
```

```
mycart=GETCOLNOTEQ(mycart,1,drec)
GOTO PAGE
>>
```

Changes are shown in bold. To handle the different shipping options, you use a `shipcode` variable, which can contain the values A, B, or C, corresponding to ground, express, or overnight delivery respectively. The `shipcode` variable is first initialized to the value A. Then, depending on the value, different shipping formulas are used.

Inside the page, a pull-down menu gives the user the ability to select a shipping option. When the user clicks Recalculate the HTML form is resubmitted, thereby setting a new value for `shipcode`. The `changecart` on-click Overlay also includes code, shown in bold, to recalculate the shipping charge when the user clicks the Checkout button.

Summary

In this chapter you learned how to extend the capabilities of shopping carts. Next, in Chapter 20, *Building Checkout Pages*, you learn how to combine the information stored in the cart with that information used to complete the ordering process. The next chapter, along with this one, gives you the ability to build a wide variety of ordering systems—an important component of e-commerce applications.

Exercises

In the following exercises you build pages that compliment those described in this chapter. Answers to these exercises are provided on this book's companion Web site as described in the book's Preface.

Exercise 1

In the "Saving Shipping Carts Using Cookies" section of this chapter, you learned that placing thousands of files in a single directory is not advisable. Build a function that takes any filename and places it in one of two hundred directories. Hint: To do this, add up the ASCII values of the characters in the filename (use the GETASCII and MIDDLE tags) and find modulus 200 of the sum, in other words, the integer portion of the sum divided by 200. (Use the MOD tag.) Use this to determine the directory name in which to place the file.

Exercise 2

The "Building Advanced Shipping Options" section of this chapter used calculations hard-coded into the Web page. Modify the page so shipping options are read from a delimited text file. Place in the columns a shipping code, a shipping title, and the parameters X, Y, and Z used in the formula `shipping=MAX(Z,X + Y*rows(mycart))`. Modify the Web page so modifications to the shipping file change the shipping options and shipping calculations presented to users.

Exercise 3

Starting with the code provided in the "Fifteen-Line Spreadsheet Editor" section of Chapter 10, *HTML Forms Processing*, build an editor for the shipping parameters of Exercise 2. Now you have a back-end page that gives staff members the ability to edit shipping options and shipping calculations.

## CHAPTER 20

Building Checkout Pages

Order checkout is the part of an e-commerce site associated with the completion of a customer transaction. At the least, checkout pages include the features discussed in the "A Nine-Line Checkout Page" section of Chapter 16, *Designing E-Commerce Systems*. But as the sophistication of the e-commerce site grows, so too does the feature list of this type of page.

Sophisticated e-commerce sites spread the checkout pages across multiple pages, which increases the number of pages a user must navigate and goes against the Web design rule: *Don't have the user navigate unnecessary pages*. However, in this particular case, the design rule is superceded with a more important design rule: *Don't make the user think about more than one transaction at a time*. Since advanced e-commerce sites provide users more options, requiring users to make more decisions and supply more information, it is best to split the order checkout process into distinct pages, each encompassing a smaller transaction.

In this chapter the checkout process is spread across a shipping page, a payment page, a review page, and an order confirmation page. You look at the code needed for each page and the sophisticated features you may add to them.

A Six-Line Shipping Page

The shipping page is where you collect the shipping address information. In this chapter you look at a checkout process split across multiple pages. As a result, users need page navigation options, which we accomplish here with Previous and Continue buttons. You place these buttons in the HTML form so changes made to that form are captured, even if the user clicks a button. The Continue button directs the user to the `review.html` page, if they have been to that page. Otherwise the Continue button directs the user to the next page. A six-line shipping page follows:

```
<html>
<title>Six-Line Shipping Page</title>
<b>My Database-Driven Store</b><br>
<b>Checkout</b><br>
```

```
Shipping Information (Page 1 of 3):<br>
<form method=post ACTION=postpage>
Enter shipping address below.<br>
<table bgcolor=#CECECE border=0 cellspacing=0>
<tr><td align=right>Street</td>
<td><input type=text name=ck_street1></td></tr>
<tr><td align=right> </td>
<td><input type=text name=ck_street2></td></tr>
<tr><td align=right>City, State, Zip</td>
<td><input type=text name=ck_city size=20>
    <input type=text name=ck_state size=4>
    <input type=text name=ck_zip size=10></td></tr>
<tr><td align=right>Country</td>
<td><input type=text name=ck_country></td></tr>
<tr bgcolor=#FFFFFF><td colspan=2 align=center>
<input type=submit name=mybutton value="Previous">
<input type=submit name=mybutton value="Continue">
</td></tr></table></form>
</html>
<<overlay postpage
  IF mybutton="Previous" THEN GOTO "cart.html"
    ELSE
      IF review_flag="TRUE" THEN GOTO "review.html"
        ELSE GOTO "purchase.html"
      /IF
  /IF
>>
```

This page contains an HTML form to capture shipping information and Previous and Continue buttons. When a user clicks a Previous button the `postpage` on-click Overlay runs and directs the user to `cart.html`. A user who clicks the Continue button is directed to `review.html` if the `review_flag` variable is TRUE (which is set to TRUE on the `review.html` page). Otherwise the user is directed to `purchase.html`, the next checkout page.

On an advanced e-commerce site you also want to add data validation. To do that use the techniques described in the "Commonly Used Validation Schemes" section of Chapter 10, *HTML Forms Processing*. If you want the user to select a shipping method, use the technique discussed in the "Building Advanced Shipping Options" section of Chapter 19, *Building Shopping Cart Pages*.

This shipping page is where you place other kinds of information or features pertaining to shipping. As an example, you may want to add to this page an option that allows the user to determine whether to split orders if one of the items is backordered. Or you may want to give the user the ability to save the shipping address for future use or load a shipping address from previously saved addresses.

A Twelve-Line Payment Page

The payment page is where you capture contact information and payment information. The page is similar to the shipping page in the preceding section except you seek to capture payment information rather than shipping information. You also want to place a billing address on the page in case the address is different from the shipping address. The page is as follows:

```
<html>
<title>Twelve-Line Payment Page</title>
<b>My Database-Driven Store</b><br>
<b> Checkout</b><br>
Payment Information (Page 2 of 3):<br>
<form method=post ACTION=postpage>
Full Name:<br>
<input type=text name=ck_bname><br>
E-Mail Address:<br>
<input type=text name=ck_bemail><br>
Enter Billing Address or click <a href=sameas>same as
shipping</a>.<br>
<table bgcolor=#CECECE border=0 cellspacing=0>
<tr><td align=right>Street</td>
<td><input type=text name=ck_bstreet1></td></tr>
<tr><td align=right> </td>
<td><input type=text name=ck_bstreet2></td></tr>
<tr><td align=right>City, State, Zip</td>
<td><input type=text name=ck_bcity size=20>
    <input type=text name=ck_bstate size=4>
    <input type=text name=ck_bzip size=10></td></tr>
<tr><td align=right>Country</td>
<td><input type=text name=ck_bcountry></td></tr>
<tr><td colspan=2>Payment Information:</td></tr>
```

```
<tr><td align=right>Credit Card</td>
<td><input type=text name=ckb_card size=15>(MM/YYYY)</td></tr>
<tr><td align=right>Exp Date</td>
<td><input type=text name=ckb_expdate
size=15>(MM/YYYY)</td></tr>
</table>
<input type=submit name=mybutton value="Previous">
<input type=submit name=mybutton value="Continue">
</form>
</html>
<<overlay postpage
   IF mybutton="Previous" THEN GOTO "cart.html"
     ELSE
       IF review_flag="TRUE" THEN GOTO "review.html"
         ELSE GOTO "purchase.html"
       /IF
   /IF
>>
<<overlay sameas
ck_bstreet1=ck_street1
ck_bstreet2=ck_street2
ck_bcity=ck_city
ck_bstate=ck_state
ck_bzip=ck_zip
ck_bcountry=ck_country
GOTO PAGE
>>
```

The page requests contact information and a billing address and provides a Same As Shipping link so the user can load the shipping address. When the user clicks that link, the sameas on-click Overlay, from which the variables are loaded from the prior page, runs. Below this you capture the billing address credit card information and provide Previous and Continue buttons. Users who click the Previous button are directed to shipping.html, the previous page. When users click the Continue button they are directed to review.html, the next checkout page.

As on the shipping page, you will want to add data validation to this page. Here too, like the shipping page, you may want to give the user the ability to save multiple addresses for future use. This is left as an exercise at the end of this chapter.

A Twelve-Line Final Review Page

Once the order information has been captured you want to give the user the ability to review and make any necessary changes needed to the ordering information before completing the order. To do this, provide a page that summarizes the content of the cart, the shipping information, and the payment information. Next to each type of information provide links to the corresponding pages where the information can be edited. A sample page is shown in Figure 20.1.

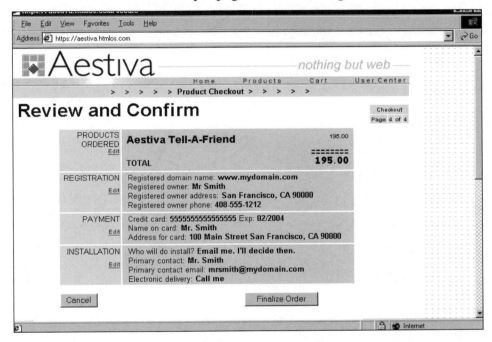

Figure 20.1: The checkout pages of this software company include this review page so a user can edit the order before finalizing it.

Assuming the same variables as the cart described in the "Twenty-Line Shopping Cart Page" section of Chapter 16, *Designing E-Commerce Systems*, the code for the page shown in Figure 20.1 is as follows:

```
<<review_flag="TRUE">>
<html>
<title>Twelve-Line Final Review Page</title>
<b>My Database-Driven Store</b><br>
<b> Checkout</b><br>
```

```
Final Review (Page 3 of 3):<br>
Review information below. Click Complete Order when
done.<br><br>
<a href=cart.html>Products</a>:<ul>
<table border=0><tr>
<td>Product</td><td>Unit
Cost</td><td>Quantity</td><td>Subtotal</td>
</tr>
<< FOR NAME=mycart ROWNAME=x DO
      DISPLAY

"<tr><td>"+x[2]+"</td><td>"+x[4]+"</td><td>"+x[3]+"</td>"+
        "<td
align=right>"+FORMAT((x[3]*x[4]),"comma")+"</td></tr>"+LF
      /DISPLAY
    /FOR
>>
<tr><td colspan=3>Subtotal</td>
<td align=right><<FORMAT(subtotal,"comma")>></td></tr>
<tr><td colspan=3>State Sales Tax:
</td><td align=right><<FORMAT(tax*subtotal,"comma")>></td></tr>
<tr><td colspan=3 name=shipping>Delivery:
</td><td align=right><<FORMAT(shipping,"comma")>></td></tr>
<tr><td colspan=3>TOTAL</td>
<td align=right>
<<FORMAT(subtotal+tax*subtotal+shipping,"comma")>></td></tr>
</table>
</ul>
<a href=shipping.html>Shipping Information</a>:<ul>
<table border=0 cellspacing=0>
<tr><td align=right>Street</td><td><<ck_street1>></td></tr>
<tr><td align=right> </td><td><<ck_street2>></td></tr>
<tr><td align=right>City, State, Zip</td><td><<ck_city>>,
<<ck_state>> <<ck_zip>></td></tr>
<tr><td align=right>Country</td><td><<ck_country>></td></tr>
</table>
</ul>
```

```
<a href=payment.html>Payment Information</a>:<ul>
Full Name: <<ck_bname>><br>
E-Mail Address: <<ck_bemail>><br>
<table border=0 cellspacing=0>
<tr><td>ADDRESS</td></tr>
<tr><td align=right>Street</td><td><<ck_bstreet1>></td></tr>
<tr><td align=right> </td><td><<ck_bstreet2>></td></tr>
<tr><td align=right>City, State, Zip</td><td><<ck_bcity>>,
<<ck_bstate>> <<ck_bzip>></td></tr>
<tr><td align=right>Country</td><td><<ck_bcountry>></td></tr>
<tr><td>Credit Card</td>
<td><<ckb_card size=15>> Exp: <<ckb_expdate>></td></tr>
</table>
</ul>
<form method=post ACTION=order.html>
<input type=submit value="Complete Order">
</form>
</html>
```

The first instruction sets `review_flag` to TRUE so users editing the ordering information with `shipping.html` or `payment.html` return to `review.html` when they click the Continue button on those pages. Then cart information is displayed along with a link to `cart.html`. After that shipping and payment information is displayed, with links to `shipping.html` and `payment.html` respectively. After that a Complete Order button links to `order.html`, the page that processes the order.

Order Processing

Final order processing takes place after the user clicks the Complete Order button in the code presented in the preceding section. This is the point where you can assume the order is final. During order processing, you need to perform a number of tasks, after which you provide the user a *Thank-you* notice and perhaps a receipt. These tasks need to be done quickly, since they are done between the instant the user clicks Complete Order and receives the *Thank-you* page. The tasks can involve any of the following, in the order shown here:

1. Check product inventory to ensure items in the cart are in stock.
2. Post order to a real-time transaction processor (such as **Authorize.net**).

3. Post order to backup log.
4. Add records to order history and transaction databases.
5. Add or edit customer database record.
6. Compose and send e-mail confirmation to order desk.
7. Compose and send e-mail confirmation to user.

To check product inventory, the first task listed, use a FOR loop to scan the items in the cart. If inventory on an item is insufficient, abort order processing, compose a message for the user, adjust the order to reflect what is available for ordering, and then direct the user to a page for posting the adjusted order.

Orders can be posted to a real-time credit card processor bureau, such as **Authorize.net** (http://www.authorize.net/), if you have contracted for such a service. This is a Web-based version of a credit card swiping machine you see in restaurants. Using instructions provided to you by the real-time credit card processing bureau, you send credit card and price information over the Web. The bureau processes these requests in real time, returning a result to you in a fraction of a second. The result you receive tells you whether the transaction succeeded. You use this result to continue your order processing or abort the transaction.

In general, credit card processing services bureaus provide two ways to interact with them. Either they tell you how to organize your information and post it to them over the Web (using the NETWEB tag, for example) or they provide you software to run at your site. The NETWEB tag is described in the Official HTML/OS Print Manual. Code examples for hooking up to real-time processing bureaus, such as **Authorize.net**, can be found in the knowledge base on the **Aestiva** Web site at http://www.aestiva.com/support/.

It should be noted that many e-commerce sites do not need real-time credit card processing, because it is often against the policies of the bank to deduct money from customer credit card accounts until the ordered item is shipped. Many e-commerce sites deal in physical goods where real-time credit card processing does not make sense.

Tasks 3, 6, and 7 in the numbered list earlier in this section have been described in previous chapters. You accomplish Task 3, posting the order to a backup log, by using the APPEND tag as shown in the "Ten-Line E-Commerce Web Site" section in Chapter 16, *Designing E-Commerce Systems*. Tasks 6 and 7, composing and sending e-mail confirmations to the order desk and user are examples of sending e-mails. Composing a sales e-mail is described in the same "Ten-Line E-Commerce Web Site" section. Extending this so the e-mails sent out can be defined using a template, is described in the "Using an E-Mail Template" section of Chapter 9, *Building Login Pages*.

Tasks 4, adding records to order history and transaction databases, and 5, adding or editing customer database records, depend on your back-end system. Task 4 is required if you keep an order history for your staff or users. Typically you save your order history in two database tables, one that saves basic order information and the other for the items ordered. You use an order number unique for each order to cross-reference the tables. If you use real-time credit card processing, you may also want to post the payment in a database reserved for financial transactions. Later, in a back-end system, you will need this database to obtain payment history for the customer or post credits and other payment adjustments, if it becomes necessary.

Once some or all of Tasks 1 through 7 are completed, assuming the transaction is successful, the user is directed to a thank you or confirmation page.

Order Confirmation

During order confirmation, you provide the users with a *Thank-you* message and explain how to contact you in the event they experience a problem. The *Thank-you* message reinforces to the user that the order has been successfully processed. This feedback is important since it gives the user a sense of closure. The page can be extremely simple, like that presented in the "One-Line Confirmation Page" section of Chapter 16, *Designing E-Commerce Systems*. Or you can be more helpful by providing the user a printable receipt.

To provide a printable receipt, add a link to the thank you page directing users to a new Web page. On the page, organize the ordering information the way a typical receipt would look and provide a Print This Page message at the top.

Summary

In this chapter you learned about checkout pages organized as a sequence of pages that capture ordering information followed by a review page where the user can either go back and edit the information or post the order. Of course, this particular design is not the rule. You have the freedom to organize checkout pages any way you want.

You may want the user to log in and provide shipping and payment information before being able to submit an order. This is a good way to organize your pages if you expect a lot of repeat business. It makes it easy for you to add quick-order buttons and single-step checkouts that take advantage of the information already on file for a user.

If orders include soft items, such as information packets or software that can be downloaded from the Web, you want your checkout pages to include a way to download the items purchased.

In general, the way you organize your checkout page will depend on the nature of your products and services, the kinds of customers you have, and your own creativity.

Next, in Chapter 21, *Building Back-End Management Systems*, you explore the kinds of systems used by staff to manage e-commerce sites. The chapter completes this discussion on e-commerce leaving you with an appreciation for the intricacies of e-commerce development and more importantly, the tools to build advanced e-commerce sites.

Exercises

In the exercises that follow you build many of the components discussed in this chapter. Answers to these exercises are provided on this book's companion Web site as described in the book's Preface.

Exercise 1

Add data validation to the six-line shipping page and the twelve-line payment pages described at the beginning of this chapter. Hint: Use the code described in the "Commonly Used Validation Schemes" section of Chapter 10, *HTML Forms Processing*.

Exercise 2

Sophisticated Web sites such as **Amazon.com** (http://www.amazon.com/) give users the ability to keep multiple shipping and delivery addresses on file. Using cookies gives users such an option. Add a pull-down menu followed with Save, Load, and Delete buttons. Clicking Save should add the current entry to the list. Clicking Load should load the selected entry into the HTML form. Clicking Delete should delete the selected entry. Save the list in a comma-delimited file using the HTMLOS.COOKIE ID describe in the "Saving Shopping Carts Using Cookies" section of Chapter 19, *Building Shopping Cart Pages*.

Exercise 3

Some sophisticated e-commerce sites require users to log in before making a purchase. Using what you learned in Chapter 9, *Building Login Pages*, precede the shipping and payment page described in this chapter with a login page. Hook this up to a `cart.html` page so, upon checking out, users must log in, if they have not already done so.

CHAPTER 21

Building Back-End Management Systems

No book on advanced Web sites would be complete without a discussion of back-end systems. *Back-end* means the part of the Web site used for performing office tasks, such as those associated with maintaining the pages for users of the Web site. We use the terms back-end and back-office interchangeably.

As a site gets more advanced, so does the need for Web pages office workers can use to maintain the site. As a site takes on more functions and provides more kinds of information, the production department imparts the maintenance of that information to other individuals in the organization.

The tasks performed by these other individuals are done with back-office Web pages that correspond to pages or features of the Web site. For example, product capsules appearing on the home page would correspond to back-end pages for selecting the products to be placed on that page. Or the automated e-mail messages sent to customers when they order a product would correspond to a back-end Web page for editing the e-mail template used to compose the automated e-mail.

This chapter concentrates on back-end Web pages for maintaining Web sites. But you could easily apply the concepts here to the construction of any kind of back-office system.

Web-based computing is ideally suited to the construction of Web-based offices since office tasks are most often related to communication and the handling or processing of information—two tasks ideally suited to Web-based computing.

Collaboration, document updates, document exchange, e-mail broadcasts, calendars, database lookup, workflow systems are tasks that can be handled by Web-based systems. With Web-based computing you can customize the tasks and combine them in different ways.

This chapter serves not only as an introduction to back-end systems as they pertain to e-commerce sites, but also as an introduction to how you build Web-based offices in general. First, we look at the benefits of running a Web-based office. Then, in the "The SBS Back-End System" section, we describe the features of a fictitious back-end system for managing an e-commerce site. The SBS system described in this chapter provides pages for updating product information, editing the Web, picking up and processing orders, and editing e-mail templates.

Benefits of Web-Based Offices

One of the main benefits of Web-based offices is the ability to customize the automation of office tasks. Web-based offices can be built, rebuilt, and adapted to changing operational needs in the way you update Web sites constantly to keep up with changing business needs.

The Web-based development environment gives businesses of all sizes the ability to build sophisticated solutions customized to meet their current and future organizational needs. Unlike approaches based on canned solutions, where the software purchased dictates offices tasks, custom solutions enable office workers to perform tasks more efficiently. For example, suppose an equipment retailer needs to provide office workers with the ability to search for customers whose orders are late so the customers can be alerted by e-mail of the delays. The retailer with a canned solution would need this feature built into the canned system. But the software may not have that feature, or the e-mails that go out may need to be combined with information in another product. The result is an inability to serve the customer to the detriment of customer and business.

Although canned solutions help businesses in the short term, custom solutions (provided they can be modified quickly) offer greater long-term benefits. The Web-approach frees the organization from the canned software mentality that systems cannot be given new features when necessary, and that manual intervention is needed when transferring information back and forth between different software products.

Another benefit of Web-based offices is that the business tasks are performed using a Web browser. This frees office workers to use any computer in the office or work from home. It means a PC can break or fail without disrupting business operations.

Customizing internal business operations using Web-based systems is an empowering experience that allows you to build a more flexible organization and take advantage of market opportunities that you may otherwise not explore. For example, any opportunity that includes the need to exchange data with another organization can benefit from the construction of custom systems. Most legacy systems suffer from development cycles of 90 to 120 days or more. New features can be added to a Web-based system in as little as a day.

Customizing your back-end systems also forces you to analyze and understand the operations in your organization. When building a back-end system you often find needless operations that you can streamline. It's a cleansing process with benefits that often yield unexpected rewards. For example, in the course of constructing a back-end system to process customer support requests you might find you already have the answers to many customer questions and can make them available over the Web. Reexamining your operations often leads to improvements in customer relations and business operations. The construction of Web-based systems involves re-examining your operations.

Perhaps the most interesting aspect of back-office Web development is that the quick-development process often makes implementation of advanced back-office pages less costly than purchasing out-of-the-box enterprise solutions. You can have your cake and eat it too. On one hand you get the customization capabilities. On the other hand you get something affordable. What many don't realize is that the development of back-end Web pages is often easier than building Web sites. Here's why:

- Back-end systems rarely need to support as many users as a high-access Web site. You may have thousands of users on your Web site but you don't have that many people on a back-end system.

- Back-end systems do not need large amounts of graphical design. Most often a list of tasks is all that's needed (although placing a nice header and footer on your pages won't hurt.)

- Only one task needs to be handled per Web page. This separation of duties makes the pages fast to develop or modify. HTML editors are not needed either. Contrast this with the pages of an advanced Web site that often perform many tasks (providing users product navigation, search, product detail, and promotional information, for example) and may contain many graphical design elements.

Back-End Design Considerations

The design of back-end systems varies from organization to organization. And, of course, the design of such systems involves many topics unique to your situation, so they cannot be discussed in this book. But some common issues directly related to Web development are important and worthy of mention. In this section we discuss the need to distribute control between users, the need to modularize and document development work, and the need to protect your code from future changes outside of your control.

Distributing Control

If you operate in a large organization you need to be keenly aware of security and that different departments may need control over their own information, their own systems, and perhaps their own development. A technical support department may not want to give other departments the ability to edit or change its information. A sales department does not want to give other departments access to its coupon databases. In these business environments you want to set up copies of HTML/OS in each department. This topic is discussed in the "Serving Network Databases" section of Chapter 15, *Database Networking*. In general, each department can maintain its own databases and give access to its respective databases by opening read or read/write access to other users in the organization on a per-request basis.

Keeping Tasks Limited

When building back-end system components keep the tasks simple. You may not be the last one modifying the page.

As an example, if you are building a page to collect incoming orders you can provide a page to view orders and another to pick up and print orders. Using different pages for each of the tasks makes it easier for someone else to make changes later.

Document, Document, Document

It is important to document your Web pages. Although HTML/OS code is easy to read (since it's English-like), you should document each task in your code and add a description within your code of the fields used in the database. This is helpful to you or anyone modifying the page later. Liberal use of *Read Me* files is helpful as well. If code in your back-end application connects to a database in another department, make sure the parameters used to access the network database are clearly accessible so they can be changed if necessary.

Using HTML Editors Carefully

HTML editors can build Web pages that don't work properly on some browsers. Since back-end systems rarely go through the compatibility testing that Web sites go through, it may make more sense to avoid using HTML editors. There is little excuse for building systems that suddenly don't work when you try to log into them with a Macintosh, for example. See the accompanying note, "Don't Tolerate Browser Bigotry."

Don't Tolerate Browser Bigotry—*People who tout one browser over another, or one computer over another hurt organizations since they place greater importance on their biases than on whether a system works. Such people should be reminded that companies are better served by making the Web their standard than the software from a single company.*

Assume Databases Will Change

Design your databases and Web pages with the expectation that fields will be added in the future. To do this, avoid using Overlay tags that are dependent on field structure. In this book we avoided tags that depend on field structure so this is not a tough thing to watch out for, but such dependent Overlay tags do exist. For example, you want to use DBFIND, not DBSEARCH. The DBFIND tag, as you have seen in the code examples in this book, has a field list parameter. If you add new fields to the database, the tag returns the same result. This is not true for DBSEARCH, which relies on the order of the fields in the database.

The SBS Back-End System

In this section you look at the back-end pages for managing a fictitious e-commerce site that sells retail products. The system is called Simple Back-End System or SBS. You can download the SBS system along with its front-end Web site from the companion Web site of this book. (See the Preface for details.) The home page of the SBS system is shown in Figure 21.1.

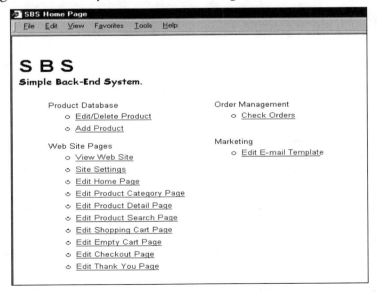

Figure 21.1: The SBS system automates the tasks needed to maintain a Web site.

The SBS system provides four main functions. A Product Database section allows marketing staff to edit, delete, and add products. A Web Site Pages section allows staff in a production department to edit and view the HTML documents that make up parts of the Web site. An Order Management section allows an order processing department to pick up and manage orders. A Marketing section allows staff to edit the automated e-mail template used to define confirmation e-mails.

The SBS pages reside in the `/apps/sbs/bin` directory. The Web site itself resides in the `/apps/sbs` directory. A directory list of the SBS pages is shown in Figure 21.2.

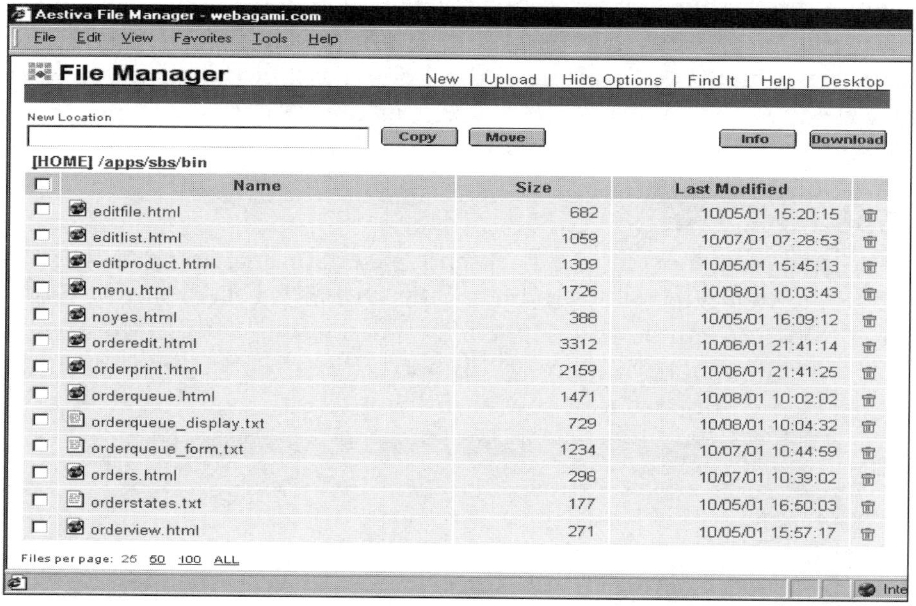

Figure 21.2: The SBS system uses only the HTML documents shown in this listing.

The Order State*—The order state is a code that represents the status of an order in a workflow system. When an order first arrives it is in one state. After it is taken out of inventory it is in another state. After it has been shipped it is in yet another state. The order states are stored in an* `orderstates.txt` *file. You associate an order coder with each order to use when you are building screens that list products at specific points of the workflow process.*

In this section you will be looking at several SBS documents to get a taste of how to build back-end systems. The files used by the SBS system and their functions are shown in the following list. The files shown in bold are described in this chapter.

`menu.html`	Back-end options menu (see Figure 21.1)
`editlist.html`	List products to edit
`editproduct.html`	Edit product in products database
`noyes.html`	Delete product confirmation page
`editfile.html`	Generic text file editor
`download.html`	Download orders
`orderstates.txt`	Display valid order states
`orders.html`	Select order by order state
`orderqueue.html`	View orders in an order state
`orderqueue_form.txt`	HTML code to display a search form
`orderqueue_display.txt`	HTML code to display an order
`orderedit.html`	Edit order record
`orderprint.html`	View print-ready order record
`orderview.html`	View archived order

The SBS system uses two databases: a `products` database and an `orders` database. The `products` database stores products that can be ordered on the Web site. The fields for the `products` database are as follows:

`PRODNAME`	Name of product
`PRODNUMBER`	Product number
`PRODPRICE`	Product price
`PRODTITLE`	Product title
`PRODDESC`	Product description
`PRODIMAGEFILE`	Product image file
`PRODSHIPPING`	Product shipping surcharge

The `orders` database stores the information about each order (such as credit card number and shipping address) as well as the individual items ordered (product name and price, for example). Each record has room for only a single item ordered, so an order with four items, for example, would occupy four records in the database. Note that many ordering systems would place the items ordered in a separate `orderitems` database. To keep this system simple a single database is used. The fields for the `orders` database are as follows:

`ORDER_NUMBER`	Order number
`ORDER_STATUS`	Order state
`ORDER_EMAIL`	Order e-mail address
`ORDER_DATE`	Date order placed
`ORDER_SHIPTYPE`	Shipping method requested

```
ORDER_CC                  Credit card number
ORDER_CCEXP               Credit card exp date
ORDER_NAME                Credit card holder name
ORDER_ADDRESS             Shipping street address
ORDER_CITY                Shipping city
ORDER_STATE               Shipping state
ORDER_ZIP                 Shipping Zip code
ORDER_PHONE               Shipping phone number
ORDER_TAXABLE             Order item tax flag
ITEM_ID                   Order item id
ITEM_QTY                  Order item quantity
ITEM_NAME                 Order item name
ITEM_PRICE                Order item price
ITEM_OPTIONS              Order item options
ITEM_SHIPPING             Order item shipping charge
ITEM_DELETE               Order item delete flag
```

Editing the Product Database

E-commerce systems with many products require a way for office staff to edit the list of products. Product information can be stored in a legacy spreadsheet or database and periodically uploaded, which requires maintaining two product databases. An alternative approach is to let office staff edit the Web-based product database directly. That is done here. Two menu options for editing the product database are provided as shown in Figure 21.1. The code for this menu page is as follows:

```
<html>
<title>SBS Home Page</title>
<br><font size=6 face=arial>
<b>S B S</b></font><br>
<b>S</b>imple <b>B</b>ack-End <b>S</b>ystem.</font><br><br>
<table border=0><tr><td valign=top>
<ul><font size=2 face=arial,helvetica>
Product Database<ul>
 <li><a href="editlist.html">Edit/Delete Product</a>
 <li><a href="addproduct">Add Product</a><br><br>
</ul>
Web Site Pages<ul>
<li><a href="../index.html">View Web Site</a>  
<li><a href="editfile.html" name=e value="data/settings.txt">
```

```
Settings</a>
<li><a href="editfile.html" name=e value="index.html">Edit Home
Page</a>
<li><a href="editfile.html" name=e value="category.html">Edit
Product Category Page</a>
<li><a href="editfile.html" name=e value="product.html">Edit
Product Detail Page</a>
<li><a href="editfile.html" name=e value="search.html">Edit
Product Search Page</a>
<li><a href="editfile.html" name=e value="cart.html">Edit
Shopping Cart Page</a>
<li><a href="editfile.html" name=e value="cart_empty.html">Edit
Empty Cart Page</a>
<li><a href="editfile.html" name=e value="checkout.html">Edit
Checkout Page</a>
<li><a href="editfile.html" name=e value="confirm.html">Edit
Thank You Page</a><br></ul>
</td><td valign=top>
<ul><font size=2 face=arial,helvetica>
Order Management<ul>
<li><a href="orders.html">Check Orders</a></ul><br><br>
Marketing<ul>
<li><a href="editfile.html" name=e value="data/email.txt">Edit
E-mail Template</a>
</ul></ul></td></tr></table>
</html>
<<overlay addproduct
   PRODNAME="Untitled."
   PRODNUMBER=""
   PRODPRICE=""
   PRODTITLE=""
   PRODDESC=""
   PRODIMAGEFILE=""
   PRODSHIPPING=""
   sc_conf=""
   sc_rec="ERROR"
   GOTO "editproduct.html"
>>
```

The menu page contains the Edit/Delete Product and Add Product options. When users select the Add Product option, they are directed to the addproduct on-click Overlay, which sets up the variables for a new product record and launches editproduct.html. The editproduct.html page is used for editing new as well as existing records.

When users select the Edit/Delete Product option, they are directed to editlist.html to select a product record. The editlist.html page is as follows:

```
<<
  IF button="Menu" THEN button="" GOTO "menu.html" /IF
  sc_products=DBFIND("/apps/sbs/data/products",
    "",1,500,'RECORD,PRODNAME,PRODNUMBER,PRODPRICE')
>>
<html>
<form method=post action=<<page>>>
<input type=text name=sc_search size=20>
<input type=submit name=button value="Menu">
</form>
<table border=1 cellpadding=2 cellspacing=0>
<tr>
 <td><b>Product Name</b></td>
 <td><b>Product ID</b></td>
 <td align=right><b>Price</b></td>
 <td> </td>
</tr>
<<
  FOR NAME=sc_products ROWNAME=sc_product DO
    DISPLAY
      '<tr>'+
        '<td><a href="editproduct.html" name=sc_rec '+
        'value='+sc_product[1]+'>'+sc_product[2]+'</a></td>'+
        '<td>'+sc_product[3]+'</td>'+
        '<td align=right>'+sc_product[4]+'</td>'+
        '<td align=right><a href="noyes.html" name=sc_delno '+
        'value='+sc_product[1]+'>delete</a></td></tr>'
    /DISPLAY
  /FOR
>>
```

```
</table>
</html>
```

The first Overlay on the page uses DBFIND to fill the sc_products variable with the records in the products database. Then a FOR loop displays the products on the page. Each product name is a hypertext link to editproduct.html. In addition, a Delete hypertext link, which links to the noyes.html page, is placed next to each product name. The page is a four-line confirmation page that gives the user a chance to confirm the delete. The code is as follows:

```
<html>
<title>Four-Line Confirmation Page</title>
<< sc_stat=DBGETREC("/apps/sbs/data/products",sc_delno)>>
Delete <u><<prodname>></u>?<BR><BR>
<a href="doit" name=sc_delno value=<<sc_delno>>>Yes</a>
      <a
href="editlist.html">No</a>
</html>
<<overlay doit
  stat=DBDELETE("/apps/sbs/data/products",sc_delno)
  sc_delno=""
  GOTO "editlist.html"
>>
```

When a user clicks Delete, the sc_delno variable is set. The noyes.html page asks whether to delete the record. If the user clicks Yes, the doit on-click Overlay is called and the DBDELETE tag deletes the record. If the user clicks No, the user returns to the editlist.html page.

When the user selects a record on the editlist.html page, the editproduct.html page launches. This is the Web page staff use when editing new or existing records. The code for the page follows:

```
<html>
<title>Eight-line SBS Product Editor</title>
<<sc_stat=DBGETREC("/apps/sbs/data/products",sc_rec)>>
<br><form method=post action=editrec>
<table border=1 cellpadding=2 cellspacing=0>
<tr><td colspan=2 align=right>
```

```
<input type=submit name=button value="Save">
<input type=submit name=button value="Quit">
<input type=submit name=button value="Quit To Products"></td>
</tr><tr><td><b>Name</b></td><td>
<input type=text name=prodname size=20></td></tr>
<tr><td><b>ID</b></td><td>
<input type=text name=prodnumber size=10></td></tr>
<tr><td><b>Price</b></td><td>
<input type=text name=prodprice size=20></td></tr>
<tr><td><b>Title</b></td><td>
<input type=text name=prodtitle size=20></td></tr>
<tr><td valign=top><b>Description</b></td><td>
<textarea name=proddesc rows=4 cols=50></textarea></td></tr>
<tr><td><b>Image file</b></td><td><input type=text
name=prodimagefile size=20></td></tr>
<tr><td><b>Shipping</b></td><td>
<input type=text name=prodshipping size=20></td></tr>
</table></form>
</html>
<<overlay editrec
 IF button="Quit" THEN
   GOTO "menu.html"
 ELIF button="Quit To Products" THEN
   GOTO "editlist.html"
 ELSE
   IF ISINTEGER(sc_rec) THEN
     stat=DBEDIT("/apps/sbs/data/products",sc_rec)
   ELSE
     stat=DBADD("/apps/sbs/data/products")
   /IF
 /IF
 GOTO PAGE
>>
```

At the top of the page a DBGETREC loads the record into the variable environment. Once loaded, it fills the HTML form displayed on the page. A similar technique is used in the "Eight-Line Database Record Editor" section of Chapter 11, *The Web Database*.

The HTML form on the page is preceded with Save, Quit, and Quit to Products buttons. When the user clicks a button, the `editrec` on-click Overlay runs. If the user clicks Quit or Quit to Products, the user is directed to `menu.html` or `editlist.html` respectively. If the user clicks Save, the `sc_rec` variable is inspected. If it's a number, you assume you are editing an existing record and hence, you save the record with a DBEDIT tag. If not, you can assume you are editing a new record and hence you create the new record with a DBADD tag.

Editing Documents

The SBS system also includes options to edit the HTML documents that make up the Web site. To provide this feature you build an `editfile.html` page similar to that described in the "Six-Line Text Editor" section of Chapter 8, *Building Text Editors*. The page is as follows:

```
<< sc_editfile="/apps/sbs/"+e
 COPY FILE=sc_editfile TO sc_editdata /COPY
>>
<html>
<form method=post action=editstuff>
<table border=0 cellpadding=0 cellspacing=0>
<tr><td><b>File: <<e>></b></td>
<td align=right>
<input type=submit name=button value="Save">
<input type=submit name=button value="Reload">
<input type=submit name=button value="Menu"></td>
</tr><tr><td colspan=2>
<textarea name=sc_editdata rows=17 cols=69></textarea>
</td></tr></table>
</form>
</html>
<<overlay editstuff
 IF button = "Reload" THEN
  GOTO PAGE
 ELIF button = "Save" THEN
  COPY sc_editdata TO FILE=sc_editfile /COPY
  GOTO PAGE
 ELIF button = "Menu" THEN
   GOTO "menu.html"
```

```
/IF
GOTO PAGE
>>
```

The variable `e`, which contains the name of the file being edited, is set in `menu.html` when a file is selected. The editor assumes filenames in `menu.html` are specified relative to the `/apps/sbs` directory. It sets `sc_filename` at the top of the file accordingly. Like the text editor described in Chapter 8, when a user clicks an option, the appropriate action is taken in the on-click Overlay at the bottom of the document.

This editor gives product staff quick access to the HTML documents that make up the Web site. It is also used for editing the e-mail template—the file that defines the automated e-mail message sent when a product is ordered. It is always a good idea to give office staff the ability to edit this document.

The Ordering System

Ordering systems gives office staff the ability to manage incoming orders. In this section we describe a sophisticated ordering system that includes workflow. The concept of workflow was first discussed in the "Document Collaboration" section of Chapter 8, *Building Text Editors*, which described a system based on text files. Here a database-based system is described.

The workflow system works as follows: All orders include a field called `order_status`. The field is set to QUEUE when an order is placed. The field can also have the values CANCEL, SHIP, HOLD, or DONE. When office staff members pick up incoming orders, they can selectively view orders depending on the order's order state. They can view orders in the incoming queue (orders with `order_status` equal to QUEUE), or they can view orders on hold, orders completed, and so on. In addition, staff members can move orders between one state and another. After they ship an order, for example, they would move the order to the DONE state. If they cancel orders, they move them to the CANCEL state. If they must put an order on hold, they move it to the HOLD state.

From a programming perspective, the process of moving orders between order states is simply a matter of changing the contents of the `order_status` field. Viewing orders of a specific order state is a matter of setting up the query on the `orders` database so the page displays only those records with an `order_status` equal to the specified order state.

In the SBS system, the order states are stored in the `orderstates.txt` file. The file is a two-column, delimited text file with the following contents:

```
QUEUE,"Input Queue"
SHIP,"Orders To Ship"
DONE,"Orders Shipped"
CANCEL,"Cancelled Orders"
HOLD,"Order On Hold"
```

The file defines five order states. Different workflow systems can use different sets of possible states. The first column contains the codes you store in the `order_status` field of the `orders` database. The second column contains a text description you used on Web pages and in links to describe the order state. The ordering system is launched from the `menu.html` page, which provides a Check Orders hypertext link to `orders.html`.

The `orders.html` page gives office workers the ability to access orders in different order states. They may wish to view only incoming orders. At other times, they may need to search completed orders. The `orders.html` page used in this SBS system is dynamically created using the `orderstates.txt` file. The code for the page is as follows:

```
<html>
<title>Three-Line SBS Order States Page</title>
<< COPY FILE='orderstates.txt' TS=',' TO sc_states /COPY >>
<a href="menu.html">Menu</a>
<ul>
<< FOR NAME=sc_states ROWNAME=sc_row DO
     DISPLAY '<li><a href="orderqueue.html" '+
       'name=sc_state value="'+sc_row[1]+'">'+
       sc_row[2]+'</a>'+LF /DISPLAY
 /FOR
>>
</ul>
</html>
```

The page reads the `orderstates.txt` delimited text file into the `sc_states` variable. Then, using a `FOR` loop, it displays hypertext links to each state. When the user clicks a state, the `sc_state` variable is set to the order state and the page `orderqueue.html` runs.

The `orderqueue.html` page is the main page used to view orders. The page lists products for a specified order state and contains options to move orders to different order states. A sample screen shot is shown in Figure 21.3. The code for the page follows.

Figure 21.3: The workflow system used by SBS includes a page where staff can move orders among different order states.

```
<<
IF sc_day="ERROR" THEN
  sc_searchdate=TODAY
ELSE
  sc_searchdate=sc_month+'/'+sc_day+'/'+sc_year
 /IF
 sstr='ORDER_DATE>="'+sc_searchdate+'" AND '+
      'ORDER_STATUS="'+sc_state+'"'
 flist='ORDER_NUMBER,ORDER_NAME,ORDER_DATE,ITEM_QTY,'+
       'ITEM_PRICE,ORDER_TAXABLE,ITEM_DELETE'
 sc_orders=DBFIND('/apps/sbs/data/orders',sstr,1,100,flist)
 sc_linkstates=GETCOLNOTEQ(sc_states,1,sc_state)
>>
<html>
<title>Thirty Five-Line Order List Page With Workflow</title>
<b><<GETTABLE(GETCOLEQ(sc_states,1,sc_state),2,2,1,1)>></b><br>
<a href="menu.html">Menu</a>  <a
href="orders.html">Orders</a>
<< DISPLAY FILE="orderqueue_form.txt" /DISPLAY >>
```

```
<table border=0>
<<
i=0 sc_total=0 lastorder="ERROR"
IF sc_orders!="" THEN
 DISPLAY "<tr bgcolor=#EEEEEE>"+
         "<td><u>Order Number</u></td>"+
         "<td><u>Name</u></td><td><u>Date</u></td></tr>"
 /DISPLAY
 FOR NAME=sc_orders ROWNAME=sc_order DO
   IF lastorder != sc_order[1] THEN
     IF lastorder!="ERROR" THEN
       EXPAND FILE="orderqueue_display.txt" /EXPAND
     /IF
     sc1=sc_order[1] sc2=sc_order[2] sc3=sc_order[3]
     lastorder=sc_order[1]
   /IF
 /FOR
 IF lastorder!="ERROR" THEN
   EXPAND FILE="orderqueue_display.txt" /EXPAND
 /IF
/IF
>>
</table>
</html>
<<OVERLAY changestate
 sc_newstate=CUT(CHOPRIGHT(sc_orderdata,'|'),'|')
 sc_ordernum=CUT(CHOPLEFT(sc_orderdata,'|'),'|')
 sstr='ORDER_NUMBER="'+sc_ordernum+'"'

stat=DBFILL('/apps/sbs/data/orders',sstr,'ORDER_STATUS',sc_newst
ate)
 GOTO PAGE
>>
```

The Underlay at the top of `orderqueue.html` page composes a search string to determine which orders should be listed on the page. The DBFIND tag extracts orders. The instruction `sc_linkstates=GETCOLNOTEQ(sc_states,1,sc_state)` fills `sc_linkstates` with a column of order states with all states other than the current state. The variable is used later in the code to generate a list of order states to which an order may be moved.

Below this Underlay is the display part of the Web page. The page uses the following Overlay to generate its page title dynamically. Depending on the current order state, a different title is displayed. Note that sc_states was filled in a prior page with the contents of the orderstates.txt file, so the Overlay effectively displays the title associated with the current order state.

```
<<GETTABLE(GETCOLEQ(sc_states,1,sc_state),2,2,1,1)>>
```

Below this Underlay an HTML form is placed on the page, so the user can list only orders since a specified date. The HTML form is stored in the orderqueue_form.txt file and placed in the page using the instruction:

```
DISPLAY FILE="orderqueue_form.txt" /DISPLAY
```

The contents of this file could have been written directly into the page, but here, as a way to cut down the size of the page, the code for the search box is stored in a separate file. The contents of the file follow:

```
<form method=post action=orderqueue.html>
Show orders after <select name=sc_month>
<option value=01>Jan<option value=02>Feb<option value=03>Mar
<option value=04>Apr<option value=05>May<option value=06>Jun
<option value=07>Jul<option value=08>Aug<option value=09>Sep
<option value=10>Oct<option value=11>Nov<option value=12>Dec
</select>
<select name=sc_day>
<option value=01>01<option value=02>02<option value=03>03
<option value=04>04<option value=05>05<option value=06>06
<option value=07>07<option value=08>08<option value=09>09
<option value=10>10<option value=11>11<option value=12>12
<option value=13>13<option value=14>14<option value=15>15
<option value=16>16<option value=17>17<option value=18>18
<option value=19>19<option value=20>20<option value=21>21
<option value=22>22<option value=23>23<option value=24>24
<option value=25>25<option value=26>26<option value=27>27
<option value=28>28<option value=29>29<option value=30>30
<option value=31>31</select>,
<select name=sc_year>
```

```
<option value=2001>2001<option value=2002>2002<option
value=2003>2003
<option value=2004>2004<option value=2005>2005<option
value=2006>2006
</select>
<input type=submit name=button value="Go">
</form>
```

When the user specifies a date with this HTML form and clicks the Go button, the page redisplays, a new search string is calculated, and the orders after or on the selected date are displayed.

Below this portion of the page the orders are displayed. A FOR loop loops across sc_orders, the records obtained using the DBFIND tag in the Underlay. This FOR loop is a bit tricky since the orders database contains records for each order item, not simply one record per order. You want to display only one link per order. To do that you use a variable called lastorder, which is initialized to ERROR. As you loop across sc_orders, when the order number of the order in the loop changes from the previous, you display the order line. The code to display the order line could be placed in the Web page, but to save space, the code is expanded into the Overlay using the EXPAND tag. The code is stored in the orderqueue_display.txt file. The code is as follows:

```
DISPLAY
'<tr><td>'+sc1+'</td><td>'+sc2+'</td><td>'+sc3+'</td></tr>'+
'<tr><td colspan=3><br>Options: '+
'<a href="orderedit.html" name=sc_ordernum value="'+sc1+'">'+
'Edit order</a> | '+
'<a href="orderprint.html" name=sc_ordernum value="'+sc1+'">'+
'Print order</a> | '+
'<a href=orderview.html name=sc_ordernum value="'+sc1+'">'+
'View original</a>'+
'<br>Move To:'
/DISPLAY
DISPLAY
   LAYOUT(sc_linkstates,' | ',
          '<a href="changestate" name=sc_orderdata value="',
          [1],'|',sc1,'">',[2],'</a>')
/DISPLAY
DISPLAY
```

```
'</td></tr><tr><td colspan=3><hr size=1></td></tr>'
/DISPLAY
```

This code displays the order number and the name of the contact associated with the order. Below it, the Edit, Print, and View options display. Each option is a link to a different Web page. Below that LAYOUT tag displays a series of links, each connecting to the changestate on-click Overlay. When the user clicks a link, the sc_orderdata variable is set to the order number followed by a vertical bar and the name of the desired order state. The changestate on-click Overlay contains the following code:

```
sc_newstate=CUT(CHOPRIGHT(sc_orderdata,'|'),'|')
sc_ordernum=CUT(CHOPLEFT(sc_orderdata,'|'),'|')
sstr='ORDER_NUMBER="'+sc_ordernum+'"'

stat=DBFILL('/apps/sbs/data/orders',sstr,'ORDER_STATUS',sc_newst
ate)
  GOTO PAGE
```

Using the CUT tag and CHOPRIGHT tags the new order state and order number are extracted from the sc_orderstate variable. Then a search string is set to select the records belonging to the specified order number and used in the DBFILL tag to change the ORDER_STATUS variable to its new order state. The DBFILL tag is a DB tag used to change a particular field across a selection of many records. It is described in the knowledge base on the **Aestiva** Web site at http://www.aestiva.com/support.

Other Potential SBS Options

You can expand the SBS back-office application to provide additional functionality. For example, you can limit access to the pages with login pages like those described in the Chapter 9, *Building Login Pages*. By adding a login page, you can limit the tasks office staff can perform.

Order options may be split between a shipping department, which can complete an order, place it on hold, or send it back to the input queue, but not edit the order—a task reserved for order takers or managers. Tasks for the computer department can be added so they can issue login IDs and access rights to different Web pages (applications). Additional options to manage additional features on the Web site may also be needed.

Another option that you can add to the SBS system is an e-mail broadcast page. The option can give individuals in the marketing department the ability to send mass e-mails to people who ordered before. The Web pages to send a broadcast e-mail are divided into the following three tasks:

Database selection—Database selection involves setting up query pages that pull records from databases containing customer or prospective customer information. The purpose of these pages is to create a list of e-mail addresses and related information for use in an e-mail merge broadcast system. These pages are built using the same techniques described in Chapter 12, *Building Query Pages*.

E-mail template management—E-mail template management is a matter of giving the user the ability to set up a directory of text files containing the kinds of e-mails you wish to broadcast. That directory is displayed on the screen in a pull-down menu. The files can contain placeholders as described in the "Using an E-Mail Template" section of Chapter 9, *Building Login Pages*, so they can be used with an e-mail broadcast system.

E-mail merge broadcast—E-mail broadcast systems use a specified e-mail template file and a variable or file containing e-mail addresses and information that need to be merged into the e-mails (such as customer name) and broadcasts it to the e-mail addresses on the list.

As an example of e-mail broadcasting, suppose the name of your template file is stored in the `mytemplate` variable and your e-mail addresses are stored in a two-column variable called `myemails` with the e-mail addresses in the first column and customer names in the second. Then the page to broadcast e-mails can be as follows:

```
<< # Ten-Line E-Mail Broadcast Page
   # Incoming Variables:
   #  Email variable: myemails
   #  Template file: mytemplate
   #  Subject: mysubject
   /#
   IF ISINTEGER(email_row)="FALSE" THEN email_row=1 /IF
   IF myemails[1,email_rowno] != "" THEN
      temp=myemail[1, email_rowno]
      mymetalink='<META HTTP-EQUIV="REFRESH"' +
          'CONTENT="1;URL='+PAGE+'">'
      myletter=REPLACEALL(myletter," [name]",
myemails[2,email_rowno])
```

```
    MAIL myletter TO ADDRESS=temp SUBJECT=mysubject /MAIL
    msg="Message #"+email_row+" sent."
    email_rowno = email_rowno + 1
  ELSE
    mymetalink=""
    email_row="ERROR"
    msg="Broadcast Complete"
  /IF   >>
<html>
<title>Ten-Line E-Mail Broadcast Page</title>
<<mymetalink>>
<<msg>>
</html>
```

This page sends one e-mail message and then redisplays itself, each time sending the next e-mail in the myemails variable, until all e-mails have been sent. The tricky part of this page is knowing you cannot simply send mass e-mails using a FOR loop since this places too much load on an outgoing mail server and, further, may take so long the Web page may time out. Instead, e-mails should be sent one at a time with a couple of seconds of a pause between them. Sending out an e-mail, redisplaying the page, and repeating the process with the next e-mail is a good way to broadcast multiple e-mails.

The code for this page begins by initializing email_row, if necessary. This is the row in the myemails variable (which contains a list of e-mail addresses) to send. Then you see whether the e-mail in the row is empty. If it's not empty, another e-mail needs to be sent: In this case the mymetalink variable is filled with the HTML needed to redisplay the page. The HTML command to redisplay a Web page is written as follows, where URL is the name of the Web page to display and seconds is the number of seconds to wait before bouncing to the specified URL. The command can be placed just below the <TITLE>...</TITLE> tags in the HTML document.

```
<META HTTP-EQUIV="REFRESH" CONTENT="seconds;URL=URL">
```

After the mymetalink variable is set, an e-mail message is composed and the message is emailed with the MAIL tag. Note the use of the REPLACEALL tag for swapping [name] with the name of the recipient. You can extend this e-mail merge feature by adding additional REPLACEALL instructions.

Summary

In this chapter we covered the nature of back-end management systems and viewed a sample system for managing an e-commerce site. You learned that back-end systems and Web-based offices are built from the same components already discussed in this book. Indeed, an understanding of the techniques used in this book is what you need to build both advanced Web sites and Web-based offices.

In Appendix C, *The Next Generation: Web-Based Products*, you look beyond advanced Web development—to the next generation of Web-based computing. You learn that Web-based computing is also about building products that can be sold and installed in hosting accounts all across the Web.

Exercises

In the exercises that follow you apply the concepts described in this chapter. Answers to these exercises are provided on this book's companion Web site as described in the book's Preface.

Exercise 1

The "Other Potential SBS Options" section of this chapter included a ten-line e-mail broadcast page. Complete the application by setting up a page that allows you to select templates stored in a directory, define a subject line for your e-mails, and launch the e-mail broadcast application.

Exercise 2

Add a login page to the SBS system discussed in this chapter. Have the page divide marketing staff from order processing staff. Replace menu.html with one that works with your login page to give different users different sets of options.

Exercise 3

Add a download option to the SBS system so orders being viewed can be downloaded. Hint: Add the option to the top of orderqueue.html page. When a user clicks the link, create a delimited text file with the orders and use the FILEPUSHLINK tag to push the file to the user. Information on setting up download options and the FILEPUSHLINK tag is available in **Aestiva** knowledge base at http://www.aestiva.com/support.

HTML/OS Resources

Aestiva Web site
http://www.aestiva.com/
The home page for Aestiva. Features product and sales information on HTML/OS and other Web-based products and information on Aestiva.

Companion Web Site for *Advanced Web Sites Made Easy*
http://www.topfloor.com/advanced/
Information of interest to readers of this book. Includes answers to exercises, sample code, book notes, and reviews.

30-Day Free Trial Sign-Up for *Advanced Web Sites Made Easy*
http://dev.aestiva.com/freetrial/
The sign-up page for your reserved copy of HTML/OS.

User Forum for *Advanced Web Sites Made Easy*
http://dev.aestiva.com/advanced/forum/
An interactive user forum for getting answers to development questions. Reserved for readers of this book.

Aestiva Freeware Library
http://www.aestiva.com/freeware/
A code library containing dozens of freeware applications. Includes sample e-commerce sites, Web-based utilities and back-office applications.

Aestiva Knowledge Base
http://www.aestiva.com/support/
A database of answers to development questions. Includes answers to questions on more topics, sample code, and reference pages on tags not described in this book.

Aestiva Clips Library

http://www.aestiva.com/freeware/

A code library containing dozens of document sets for performing specific tasks. Includes login pages, sample HTML forms processing pages, database pages, HTML editors, and more.

Major HTML Tags

This appendix provides a crash minicourse in HTML. Without a knowledge of these tags you won't become an accomplished Web developer even if you're an experienced programmer, because Web developers must *think* in HTML. Producing on-the-fly documents is about visualizing the end result—documents containing HTML tags rendered by the browser.

Luckily, almost anyone can get comfortable with HTML in a few hours. Most HTML tags don't work across different kinds of browsers, browser versions, and different hardware. Learning HTML is not about learning all the tags available. It's about learning the limited number of HTML tags that work.

To learn HTML, take the tags listed here and play with them in an HTML document on your copy of HTML/OS. Spend a few hours testing these tags. Test all the tags until you feel comfortable with them. After you're done you'll have enough knowledge of HTML to use this book. The HTML tags discussed in this appendix fall into the following four categories, which are discussed in the sections that follow:

- Text tags
- Page attributes
- HTML tables
- Links and images

After learning these tags, you will also want to learn how to place input boxes and other input elements on the page, which involves another set of HTML tags. They are described in Chapter 10, *HTML Forms Processing*.

In this appendix you start by looking at how HTML tags are written. Then you look at the most common tags used, presented in the four categories we've just noted. Note that the tags and attributes presented in this appendix are not intended to be complete but serve as a quick introduction to HTML. For example, HTML style tags and tags that work only in the latest browsers are not listed here. For further information see the resources listed in the "Further Reading" section at the end of this appendix.

Writing HTML Tags

By convention all HTML tags begin with a < character and end with a > character. The tags are sequences of text placed in HTML documents, which are themselves text documents. The first word in every HTML tag is the name of the tag. The name of the tag is then followed with one or more *name-value* pairs. Most tags have a corresponding end tag. These ending tags always begin with </ characters followed by the name of the tag and the > character. They never contain *name-value* pairs. As an example, consider the following HTML:

```
<font size=3 color=red face=helvetica>Hello World</font>
```

This prints "Hello World" on the page. The tag preceding these words is `<font>`. It has three `name-value` pairs. The *names* in these *name-value* pairs are called attributes and are predefined for the tag. In this `<font>` tag, the first attribute is `size`. It is set to 3. The second attribute is `color`. The last attribute sets the typeface of the text. The ending tag to the `<font>` tag is the `</font>` tag. The pair of tags affects only the text between them.

As a rule, all HTML tags are built this way. To fully understand how a tag is written, you need to know the name of the tag and the possible *name-value* pairs it may contain. The order of the *name-value* pairs in the tag is unimportant and, as the examples in this appendix suggest, *name-value* pairs are often optional—that is, you don't have to use all options. A tag's name and its attributes can be written in either upper or lower case. HTML is not case-sensitive.

Text Tags

Text tags are the easiest tags in HTML. You use them to change how your text looks on the page. The most important ones to know are discussed in the sections that follow.

...

Place text between `<b>` and `</b>` tags and your text will appear bold when the browser displays it. Browsers also allow you to use the tags `<i>` and `</i>` to make your text italic, and `<u>` and `</u>` to underline your text. These tags always appear in pairs.

Example: `This is <b>bold</b> text.`

<font size=size color=color face=typeface>...</font>

Text that you place between these tags resizes to a specified *size* and the color of the text changes to the specified color. Browsers accept sizes that start at 1 (very small). The default size is 3. A very large font would be 6. The color you specify can be certain, predefined English word such as red, or a set of three two-digit hexadecimal numbers from 00 to FF representing the amount of red, blue, or green in the color. White is #FFFFFF and black is #000000. The font tag can also contain a typeface. Popular typefaces are Arial and Courier. The default font (if not specified) is Times Roman. These tags always appear in pairs.

Example: This is <font color=red>red</font> text.

<center>...</center>

Place text between the <center> and </center> tags to center the line they are on. Funny thing though, there are no <right>...</right> tags in HTML. Who knows why. In any event, we describe right justification using HTML tables in the "HTML Tables" section, later in this appendix. These tags appear in pairs.

Example: <center>This line is centered.</center>

You can place <br> at the end of lines or paragraphs as a page-break tag. Everything after the tag appears on lines below the tag. This tag is needed since browsers ignore end-of-line characters in raw HTML text, because end-of-line characters are different on the Macintosh, Unix, and Windows systems. Since browsers work with all kinds of text files from all kinds of computers, they treat conventional end-of-line characters (and sequences of these characters or spaces) as if they were a single space. If you need a line break you must supply it. This tag does not need an ending tag.

Example: This is line one.
This is line two.
This is line three.

Page Attributes

Page attributes are HTML tags that tell the browser how to build the page. For example, you can tell the browser what background color to use for the page, what to write in the title bar across the top of a browser, and so on. The most common page attribute tags follow.

<html>...</html>

Put all of your text and HTML tags between these two tags. In other words, place the <html> at the top of the document and </html> at the end of the document. Note that HTML/OS programming can appear above and below these tags. The `<html>` and `</html>` tags surround the display portion of the page.

<title>...</ title>

Follow the `<html>` tag with a line of text between the `<title>` and `</title>` tags. This is the text you want to appear in the title bar of a visitor's browser. If you do not define a title for your document, browsers will either leave the title line blank or use your document name as the title.

Example: `<title>Home Page</title>`

<body bgcolor=color> or <body background="image">

Follow the `<title>...</title>` line with one of these two tags if you want a background color or image for the page. When specifying an image file, use a URL or a filename. Only `.gif` or `.jpg` image types are supported universally on the Web. This tag does not need an ending tag.

Example 1: `<body background="/images/mylogos.gif">`
Example 2: `<body bgcolor=white>`

HTML Tables

HTML enables users to organize information in grids with rows and columns, meaning in tables. To accomplish this, you need three kinds of tags: you use a `<table>` tag to surround the entire grid, a `<tr>` tag to surround each row of a table, and a `<td>` tag to surround a cell containing data in the table. `<table>` tags surround `<tr>` tags, which surround `<td>` tags, which surround text, images, and content on the page. The following sections discuss each of these tags in more detail.

<table border=border bgcolor=color>...</table>

The `<table>` and `</table>` tags are the starting and ending tags for a whole table. The border attribute in the tag sets the width of the border around the grid. Note that this pair of tags must surround one or more table row and end table row tags, as described in the following section. These tags appear in pairs.

<tr bgcolor=color>...</tr>

The `<tr>` and `</tr>` tags are the starting and ending tags for rows in a table. The `bgcolor` attribute sets the background color for all of the cells in the row. It overrides any `bgcolor` setting specified in the table tag. That is, a row's `bgcolor` attribute defines the color for the current row, while the table's `bgcolor` attribute defines the color for remaining rows. Note that this pair of tags must surround one or more table cell tags, as described in the next section. These tags appear in pairs.

<td align=*value* valign=*value* color=*color*>...</td>

The `<td>` and `</td>` tags are the starting and ending tags for a cell in a row in a table. The `bgcolor` attribute sets the background of the cell. It overrides any `bgcolor` setting specified in the table row or table tags. These tags appear in pairs.

    Example:
```
<table border=1>
    <tr><td>Cell 1</td><td>Cell 2</td></tr>
    <tr><td>Cell 3</td><td>Cell 4</td></tr>
    </table>
```

Links and Images

Perhaps the most important aspect of HTML documents is their ability to contain hypertext links and images. After all, the acronym HTML stands for HyperText Markup Language. Here you learn how to write links and embed images in documents.

<img border=*border* src=*"image"*>

You use the `<img>` tag to display images inside a document. The image is the name of the image you want to display. The border sets up a border around the image. Setting it to `0` removes any border. This tag does not need an ending tag.

    Example: `<img border=0 src="/images/logo.gif">`

<a href=*"LINK"*>...</a>

The `href` tag is called a hypertext link. When you place it and its closing tag around text, a browser makes it a link to the specified file. By default the link displays as blue, underlined text. HTML also allows you to place images between these tags. Click the text or image between the tags and the browser changes the document to the one specified. In HTML/OS, the link can be the name of an HTML document, a URL to a page somewhere else on the Web, or a link to an on-click Overlay at the bottom of the same Web page.

    Example: `<a href="/work/cart.html" >View Shopping Cart</a>`

Further Reading

Visit sites like **Yahoo!** (http://www.yahoo.com/) to see how other sites write their HTML pages. Also, you may wish to look at the following books on the subject.

Chuck Musciano and Bill Kennedy. *HTML and XHTML: The Definitive Guide,* Second Edition (O'Reilly & Associates, 2000) ISBN 059600026X.

Steve James and Ed Tittel. *HTML for Dummies, Third Edition* (Hungry Minds, Inc., 1997) ISBN 076450214X.

The Next Generation: Web-Based Products

This appendix digresses from the book's main purpose, which is the development of your Web-construction skills. Here you learn how to build commercially salable products that run across the Web.

The ability to build a Web-based product and sell it to any business on the Web represents a huge opportunity for developers. But the systems-integration approach to Web development, as discussed in the "Legacy Beast" section of Chapter 1, *Introduction*, is once again a problem. Whereas systems integration creates development complexities, upgrade problems, and reliability nightmares, that pales in comparison to the complexities encountered by Web developers interested in creating products that run not only on their own equipment, but also across the wide spectrum of environments on the Web. Most Web developers encounter so many installation and compatibility problems that they find they cannot sell their products at all. They literally give up and opt instead to rent their applications rather than sell them. This model of renting software is known as the application service providers (ASP) model. Unfortunately, this way of providing software (no matter how financially attractive it may appear) is not attractive to customers who dislike the pay-forever model of computing. Given a choice to buy or rent, many would rather buy. There is historical precedent for this as mentioned in the accompanying "Is History Repeating Itself?" note.

Is History Repeating Itself?—*Prior to 1985 most corporate software was rented and hosted on large time-sharing computers. Why did companies rent software? Because, like today, development was too costly and packaged solutions were not yet available. In 1985 the industry suddenly collapsed when these billion dollar companies could no longer compete with the new generation of young software developers selling vertical solutions for just about every industry segment. Will application service providers suffer the same fate as these timer-sharing companies? Only history can answer this question.*

In this appendix you learn how to build Web-based products people can buy and install on their own equipment or their own hosting accounts. First you look at the development precautions you need to take. Then you are shown how to package a product using Bundle Bee, a wizard that walks you through a dozen steps, from defining the icon for your application to defining which files should be copy-protected. By the end of this appendix you'll know how to build Web-based products that can be run anywhere on the Web.

Preparing Your Product

When building a Web-based software product, you follow the same steps you follow when you build any advanced Web site except that you design your Web pages so they satisfy the following requirements:

- The Web pages must be installable into any directory.
- The Web pages must be configurable by the user.
- The Web pages must *not* contain server-specific components.

The first requirement, that the users must be able to install Web pages into any directory, is needed since the HTML/OS installer gives users of HTML/OS the ability to set their own installation directory. When users install your set of documents, they may place them in any directory, so you need to design them to run from any directory. To do so, you simply need to specify directory, file, and database names with relative paths. You should not use absolute references to filenames.

The second requirement, that the user must be able to configure the Web pages, is needed since one product must serve many different customers. Parts of Web pages with customer-specific information must be placed in text files or databases. You must give the user the ability to change those settings using settings or configuration pages.

The last requirement, that Web pages must *not* contain server-specific components, is needed so the product runs on any kind of platform. In general this is an easy requirement to satisfy since HTML/OS tags, in general, do not contain server-specific parameters. Such parameters, like the name of an outgoing mail server, are defined in the HTML/OS Control Panel, not in your application. However, when it comes to file naming, it is important to realize that Unix and Linux file systems are case sensitive, whereas the Windows system is not. To ensure your application works the same across these different file systems, it's a good idea to use only lower-case filenames.

Once you have completed a set of Web pages satisfying these requirements, you can bundle the files into a single file that users can install with the Install option in the HTML/OS Control Panel. To do this you use an application called Bundle Bee. The product produced by Bundle Bee is a single binary file that can be transported across the Web and installed on any copy of HTML/OS, regardless of the server configuration or server hardware.

To understand the process of building a Web-based software product let's follow the packaging of a Web-based game called Aestiva Landmines. The game is shown in Figure C.1.

Figure C.1: Landmines is a Web-based software product packaged with Bundle Bee.

The files and directories for the game can be found in the /apps/bundlebee/ sample directory. Copy them to the /apps/mygame directory. A total of seven files are used in the game. They are as follows:

- mines.html
- lib/functions.lib
- lib/genmines.lib
- gifs/app_icon_landmines.gif
- gifs/landminelogo.gif
- gifs/mine.gif
- gifs/minehit.gif

Note how the files are organized. These pages use the following conventions. While these conventions are optional, they are recommended since they help make your application tidy and easy to manage:

- Place images in their own directory. Name the directory gifs or images.
- Place files containing functions in a lib directory. Give each a .lib extension.
- Place databases in their own directory. Name the directory dbs or data.
- Place product settings files in their own directory. Name it settings or lib/settings.
- Place the entry document in the highest-level directory of the product. Clear the directory of other files, so it contains only the entry document, other subdirectories, and perhaps a *ReadMe* file.

- Use lowercase file and directory names.
- Put the word `icon` in the name of the image for your product's icon image.

Using Bundle Bee

After you set up and test your files, you're ready to bundle them into a product with the Bundle Bee program as follows:

1. Click the Bundle Bee icon on the HTML/OS desktop.
2. Click **Bundle** on the Bundle Bee menu bar. This will provide you the first screen of Bundle Bee's Application Bundling Wizard. The wizard allows you to step through the process of creating a product.
3. First you determine the base directory for the files of your product. All product files must be in this directory. The Landmines game files are stored in the /apps/mygame directory, so that is your base directory. Change to that directory. You should now see a screen like that shown in Figure C.2.

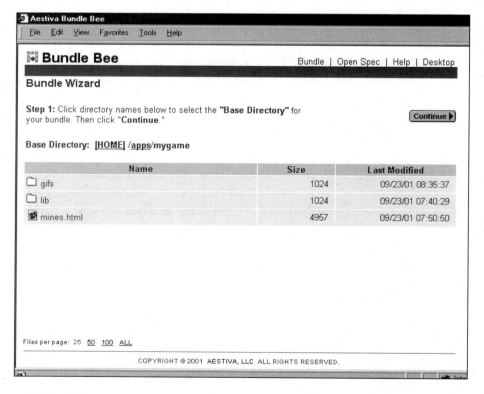

Figure C.2: When packaging a product you first select your base directory.

4. Click **Continue.** Here you select the files in /apps/mygame that you want in your product. Since you wish to include all the files click **All.** This will place all the files and directories in /apps/mygame into a Bundle List—shown on the right side of the page. You should now see a screen like that shown in Figure C.3. Click **Continue.**

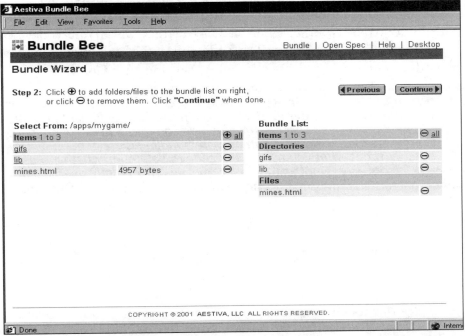

Figure C.3: Your next step in packaging a product is selecting the files to place in your product.

5. Now you select the image for your HTML/OS desktop icon. If you already have one, select that. If not, use the Select From System Icons link and click **Continue.**

6. You will be asked to enter the desktop title for the icon. Enter Land Mines and click **Continue.**

7. The wizard asks you which HTML document to use as your entry document. Select mines.html and click **Continue.**

8. Next you select files that should not be overwritten at installation time. This is where you select settings and configuration files so your users can safely install the bundle on top of a pre-existing version of your product without disrupting the user's product settings. All files you select here will

not be installed if they already exist. The Landmines product has no settings or configuration files, so click **Continue**.

9. Now the Bundle Bee Wizard asks for a product code, which Bundle Bee uses when copy-protecting products. If you decide to restrict access to your product with a product registration key, you must enter the product code, along with a product registration key, in the HTML/OS Control Panel when you install the product. If you don't correctly enter the product code and registration key, your program can detect that within the code. See the accompanying note "Adding Product Registration Keys." For this Landmines product, enter the product code landmines and click **Continue**.

Adding Product Registration Keys—*Registration keys are multidigit numbers a user must enter into the Register Product option in the Control Panel to run products that check for these keys. The registration key can be generated on a copy of HTML/OS registered to the domain name where bundling is done, but not elsewhere. The* ISGOODKEY *tag is what you use in your code to determine whether a user has a valid key. If* ISGOODKEY *is not* TRUE, *for example, you can limit specific features or display an unregistered message. As an example, consider the following Underlay:*

```
<<
IF ISGOODKEY != "TRUE"
THEN GOTO "register.html"
/IF
>>
```

You can place this code at the top of the entrance document of the application. It directs unregistered users to register.html. Note that product registration is only useful if the Web pages in your product are copy-protected (stopping users from being able to view or modify the source code of your application). Copy protection is done in Step 11 of the procedure in the main text of this section.

---

10. Next you set the default install directory for your application. Note that this is the suggested install directory. It is not necessarily where your application will run, since the user can change this at installation time. That is why it is important to design your application so it can run from any directory. Also note that you should not necessarily set this directory to the directory where the source files are located. Enter /apps/landmines and click **Continue**. The users installing this application will see this as their default installation directory. By convention, products are installed in a subdirectory of the /apps directory. The word *apps* is short for applications.

11. Next you select the extensions of files that should be copy-protected. By default, Bundle Bee copy protects files with .html, .htm, and .lib extensions. Copy protection is a method of encrypting documents so they

cannot be viewed. In HTML/OS this is known as *scrambling*. The HTML/OS Professional engine can run either source code or scrambled documents. The HTML/OS Runtime engine, as discussed in the section "The Runtime Engine," later in this appendix, can run only scrambled pages. Select the .html, .htm, and .lib extensions and click **Continue**.

12. Next you select the HTML/OS desktop menu for your product's icon. You may want your application icon to be placed in its own menu. Or, if you leave the setting blank, your product icon will be installed in the Main Menu. Note that products can contain other bundled products. If this occurs, the HTML/OS installer, at installation time, will install all the icons in the menu you select here. Click **Continue** since you do not need to build a custom menu.

13. You'll see the last setting page. Here the wizard asks you to enter a filename for your product file. By convention, product files are given the .bb file extension. Enter a filename and click **Continue**. You'll be placed on a summary screen that shows all the settings you've entered for your product. To go back and make changes to the specifications of your bundle, click the **edit link** next to the setting you wish to modify. This summary screen is shown in Figure C.4.

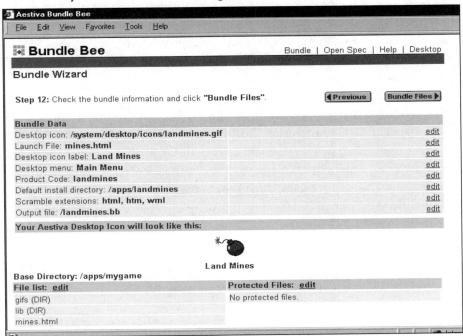

Figure C.4: Before final bundling you can review your settings and make necessary changes.

14. To complete the bundling process, click **Bundle Files**. Bundle Bee will ask you whether you wish to save the settings for the future and then bundle your files into a single file or bundle. This usually takes a few seconds. When done, you have a product that can be installed onto any copy of HTML/OS.

Further information on building registered copy-protected software is available in the on-line help pop-up box in the Bundle Bee application. There you'll find complete descriptions of the previous steps.

Installing a Product—*To install a Bundle Bee file use the Install option in the HTML/OS Control Panel. Click* Control Panel *from the menu bar on your HTML/OS desktop. Select* Install. *Then click* Install Product. *You can then upload a Bundle Bee file or browse the HTML/OS file system for one. After selecting a Bundle Bee file, click* Install. *When installation is complete you'll get a successful installation message. You can now return to the HTML/OS desktop to view the icon for your new product and run it.*

The Runtime Engine

The HTML/OS engine comes in two versions: the Professional and the Runtime editions. The Professional edition is discussed throughout this book. The Runtime edition is a version of the engine designed specifically for running Web-based software products. It can run copy-protected applications that have been scrambled with Bundle Bee. The Runtime engine cannot run HTML documents with Overlays in them.

The Runtime edition of HTML/OS is generally what you want to distribute with your product. It is less costly than the Professional edition and runs only scrambled applications. It includes the standard HTML/OS Control Panel for configuring e-mail and security settings, and dbConsole, which is convenient, because it gives customers open access to the databases within your product. The ability to import and export data from databases in your product makes it more open, accessible, and easier to interface with other Web-based products.

HTML/OS Tag Reference Guide

This appendix provides each HTML Overlay tag used in this book. Each tag includes a general description of the tag, its parameters, the output returned by the tag, and values placed in TAGRESULTS, and error status variable, if any.

Each description includes a "See Also" entry that lists related tags that may or may not appear in this appendix. Related tags that don't appear in this book are marked with an asterisk. If further options are available other than those described in this appendix, then the "See Also" entry will refer to other options for the tag. Such additional options are listed in the Official HTML/OS Tag Reference. This official reference is included with purchase of HTML/OS Professional. The additional options and related tags are also available in the knowledge base on the **Aestiva** Web site at http://www.aestiva.com/support/.

The appendix begins by listing tag names by category. Thereafter, Overlay tag descriptions are listed alphabetically.

Tag Names By Category

The following are those HTML/OS Overlay tags that are used in this book grouped by categories. For a complete list of Overlay tags see the HTML/OS tag Reference provided with purchase of HTML/OS.

Learn These First

This section includes the HTML/OS tags you should know like the back of your hand. Other tags can be referenced as needed.

```
APPEND.../APPEND          IF-THEN
COPY.../COPY              LAYOUT
DISPLAY.../DISPLAY        MAIL.../MAIL
FOR.../FOR                PAGE
GOTO                      ROW
```

Text Processing
Text processing tags work with sequences of text characters.

CUT	LOWER
CUTALL	MIDDLE
FORMAT	REPLACE
LEFT	REPLACEALL
LENGTH	RIGHT
LOCATE	TRIM

Table Operations
Table operations tags work with arrays—variables containing one or more rows and columns.

APPEND.../APPEND	LAYOUT
COLTOLIST	LISTTOCOL
GETCOLBEGIN	MERGE
GETCOLEQ	ROW
GETCOLNOTEQ	SUMCOL
GETTABLE	

Database
Database tags work with databases.

DBADD	DBFINDSORT
DBDELETE	DBGET
DBEDIT	DBGETREC
DBFIND	DBREMOVE
DBFINDJ	DBUNIQUE

File System
File system tags work with files and directories in the Web file system.

APPEND.../APPEND	ISDIR
COPY.../COPY	SYSMV
FILELIST	SYSRM
ISFILE	

Programming

You use programming tags for conditionals and loops, and when performing tests, debugging, and working with special characters.

COOKIEREAD	ISMOD10
COOKIEWRITE	ISNUMBER
COUNT	LF
CR	MAX
EXPAND.../EXPAND	RANDOM
FOR.../FOR	ROUNDDOWN
FUNCTION	ROUNDUP
IF-THEN	TAB
ISGOODKEY	TRACE
ISINTEGER	WHILE.../WHILE

Date and Time

Date and time tags work with dates and time.

ADDDAYS	ISWEEKDAY
GETDATE	TIMEFROM
ISDATE	TODAY

Alphabetical Listing

The following are the HTML/OS Overlay tags that are used in this book grouped alphabetically. Each description includes the name and usage of the tag, the parameters used by the tag (known as params), a tag example, and a list of related tags, if any. For complete list of Overlay tags, see the HTML/OS Tag Reference provided with purchase of HTML/OS.

ADDDAYS

Returns the date offset from the specified input date by a number of days.

Usage: `ADDDAYS(date,days)`

Params: *date*——any valid date after 1970

                  days——number of days to add. Negative numbers allowed

Example: `nextweek=ADDDAYS(today,"7")`

See also: `ADDHOURS*, ADDMINUTES*`

APPEND.../APPEND

Appends the variable to a variable, document, or delimited file.

Usage:	`APPEND variable TO variable2 /APPEND`
	`APPEND variable TO FILE=file /APPEND`
	`APPEND variable TO FILE=file TS=delimiter /APPEND`
Params:	*variable*—input variable being appended to variable, document or file
	variable2—input/output variable. *variable1* is added as new rows to end of *variable2*
	file—input/output file
	delimiter—delimiter of file. When specified, *variable1* is appended as new rows to file. When it is not, *variable1* is appended as text to end of file
Example:	`APPEND PAGE TO myhistory /APPEND`
	`APPEND PAGE+LF TO FILE="pagelog.txt" /APPEND`
	`APPEND PAGE TO FILE="pagelog.txt" TS="," /APPEND`
See also:	Other `APPEND` options*, `MERGE`, `GETTABLE`

COLTOLIST

Converts a column in variable to a delimited list.

Usage:	`COLTOLIST(variable,col,delimiter)`
Params:	*variable*—input table
	col—column number in variable to convert
	delimiter —character separator
Example:	`scores=COLTOLIST (results,3,",")`
See also:	`LISTTOCOL`, `SPLIT*`, `ROWTOLIST*`, `TABLETOLIST*`

COOKIEREAD

Reads cookie variable from an HTML cookie.

Usage:	`COOKIEREAD(cookie_var)`
Params:	*cookie_var*——name of cookie variable
Example:	`no_cols=COOKIEREAD("windowsize")`
See also:	`COOKIEWRITE`

COOKIEWRITE

Writes to HTML cookie variable.

Usage:	`COOKIEWRITE(cookie_var,cookie_value,expiration)`
Params:	*cookie_var*—name of cookie variable
	cookie_value—value to write to *cookie_var*
	expiration—expiration date of cookie

Example: `stat=COOKIEWRITE("windowsize",no_cols`
`,ADDDAYS(today,100))`

See also: Other `COOKIEWRITE*` options, `COOKIEREAD`, and the "Using Cookies" section of Chapter 8, *Building Text Editors*.

COPY.../COPY

Copies a source variable, document, or delimited file to a destination variable, document, or delimited file.

Usage: `COPY source TO destination /COPY`

Params: *source*—the source variable, document, or delimited file where document is specified as `FILE=filename` and delimited file is specified as `FILE=filename TS=delimiter`
destination—the destination variable, document, or delimited file where the document is specified as `FILE=filename` and delimited file is specified as `FILE=filename TS=delimiter`

Example: `COPY myresults TO FILE="data.txt" /COPY`
`COPY FILE="data.txt" TO myresults /COPY`
`COPY mycart TO FILE="cart.txt" TS="," /COPY`

See also: Other `COPY` options*, `APPEND`

COUNT

Returns the number of matches of a pattern in the string.

Usage: `COUNT(variable,pattern)`

Params: *variable*—input text
pattern—pattern being searched

Example: `no_dots=COUNT(mydata,".")`

See also: `COUNTX*`, `LOCATE`

CR

Returns the carriage-return end-of-line character (ASCII 13).

Usage: `CR`

Example: `x=x+CR+LF`

See also: `LF`, `TAB`, `ASCII*`, `GETASCII*`

CUT

Removes first match of pattern from string.

Usage: `CUT(variable,pattern)`

Params: *variable*—input text
pattern—pattern being cut

Example:	x=CUT(x,"~")
See also:	CUTALL, CUTX*, CUTALLX*

CUTALL

Removes all the pattern matches from the string.

Usage:	CUTALL(*variable*,*pattern*)
Params:	*variable*—input text
	pattern—pattern being cut from text
Example:	x=CUTALL(x, "<")
See also:	CUT, CUTX*, CUTALLX*

DBADD

Adds a new record to a database using current variables. Returns a status result.

Usage:	DBADD(*dbname*)
	DBADD(*dbname*,*fieldlist*)
Params:	*dbname*—database name
	fieldlist—specific fields to place in record. If *fieldlist* is specified, only those fields in the list are placed in the record
Status:	[1,1]—TRUE or FALSE
	[1,2]—OK or error message
	[2,1]—record number of record added
Example:	stat=DBADD("/apps/work/db/mydb")
	record_added=TAGRESULTS[2,1]
See also:	DBDELETE, DBEDIT, and the "Eight-Line Database Editor" section of Chapter 11, *The Web Database.*

DBDELETE

Deletes a record from database. Returns a status result.

Usage:	DBDELETE(*dbname*,*record*)
Params:	*dbname*—database name
	record—record number of record to remove
Status:	[1,1]—TRUE or FALSE
	[1,2]—OK or error message
Example:	stat=DBDELETE("/apps/work/db/mydb",43)
See also:	DBADD, DBEDIT

DBEDIT

Updates a record in database. Returns a status result.

Usage:	DBEDIT(*dbname*,*record*)
	DBEDIT(*dbname*,*record*,*fieldlist*)
Params:	*dbname*—database name
	record—record number of record to remove
	fieldlist—specific fields to change in record. If *fieldlist* is specified, only those fields in the list are updated
Status:	[1,1]—TRUE or FALSE
	[1,2]—OK or error message
Example:	stat=DBEDIT("/apps/work/db/mydb",43)
See also:	DBADD, DBDELETE, and the "Eight-Line Database Editor" section of Chapter 11, *The Web Database*

DBFIND

Retrieves records from a database. Returns the result in table. Places the status result in TAGRESULTS.

Usage:	DBFIND(*dbname*,*query*,*from*,*to*,*fieldlist*)
Params:	*dbname*—database name
	query—Boolean search expression
	from—number of first result to return
	to—number of last result to return
	fieldlist—specific fields to return from database. Each record returned is placed in a different row. Each field is placed in a column based on its order in the field list
Status:	TAGRESULTS[1,1]—TRUE or FALSE
	TAGRESULTS[2,1]—number of records returned
	TAGRESULTS[3,1]—first match number returned
	TAGRESULTS[4,1]—last match number returned
	TAGRESULTS[5,1]—total matches in database
	TAGRESULTS[1,2]—OK or error message
Example:	data1=DBFIND("db1","age>21",1,50,"fullname,usrid")
See also:	Other DBFIND options*, DBFINDSORT, DBSEARCH*, DBSEARCHSORT*, DBFINDJ, and the "The Query String" section of Chapter 12, *Building Query Pages*

DBFINDJ

Retrieves records from a database, joining with prior search result. Returns result in table. Places a status result in TAGRESULTS.

Usage:	DBFINDJ(dbname,query,from,to,fieldlist,results,col,field)
Params:	*dbname*—database name
	query—Boolean search expression

	from—number of first result to return
	to—number of last result to return
	results—search result table
	col—join column in results table
	field—join field in database
Status:	TAGRESULTS[1,1]—TRUE or FALSE
	TAGRESULTS[2,1]—number of records returned
	TAGRESULTS[3,1]—first match number returned
	TAGRESULTS[4,1]—last match number returned
	TAGRESULTS[5,1]—total matches in database
	TAGRESULTS[1,2]—OK or error message
Example:	data2=DBFINDJ("db2","salary>25",1,50,"",data,r1,1,"usrid")
See also:	Other DBFINDJ options*, DBFIND, DBFINDSORT, DBSEARCH*, DBSEARCHSORT*, and the "On-the-Fly Joins" section of Chapter 12, *Building Query Pages*

DBFINDSORT

Retrieves records from a database sorted by field. Returns the result in table. Places the status result in TAGRESULTS.

Usage:	DBFINDSORT(*dbname,query,from,to,fieldlist,sfield,order*)
Params:	*dbname*—database name
	query—Boolean search expression
	from—number of first result to return
	to—number of last result to return
	fieldlist—specific fields to return from database. Each record returned is placed in a different row. Each field is placed in a column based on its order in the field list
	sfield—sort field
	order—sort order, "Y" or "N"
Status:	TAGRESULTS[1,1]—TRUE or FALSE
	TAGRESULTS[2,1]—number of records returned
	TAGRESULTS[3,1]—first match number returned
	TAGRESULTS[4,1]—last match number returned
	TAGRESULTS[5,1]—total matches in database
	TAGRESULTS[1,2]—OK or error message
Example:	data1=DBFIND("db1","age>21",1,50,"fullname,usrid")
See also:	Other DBFINDSORT options*, DBFIND, DBSEARCH*, DBSEARCHSORT*, DBFINDJ

DBGET

Updates current variables from a queried record in a database. Returns status result.

Usage: DBGET(`dbname`,`query`,`num`)
Params: *dbname*—database name
              query—Boolean search expression
              num—result number to return
Status: [1,1]—TRUE or FALSE
              [2,1]—number of records returned
              [3,1]—first match number returned
              [4,1]—last match number returned
              [5,1]—total matches in database
              [1,2]—OK or error message
Example: stat=DBGET("/apps/work/db/mydb","usrid=abc",1)
See also: Other DBGET options*, DBGETSORT*, DBGETREC

DBGETREC

Updates current variables from a record in a database. Returns a status result.

Usage: DBGETREC(`dbname`,`record`)
Params: *dbname*—database name
              record—database record to remove
Status: [1,1]—TRUE or FALSE
              [1,2]—OK or error message
Example: stat=DBGETREC("/apps/work/db/mydb",43)
See also: Other DBGETREC options*, DBGETSORT*, DBGET, and the "Eight-Line Database Editor" section of Chapter 11, *The Web Database*

DBREMOVE

Deletes queried records from a database. Returns a status result.

Usage: DBREMOVE(`dbname`,`query`)
Params: *dbname*—database name
              query—Boolean search expression
Status: [1,1]—TRUE or FALSE
              [2,1]—total number of records deleted
              [1,2]—OK or error message
Example: stat=DBREMOVE("/db/myusers","usrid=abc")
See also: DBDELETE

DBUNIQUE

Retrieves unique values for a field from queried records in a database. Returns results in a column. Places the status result `TAGRESULTS`.

Usage:	`DBUNIQUE(`*`dbname`*`,`*`query`*`,`*`field`*`)`
Params:	*dbname*—database name
	query—Boolean search expression
	field—name of field
Status:	`TAGRESULTS[1,1]`—`TRUE` or `FALSE`
	`TAGRESULTS[1,2]`—`OK` or error message
Example:	`data1=DBUNIQUE("db1","","category_names")`
See also:	`DBFIND`

DISPLAY.../DISPLAY

Inserts text into an HTML document.

Usage:	`DISPLAY variable /DISPLAY`
	`DISPLAY FILE=`*`file`*` /DISPLAY`
Params:	*variable*—input variable being displayed
	file—filename. When specified, contents of file are inserted into document
Example:	`DISPLAY "Hello World" /DISPLAY`
	`DISPLAY FILE="myheader.txt" /DISPLAY`
See also:	Other `DISPLAY options*`, `EXITDISPLAY*`

EXPAND.../EXPAND

Expands HTML/OS code into an Overlay from file.

Usage:	`EXPAND FILE=`*`file`*` /EXPAND`
Params:	*file*—filename. Contents of the file are inserted into the current Overlay from file and executed
Example:	`EXPAND FILE="mylibrary.txt" /DISPLAY`
See also:	Other `EXPAND options*`

FILELIST

Lists the files in a directory. Returns list of files in a five-column table. Column 1 contains file or directory names. Column 2 contains file size in bytes. Column 3 contains last modification time. Column 4 contains file type (`FILE`, `DIR`). Column 5 contains the file area (`PRIVATE`, `PUBLIC`, `MIRROR`).

Usage:	`FILELIST(directory)`
Params:	*directory*—directory path listed

Example: `myimages=FILELIST("/work/images")`
See also: `FILEINFO`

FOR.../FOR

Repeats instructions as integer increments from one value to another. Compare also with next listing.

Usage: `FOR NAME=integer VALUE = value1 TO value2 DO`
               `instructions /FOR`

Params: *integer*—variable being changed
               value1—first value of integer
               value2—last value of integer
               instructions—HTML/OS instructions repeated

Example: `FOR NAME=i VALUE=1 TO 10 DO sum=sum+a[i] /FOR`
See also: Other `FOR` options*, `BREAK`*, `CONTINUE`*, `FOR`, `WHILE`, `CASE`, and the "Working with Loops" section of Chapter 6, *Variables, Conditionals, and Loops*

FOR.../FOR

Repeats instructions as row increments from top row of table to bottom row of table. Compare with the preceding listing.

Usage: `FOR NAME=variable ROWNAME=rowvar DO instructions /FOR`
Params: *variable*—table being looped across
               rowvar—name of table containing one row from *variable*
               instructions—HTML/OS instructions repeated

Example: `sum=0 FOR NAME=mycart ROWNAME=x DO  sum=sum+x[5] /FOR`
See also: Other `FOR` options*, `BREAK`*, `CONTINUE`*, `FOR`, `WHILE`, `CASE` and the "Working with Loops" section of Chapter 6, *Variables, Conditionals, and Loops*

FORMAT

Returns number reformatted based on specified format. Formats supported include `normal`, `comma`, `ledger`, and `percent`.

Usage: `FORMAT(number, format)`
               `FORMAT(number, format, decimals)`

Params: *number*—input number
               format—format type
               decimals—number of decimal places to return. When not specified defaults are used

Example: `DISPLAY FORMAT(mytotal,"comma",2) /DISPLAY`
See also: `ROUNDSIG`*

FUNCTION
Defines a function (Overlay Tag).

Usage: FUNCTION *otag(param,param...)* DO *instructions* RETURN
        variable /RETURN /FUNCTION

Params: *otag*—name of Overlay tag (function) being defined
         param—temporary name of function parameters
         instructions—instructions to be executed when function is run
         variable—variable returned by function

Example: FUNCTION bold(x) DO x=""+x+"" RETURN x /RETURN
          /FUNCTION

See also: Other FUNCTION options*, LOCALS*, EXPAND

GETCOLBEGIN
Extracts from multirow variable those rows with a column entry that begins with a pattern. Returns table with matching rows.

Usage: GETCOLBEGIN(*variable,col,pattern*)

Params: *variable*—input table
         col—column to match
         pattern—string to match to entry in column

Example: filesinwork=GETCOLBEGIN (myfiles,1,"/work/")

See also: GETCOLEND*, GETCOLNOTEND*, GETCOLEQ, GETCOLNOTEQ

GETCOLEQ
Extracts from multirow variable those rows with a column entry that equals a pattern. Returns table with matching rows.

Usage: GETCOLEQ(*variable,col,pattern*)

Params: *variable*—input table
         col—column to match.
         pattern—string to match to entry in column

Example: userdata=GETCOLEQ(loginfile,1,loginid)

See also: GETCOLEND*, GETCOLNOTEND*, GETCOLBEGIN, GETCOLNOTEQ

GETCOLNOTEQ
Extracts from multirow variable those rows with a column entry that does not equal a pattern. Returns table with nonmatching rows.

Usage: GETCOLEQ(*variable,col,pattern*)

Params: *variable*—input table
         col—column to search
         pattern—string to match to entry in column

Example: `mycart=GETCOLNOTEQ(mycart,1,sku)`
See also: `GETCOLEND*, GETCOLNOTEND*, GETCOLBEGIN, GETCOLEQ`

GETDATE

Returns a date in a specified format.
Usage: `GETDATE(date,format)`
Params: *date*—input date
              format—display format. SHORT, LONG, and NORMAL formats supported
Example: `DISPLAY GETDATE(today,"LONG") /DISPLAY`
See also: `GETDAY*, GETMONTH*, GETYEAR*, GETHOUR*, GETTIME*`

GETTABLE

Extracts a subtable from a table. Returns a subtable.
Usage: `GETTABLE(variable,col1,col2,row1,row2)`
Params: *variable*—input table
              `col1`–left most column to extract
              `col2`—right most column to extract
              `row1`—top row to extract
              `row2`—bottom row to extract
Example: `userdata=GETTABLE(mytable,1,5,1,220)`
See also: `GETCOLEQ, GETCOLNOTEQ`

GOTO

Continues the execution of code at top of specified file if the destination is a filename. Takes the user to a Web location if destination is a URL.
Usage: `GOTO destination`
Params: *destination*—URL or filename
Example: `GOTO PAGE`

IF-THEN

Executes instructions between THEN (and /IF, ELSE, or ELIF, respectively) if test returns TRUE, otherwise skips instructions and executes instructions between ELSE and /IF (if ELSE is specified) or performs next test (if ELIF is specified).
Usage: `IF test THEN instructions /IF`
              `IF test THEN instructions ELSE instructions /IF`
              `IF test THEN instructions ELIF test THEN`
              `instructions /IF`
Params: *test*—expression or Boolean test
              instructions—HTML/OS instructions being conditionally executed

Example: IF ISWEEKEND(today) THEN GOTO "home_weekend.html" /IF
              IF Age >= 21 THEN GOTO "home_weekend.html" /IF
See also: Other IF-THEN options*, BREAK*

ISDATE

Returns TRUE if the string is a proper HTML/OS date. Otherwise returns FALSE.
Usage: ISDATE(variable)
Params: variable—input variable
Example: IF ISDATE(mydate)="FALSE" THEN msg="Bad Date" /IF
See also: ISPAST*, ISFUTURE*, ISTODAY*, ISWEEKDAY, ISWEEKEND*

ISFILE

Returns TRUE if a file exists. Otherwise returns FALSE.
Usage: ISFILE(file)
Params: file—name of file
Example: IF ISFILE(myimg) THEN DISPLAY "<img src="+myimg+">"
              /DISPLAY /IF
See also: ISDIR

ISDIR

Returns TRUE if the directory is valid. Otherwise returns FALSE.
Usage: ISDIR(directory)
Params: directory—name of file
Example: IF ISDIR(myhome) THEN GOTO myhome+"/index.html" /IF
See also: ISFILE

ISGOODKEY

Returns TRUE if a valid product has been registered. Otherwise returns FALSE.
Usage: ISGOODKEY
Example: IF ISGOODKEY="FALSE" THEN GOTO "notice.html" /IF
See also: Other ISGOODKEY options*

ISINTEGER

Returns TRUE if input is a valid integer. Otherwise returns FALSE.
Usage: ISINTEGER(variable)
Params: variable—input variable
Example: IF ISINTEGER(age)="FALSE" THEN GOTO homepage /IF
See also: ISNUMBER, ISEVEN*, ISODD*

ISMOD10

Returns TRUE if variable passes "Mod 10" credit card test. Otherwise returns FALSE.

Usage: ISMOD10(*variable*)

Params: *variable*—input credit card number (no spaces or special characters)

Example: IF ISMOD10(mycard)!="TRUE" THEN msg="Bad Credit Card"
             /IF

See also: ISNUMBER, ISEVEN*, ISODD*

ISNUMBER

Returns TRUE if input is a valid number. Otherwise returns FALSE.

Usage: ISNUMBER(*variable*)

Params: *variable*—input number

Example: IF ISNUMBER(taxrate)="FALSE" THEN msg="Bad Tax Rate"
             /IF

See also: ISINTEGER, ISEVEN*, ISODD*

ISWEEKDAY

Returns TRUE if date falls on a weekday between Monday and Friday. Otherwise returns FALSE.

Usage: ISWEEKDAY(*variable*)

Params: *variable*—input date

Example: IF ISDATE(mydate)="FALSE" THEN msg="Bad Date" /IF

See also: ISPAST*, ISFUTURE*, ISTODAY*, ISWEEKEND*

LAYOUT

Returns a table based on input table and list of columns.

Usage: LAYOUT(*variable*,*col*,*col*,...)

Params: *variable*—input table

Params: *col*–contents of output column. If specified as a column number
             in square brackets, output column is taken from that column of
             the input variable. If specified as variable, entry is repeated in
             column for all rows of output

Example: mirrortable=LAYOUT(oldtable,[3],[2],[1])

See also: GETTABLE and "Using the LAYOUT Tag" section of Chapter 4,
             Your First Web Database Program

LEFT

Returns the specified left-most number of characters of a string.

Usage: `LEFT(variable,number)`
Params: *variable*—input text
             number—number of left-most characters to return
Example: `firstletter=LEFT(myname,1)`
See also: `RIGHT, MIDDLE`

LENGTH

Returns length of a character string.

Usage: `LENGTH(variable)`
Params: *variable*—input text
Example: `nochars=LENGTH(myname)`
See also: `RIGHT, MIDDLE`

LF

Returns line-feed newline character (ASCII 10).

Usage: `LF`
Example: `msg=msg+LF+LF`
See also: `CR, TAB, ASCII*, GETASCII*`

LISTTOCOL

Converts list to one-column variable.

Usage: `LISTTOCOL(variable,delimiter)`
Params: *variable*—input list
             delimiter—character separator between items in list
Example: `mycol=COLTOLIST(listofnames, ",")`
See also: `COLTOLIST, ROWTOLIST*, TABLETOLIST*, SPLIT*`

LOCATE

Returns the position of a pattern in string. Returns 0 if not found.

Usage: `LOCATE(variable,pattern)`
Params: *variable*—input text
             pattern—pattern being searched
Example: `myposition=LOCATE(mydata," ")`
See also: `LOCATEX*, COUNT, COUNTX*`

LOWER

Returns lowercase value of input string.

Usage:	`LOWER(variable)`
Params:	*variable*—input text
Example:	`myfile=LOWER(myfile)`
See also:	`UPPER*, PROPER*`

MAIL.../MAIL

E-mails message to an e-mail address.

Usage:	`MAIL variable TO ADDRESS=address SUBJECT=subject /MAIL`
Params:	*variable*—input message
	address—e-mail address
	subject—e-mail message subject line
Example:	`MAIL "This is a test" TO ADDRESS="test@test.com"`
	`SUBJECT="testing..." /MAIL`
See also:	See other `MAIL` options*, `NETMAIL*`

MAX

Returns maximum of two or more input numbers.

Usage:	`MAX(variable,variable)`
	`MAX(variable,variable,variable...)`
Params:	*variable*—input number
Example:	`myprice=MAX(shippingmax,0.05*total)`
See also:	`MIN*`

MERGE

Returns two input tables merged horizontally.

Usage:	`MERGE(variable1,variable2)`
Params:	*variable1*—input variable being merged with variable2
	variable2—input variable being merged with variable1
Example:	`fivecoltable=MERGE(2coltable,3coltable)`
See also:	`APPEND, GETTABLE`

MIDDLE

Returns substring of character string.

Usage:	`MIDDLE(variable,number1,number2)`
Params:	*variable*—input text
	number1—position in *variable* of left most character to return
	number2—position in *variable* of right most character to return

Example: `myday=MIDDLE(today,4,5)`
See also: `RIGHT, LEFT`

PAGE

Returns filename of the current page.
Usage: `PAGE`
Example: `GOTO PAGE`
See also: `DIRNAME*`

RANDOM

Returns random integer between two values.
Usage: `RANDOM(number2)`

                `RANDOM(number1,number2)`
Params: *number1*—minimum integer to return when unspecified minimum is 1

                number2—maximum integer to return
Example: `mydraw=RANDOM(100)`
See also: Math, trigonometric, and statistical tags*

REPLACE

Returns a string with pattern in an input string substituted for another.
Usage: REPLACE(*variable,pattern1,pattern2*)
Params: *variable*—input text

                pattern1—pattern being replaced (replacement done on first
                match only)

                pattern2—pattern being substituted
Example: `myletter=REPLACE(myletter,"Mister","Mr.")`
See also: `REPLACEX*, REPLACEALL, REPLACEALLX*`

REPLACEALL

Returns a string with all patterns in input string substituted for another.
Usage: `REPLACE(variable,pattern1,pattern2)`
Params: *variable*—input text

                pattern1—pattern being replaced (replacement done on all matches)

                pattern2—pattern being substituted
Example: `myletter=REPLACEALL(myletter,LF,"[LineFeed]")`
See also: `REPLACEX*, REPLACE, REPLACEALLX*`

RIGHT
Returns the specified right-most number of characters of a string.

Usage: RIGHT(*variable*,*number*)
Params: *variable*—input text
         number—number of right-most characters to return
Example: lastletter=RIGHT(myname,1)
See also: LEFT, MIDDLE

ROUNDDOWN
Returns input number rounded down to the nearest integer.

Usage: ROUNDDOWN(*variable*)
Params: *variable*—input number
Example: myprice=ROUNDDOWN(shippingmax)
See also: ROUNDUP

ROUNDUP
Returns input number rounded up to the nearest integer.

Usage: ROUNDUP(*variable*)
Params: *variable*—input number
Example: myprice=ROUNDUP(shippingmax)
See also: ROUNDDOWN

ROW
Returns a one-row table with specified columns.

Usage: ROW(*variable*,*variable*,*variable*...)
Params: *variable*—column entry
Example: mylogentry=ROW(TODAY,userid,"Saved File")
See also: GETCOLEQ, GETCOLNOTEQ

SUMCOL
Returns sum of values in a column of a table.

Usage: SUMCOL(*variable*,*col*)
Params: *variable*—input table
         col—column number to sum
Example: mytotal=SUMCOL(mycart,5)
See also: SUMSQRCOL*, MEDIANCOL*, AVECOL*

SYSMV

Renames a file and returns a status result.

Usage: `SYSMV(file1,file2)`

Params: *file1*—source filename

                   file2—destination filename

Example: `stat=SYSMV("/work/f1.html","/archive/f1.html")`

See also: `SYSCP*, SYSMD*, SYSRD*, SYSRM`

SYSRM

Deletes a file. Returns a status result.

Usage: `SYSRM(file)`

Params: *file*—filename to delete

Example: `stat=SYSRM("/work/f1.html")`

See also: `SYSCP*, SYSMD*, SYSRD*, SYSMV`

TAB

Returns a tab character (ASCII 9).

Usage: `TAB`

Example: `COPY mydata TO FILE="data.txt" TS=TAB /COPY`

See also: `LF, CR, ASCII*, GETASCII*`

TIMEFROM

Returns the number of `minutes` or `hours` since a specified time.

Usage: `TIMEFROM(variable,units)`

Params: *variable*—input date

                   units—output units (`MINUTES, HOURS`)

Example: `IF ISDATE(mydate)="FALSE" THEN msg="Bad Date" /IF`

See also: Other `TIMEFROM` options*, `TIMEBETWEEN*, TIMETILL*`

TODAY

Returns current date.

Usage: `TODAY`

Example: `DISPLAY "Today is "+TODAY /DISPLAY`

See also: `TIME*, NOW*, YESTERDAY*, TOMORROW*`

TRACE

Performs variety of debugging tasks.

Usage: `TRACE(variable)`

Params: *variable*—control variable or variable

ON–turn on variable logging

OFF–turn off variable logging

BUFFER–turn on trace buffering

IGNORE–ignore TRACE tags

variable–place variable in trace log

Example: stat=TRACE("ON")

See also: Other TRACE options*, and Chapter 7, *Debugging Techniques*

TRIM

Returns string with no leading or trailing spaces, no multiple spaces, and no line-break characters or special (unviewable) characters.

Usage: TRIM(variable)

Params: *variable*—input text

Example: mydata=TRIM(mydata)

See also: CUTALL*

WHILE

Repeats instructions as long as test returns TRUE.

Usage: WHILE test DO instructions /WHILE

Params: *test*—Boolean test

instructions—HTML/OS instructions repeated

Example: i=1 WHILE i < 5 DO sum=sum+a[i] i=i+1 /WHILE

See also: Other WHILE options*, BREAK*, FOR, CASE, and the "Working with Loops" section of Chapter 6, *Variables, Conditionals, and Loops*

**Aestiva HTML/OS
30-Day Free Trial
Pre-installed on the Web just for you!**

ACTIVATION KEY

ADW-DKW-EEF-OHX

Instructions:
1. Visit http://dev.aestiva.com/advanced
2. Enter Activation Key above.
3. Gain instant access to your pre-installed copy of Aestiva HTML/OS*

* Once on-line, see license agreement for usage limitations.

POOR RICHARD'S WEB SITE
Geek-Free, Commonsense Advice on Building a Low-Cost Web Site, 2nd Edition

Poor Richard's Web Site is the *only* book that explains the entire process of creating a Web site, from deciding whether you really need a site—and what you can do with it—through picking a place to put the site, creating the site, and bringing people to the site. It is full of commonsense advice that Amazon.com called an "antidote to this swirl of confusion" and "straightforward information." Praised by *BYTE magazine*, *Publisher's Weekly*, and *USA Today*, *Poor Richard's Web Site* can save you thousands of dollars and hundreds of hours.

❝Poor Richard's Good Advice. With all great new things comes a proliferation of hucksters and snake-oil salesmen, and the Internet is no exception. The antidote to this swirl of confusion lies in Peter Kent's *Poor Richard's Web Site*. The analogy to Ben Franklin's volume is appropriate: the book is filled with the kind of straightforward information the Founding Father himself would have appreciated."
—Amazon.com

❝We highly recommend that you get a copy."
—Marketing Technology

❝Very well written."
—Library Journal

❝Poor Richard's offers clear advice to help you defend against jargon-happy sales people and computer magazines."
—Fortune.com

Poor Richard's Web Site is available in bookstores both online and offline, and at http://www.TopFloor.com/

Poor Richard's Web Site, Second Edition
by Peter Kent   ISBN: 0-9661032-0-3

POOR RICHARD'S INTERNET MARKETING AND PROMOTIONS
How to Promote Yourself, Your Business, Your Ideas Online, 2nd Edition

Much of what you've read about marketing on the Internet is wrong: registering a Web site with the search engines *won't* create a flood of orders; banner advertising *doesn't* work for most companies; online malls *do not* push large amounts of traffic to their client Web sites. . . .

What you really need is some geek-free, commonsense advice on marketing and promoting on the Internet, by somebody's who's actually done it! Most books and articles are written by freelance writers assigned to investigate a particular subject. *Poor Richard's Internet Marketing and Promotions* is written by a small-business person who's been successfully marketing online for a decade.

Poor Richard's Internet Marketing and Promotions uses the same down-to-earth style so highly praised in *Poor Richard's Web Site.* You'll learn how to plan an Internet marketing campaign, find your target audience, use giveaways to bring people to your site, integrate an email newsletter into your promotions campaign, buy advertising that works, use real-world PR, and more.

You'll also learn to track results, by seeing who is linking to your site, by hearing who is talking about you, and by measuring visits to your site.

❝Go now as fast as you can and get this book and soon your Web site will reach the heights of the well known."

—About.com

❝This book offers readers the ability to discipline themselves and the resources they need to succeed. It's loaded!"

—The Web Reviewer

Poor Richard's Internet Marketing and Promotions
is available in bookstores both online and offline, and at
http://www.TopFloor.com/

Poor Richard's Internet Marketing and Promotions:
by Peter Kent and Tara Calishain ISBN: 1-930082-00-2

POOR RICHARD'S E-MAIL PUBLISHING

Creating Newsletters, Bulletins, Discussion Groups, and Other Powerful Communication Tools

E-mail publishing is a powerful communications medium that anyone with Internet access can use. It's cheap, effective, and very easy to use once you learn the tricks of the trade. Electronic publishing is one of the most efficient ways to promote your products or services online, as well as being an excellent way to drive traffic back to your Web site.

Poor Richard's E-mail Publishing is your complete, step-by-step, guide to the nuts and bolts of creating newsletters and discussion groups via e-mail. Whether you're an e-mail novice or a seasoned professional, this resource belongs on your shelf.

You'll find answers to questions such as:

- How do I set up an HTML newsletter?

- Why is e-mail better than a Web site for distributing information?

- How can I communicate via e-mail without spamming?

- What is the proper e-mail etiquette?

- Where do I find subscribers and then how can I manage them?

- Where can I find a high-powered list service?

- What are the insider's tricks to hosting a successful e-mail discussion list?

- How can I generate income through advertising or ancillary product sales?

Poor Richard's E-mail Publishing is available in bookstores both online and offline, and at http://www.TopFloor.com/

Poor Richard's E-mail Publishing
by Chris Pirillo   ISBN: 0-9661032-5-4

This is the first book on a new technology known as HTML/OS. The technology promises to popularize the construction of advanced Web sites. It may be the most exciting technology since the advent of Java by Sun Microsystems.

HTML/OS is both a high-speed database engine and development environment that runs all across the Web. The HTML/OS engine reduces development by more than a factor of 250. It eliminates the need for integration tools such as ASP, JSP, and PhP, and it eliminates the need for programming languages to handle protocols such XML, Corba, and DCOM. It replaces all of these with a simple BASIC-like language you type into HTML documents. Almost anyone can use it.

This book was written for Web designers, computer programmers, and commercial product developers in all industries seeking a common-sense approach to advanced Web development. It's a must-read for every Web professional who wants an advanced Web site.

This book includes the following:

- Dozens of code examples for building shopping carts, database search pages, web-based editors, email broadcast systems, login pages, and more.
- Exercises for use by teachers of e-commerce courses.
- Companion Web site that includes exercise solutions consisting of additional code examples and a developer forum.
- Free 30-day trial of HTML/OS preinstalled on the web for every purchaser of the book. No software to install. Use with any browser from any computer.

The book is useful to anyone who wants to move beyond simple HTML development. The book assumes no more than a basic knowledge of HTML and some simple programming or scripting skills. The appendix includes a crash course on HTML for those unfamiliar with HTML but wish to use this book to build advanced Web sites and intranets.